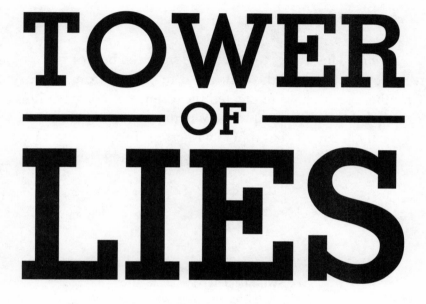

TOWER
OF
LIES

**WHAT MY EIGHTEEN YEARS OF WORKING WITH
DONALD TRUMP REVEALS ABOUT HIM**

BARBARA A. RES

GRAYMALKIN
MEDIA

Note: The stories told here are from the best of my recollection. Some of the dialogue is re-created from memory; in other cases I have re-created the essence of conversations rather than verbatim quotes. Where possible, I have tried to verify accounts that others witnessed. In some cases, I've changed names and identifying characteristics.

Graymalkin Media, LLC
11755 Wilshire Boulevard, Suite 1250
Los Angeles, CA 90025

For information about special discounts for bulk purchases, please contact Graymalkin Media at mail@graymalkin.com.

Interior design by Timothy Shaner

Manufactured in the United States of America

Library of Congress Cataloging-in-Publication data has been applied for.

ISBN 978-1-63168-304-6 (hardcover)
ISBN 978-1-63168-305-3 (paperback)
ISBN 978-1-63168-306-0 (ebook)

For my children,
Res and Peter G. Res

CONTENTS

TOWER
OF
LIES

The person I hired to be my personal representative over-seeing the construction, Barbara Res, was the first woman ever put in charge of a skyscraper in New York. She was thirty-three at the time . . . half the size of most of these bruising guys, but she wasn't afraid to tell them off when she had to, and she knew how to get things done.

—DONALD TRUMP
The Art of the Deal

INTRODUCTION

I have never been afraid of Donald, because I know who and what he is.

I was thirty years old when Donald J. Trump hired me to head construction on the building that would define him, Trump Tower. Every payment, contract, hire, question, issue, and problem with the building went through me. When I started in 1980 as a vice president at the Trump Organization, I was one of only four executives. I reported to Trump and worked for him for eighteen years in similar capacities, making deals, talking to the press on his behalf, acquiring permits on development projects, representing him before agencies and legislative bodies, and managing litigation on his projects. Throughout my years with Trump, I was a close and trusted adviser, one of the few people whom Donald listened to.

Now, whenever Donald Trump pulls a stunt, or launches an unhinged attack against someone like Nancy Pelosi or the Biden family, or he ignores a real crisis and invents a fake one, or he tells a particularly egregious lie, the media reach out to me. "Why did he do this?" they ask. "Has he ever done this before? What will he do now?" I'm a private person, but at some point I just had to share what I know with the public. In fact, Donald was the one who brought me into this.

During the 2016 campaign Trump announced that he broke the glass ceiling for women by hiring me, to show how wonderful he would be for them. Trump didn't even mention my name at first, but once he started attacking me, he sure did. It wasn't the fact that he was using me that made me speak out against his candidacy. I knew that he was not qualified or fit to be president, and I felt a duty to do whatever I could to prevent it.

As someone who knew Donald very well, I am familiar with what really happened, as opposed to the illusion he has worked so hard to create. Over time, I saw past the public persona and into the racism, sexism, and xenophobia that he carefully hid. Ironically, these things are now part of his brand.

There are people who worked with him longer, or more recently, or both. Most have chosen not to talk for their own reasons: some out of fear of recrimination, others who want to protect their privacy. Many former employees have agreed not to disparage him as a result of settlements. Others do so because they stand to or hope to gain from their relationship with Donald. Because I quit and there was no need for a severance, I am not bound by an NDA. This is rare in Trumpworld, so I am free to speak.

In print, online, and on cable news, I've offered whatever insight that I can into the character of the man I worked with for eighteen years. I don't believe what he says, but I also don't go out there to mindlessly attack him, as many are paid to or love to do. Journalists ask questions, so I share what I know, what I saw, what I understood then, and what I understand now. The press is looking for any insight into the character of our forty-fifth president—a man adored by many, reviled by many more, perplexing to just about everyone. But I see the method behind it all. The man I knew so well and worked with for almost twenty years, who gave me a break in construction at a time when women were not given such breaks, my once narcissistic but ultimately human boss is now just a hate-filled and amoral person. And he has been this way for some time.

Some people use the fact that I knew him long ago to discount my words, experience, and perspective. They say he has changed since then. They're right. He *has*. But that fact just supports my case. He's only become more himself. He is Trump raised to the nth degree, but Trump nonetheless. Donald Squared, I call him.

In the beginning Donald was glamorous and brash, even handsome. Sure, he was a showman, but he also had charm and moments of humanity, especially with some of us who worked closely with him. I saw him bully people below him and make idle threats, but what New York boss didn't—especially in the construction world? You had to be tough or you wouldn't survive one second on those sites or in those meetings. Trump thought of himself as a "killer." That's what you had to be to succeed, and he only wanted "killers" to work for him. Trump thought that I fit that mold.

In 1980 Trump hired me away from HRH Construction and put me in charge of his newest project, a state-of-the-art building on Fifth Avenue on which he would put his own name: Trump Tower. To this day, it is still his crowning achievement, the place that launched him—as a megadeveloper, a celebrity, and, ultimately, a presidential candidate. The fact that I also consider the building mine, and am immensely proud of it, complicates my feelings about him. Donald is intertwined with one of the great professional achievements of my life, and that will always be true.

For Trump, however, there has never been any room for nuance or gray. Back then, just as today, you were either the "best" or the "worst." Because he resisted firing anyone, the "worst" often stayed around. They served a purpose—he always needed people to carry out his plans with no pushback, to blame things on, to vent at, and to brutalize. If you were one of the best, you served a purpose too, beyond just making money for him. He'd call you the best mostly in *public*, where he could talk you up as a reflection of himself, where he could bask in the glory of having selected you. He did this quite frequently with people inside the company and out. I recognized this characteristic at the start of his presidency when he referred to "my generals," and "my military," and "my Justice Department." It's a way for him to swell his own legend.

During the four years when I was in charge of construction for Trump Tower, I practically lived with him. I was in contact with him multiple times a day, either on the phone, on-site, or in his office. Donald is a creature of habit and familiarity, so the office remained remarkably similar throughout the years; the only thing that changed was the number of framed awards and magazine covers of himself on the wall and the personally autographed sports memorabilia arranged on a table by the window. Again, things that reflected back onto his greatness.

In those days there was a handful of people he trusted, including me. He was demanding and sometimes nasty, but I dealt with it. I was a woman in a "man's world." And I put up with far worse than Donald's occasional eruptions.

Something changed in Donald over the years I knew him—something that magnified all his worst character traits and negated the remaining good ones. When we worked together on Trump Tower in the early 1980s, Donald and I both came to work early and walked to meetings together. Though he never treated anyone as an equal, there was a deference and basic respect in the way he communicated with many people. I left the Trump Organization in late 1984 for another job. When I returned to work for Trump again in 1987, supervising, among other things, Trump's renovation of the iconic Plaza Hotel, I could see the extent of those changes.

Now he was a different Donald. He didn't make a move without a bodyguard. People recognized him on the street—though not as much as he claimed—and the attention went to his head. Whereas he once hired only the best at what they did, now he was bringing some people in who were not of the highest caliber. They were simply yes-men.* His regard for himself had increased exponentially, as had his contempt for women. His sexism never extended to me, but it did to many others—including his wife Ivana, whom he would publicly belittle—and I came to see that I was the exception rather than the rule. His running commentary about women's bodies, faces, and interest in him became a regular conversation topic, even in business settings.

This was a new Trump and also a new Trump Organization, more spread out (he would buy an airline, a helicopter, a yacht,

---

* This means "yes-people," but the phrase is "yes-men," so I use that. It is not used here in a gendered way.

and a football team, and had launched his Atlantic City empire, among other things) with more glitz, money, egos, and fancy parties, and a different work ethic—at least on his part. Gone were the days when Donald and I would hold down the fort at seven a.m. Even though he now lived in Trump Tower, he came down to the office much later than the rest of us. Reports are that he rarely comes down to the Oval Office before eleven a.m., which is both shocking (because he's the president of the United States) and not (because he's Donald).

A couple of years later, during the Marla Maples scandal and his divorce from Ivana, his face was on the cover of tabloids all over the country and his name was on many people's lips. The constant attention further cemented this version of Donald. He got to see himself reflected in the public's eye, and though much of the attention was negative, he liked that people were talking about him. So he began to seek out the attention more and more, chasing it like an addiction. I could see how his behavior was destructive to others, to his own interests, to himself.

I watched him nurture his worst tendencies—his intolerance, his abusiveness, his dishonesty, his self-aggrandizement— and I watched as those who might speak up to him fell by the wayside. The yes-men, the inattentiveness, the taking people for granted, all became more common, while the lying and cheating accelerated. Not only did he get away with it, but he saw it as the *reason* for his success, so he kept doing it. I don't know if he looked up at the end of the 1990s—after barely surviving multiple bankruptcies—and noticed how many people had left him. Or if he cared. It's not hard to look at the trajectory of his entire life and spot an unmistakable pattern: The bigger he got as a name, the smaller he got as a person.

I'd heard Donald talking about running for office back in the 1980s. During meetings, from behind his gigantic rosewood desk on the twenty-sixth floor of Trump Tower, he would occasionally say things like "You know, Barbara, I should be president, I really should" or "These politicians don't know anything. Maybe *I* should run for president. Wouldn't that be something?" I didn't believe he was really serious; it was more like he was musing aloud to a captive audience. Whenever he'd mention it to us, everyone would nod agreeably and then laugh behind his back. Except me. "Come on, actually think about it," I said to my colleagues. "He would just hire the best people and sit back and take the credit. Like he does now."

Of course, I already knew about his lack of concentration, his penchant for diverting big decisions to other people, his collecting of ass-kissers, his mood swings, his ignorance—even in areas of his "genius," like construction and finance and real estate. But I thought maybe he could pull it off if he just acted as a figurehead, making a big to-do of signing laws and presiding over ceremonies, while letting the people under him do all the actual work.

When I put more thought into it, of course, I realized this would never work. A U.S. president has to know how the government works, commit to following the Constitution, and be willing to stand as its preeminent defender. He has to put the people's needs and interests before his own. His schedule is packed and dictated by others, and there is no money to be made on the job (or back then, we couldn't conceive that someone would try). The chief executive of the country is restrained by a million little civic norms and day-to-day functions that would drive Donald up the wall. He had been his own boss forever, didn't have to report to anyone, and regularly took time off to play golf or watch TV while leaving others to run things, which at the time seemed impossible for a president to do. *No, forget it,* I realized, *Trump couldn't handle that.* I joined the others, laughing at how preposterous it was to picture our boss in the Oval Office. That was 1987.

His musings about running for president seemed like another way of garnering publicity for a fantasy that existed only in his head, something I'd seen him do many times. This particular fantasy seems to have begun in 1987, when he flew to New Hampshire at the behest of some locals who were trying to draft him to run for president. His interest gained steam in 1999 when he toyed with running on the Reform Party ticket, and it continued through the years as something Donald would use to bring attention to himself. So toward the end of Obama's presidency, in 2015, when Donald announced he would run for the Republican nomination, I assumed it was a stunt. As he grandiosely descended the escalators in the Trump Tower atrium that I helped build, it certainly had the look and feel of one.

I'm also sure Donald didn't think he would win. He just wanted to prove to the world how smart and successful he was, maybe use the platform to bring attention to himself and feed his ego, which is always his endgame. But Trump's race-baiting found an audience, the Republican Party revealed itself to be spineless and fell into line behind him, and other factors helped get him elected. Among these were his own name recognition, FBI Director James Comey's focus on meaningless emails, and Russian interference on Trump's behalf.* It made the unthinkable a reality. So here we are.

I admit that I first gave Trump a chance, hoping that maybe the awesome responsibility of the presidency would change him. I wondered (privately and publicly) if the positive attributes I had seen would return once Donald was put in charge of 320 million people and the most powerful country on Earth. Maybe the quest for money, clout, and attention that motivated him would diminish and some larger sense of duty would arise.

As I write this in the fall of 2020, with a global pandemic still raging and with an unprepared president instigating chaos, spreading misinformation, and sowing division, I realize how deluded I was. The presidency didn't change him; *he changed it*. He didn't rise to the office; he brought it down to his level.

With his ignorance of the Constitution and of the way government works, along with his arrogant disdain for institutions, he has tried to turn himself into a king. I don't know if I'm more disgusted that he has tried or that he has largely succeeded. I get so tired of hearing politicians claim that "nobody is above the law," while doing nothing to prove it. It is a principle on which this country was built and that we once believed. But Donald Trump has revealed that the democratic system in America is only as good as the person who is entrusted with preserving it. It is sad to think that almost 63 million people thought that he would be the right person to do that. Even after nearly four years of his tenure, with his poll numbers finally dropping, I can't believe that so many still think so.

---

* As determined by U.S. intelligence and the Republican-led U.S. Senate.

The seeds of who he is today were planted back when I worked with him. He was able to control others, through lies and exaggeration, with promises of money or jobs, through threats of lawsuits or exposure. He surrounded himself with yes-men, blamed others for his own failures, never took responsibility, and always stole credit. These tactics are still at work, just deployed at the highest levels of the U.S. government, with all the corruption and chaos that necessarily ensue.

The Donald Trump of today is a creation of his own making, a man who can be understood through the lens of a handful of rules. This behavior has created the character of Donald, his family, the Trump Organization, and the Trump administration, and has now become woven into the very fabric of our nation. What Michael D'Antonio, one of Trump's biographers, wrote before the 2016 election still holds true: "What lurks in him is apparent. Less certain is what resides in us."

Donald Trump is now himself in purest form, a person with no decency or conscience—someone I hope the young people of this country are repelled by and the voters of this country will decisively reject. And I hope it's not too late. The havoc he has wreaked on the nation and its citizens will take an entire era to heal. It cannot start soon enough.

ONE

THE (GOOD) OLD DAYS

Before I met or had even seen Donald Trump, I was warned he could be trouble. I was a twenty-eight-year-old professional engineer working for HRH Construction in New York City, a female in a job and an industry where women were few and far between. (After graduating in 1972 with a degree in electrical engineering, I was one of the 1 percent of engineers who were female.) Through the 1970s, I worked for electrical contractors on sites all over New York City, from Mount Sinai Hospital to Irving Trust Bank to Citicorp Center. I held many positions for these companies, as I was promoted several times into different roles. In 1977, I was hired by HRH as an assistant project manager.

The next year, HRH was appointed general contractor on the renovation of the Commodore Hotel, which was to be Donald Trump's big splash in Manhattan real estate. Partnering with the Hyatt Corporation, he had bought the aging building with help from loans from his father and generous tax abatements from the city. The young developer was going to rescue this forgotten treasure from obscurity and remake a historic part of New York City. He would also, if allowed to, screw us.

The Commodore was a once-grand edifice that had fallen on hard times. In the 1920s and '30s, it was considered a modern marvel, magnificently regal at the corner of Lexington Avenue and 42nd Street next to Grand Central Terminal. But it fell into decay over time and in the 1970s was sold to the thirty-two-year-old developer, whose father, Fred, had made a fortune building low- and mid-rise apartments in Queens and Brooklyn. Donald said that the new project—the Grand Hyatt—was to be a Hyatt so luxurious that the name Hyatt Regency, the company's top brand, would not be good enough for it. The real story was that they didn't want confusion with the Regency Hotel on Park Avenue.

Trump claimed he was going to resurrect 42nd Street in that area, making it the hub and destination it had been fifty years prior. He sold the promise to the press and public as "the largest construction job underway in New York" at the time, though hindsight tells me that could not have been possible.

Trump was the official developer on the project, which meant that everything ran through him. He decided on all the planning, design, building, and furnishing. The vast renovation included covering the old brick building with bronze-colored aluminum and glass, while reimagining the inside with waterfalls, sculptures, and luxurious meeting spaces. And it was to be done the Trump way, which meant on a shoestring budget. Irving Fischer, HRH's chairman, would know it was going to cost a hell of a lot more than the $37 million price that HRH had guaranteed. Renovating an old building like the Commodore would require a lot of extra work due to changes that could not be anticipated.

Fischer wanted to make sure that Trump didn't fight us over every penny trying to stay under that number. The truth, as I'd learn, was also the Trump way: a mix of the nefarious and the ignorant. Donald had no idea what he was getting into *and* he might try to screw us.

The day I started working on the Grand Hyatt, Irving Fischer was also on-site. Fischer was a small, wiry man, a smart guy who came out of the financial side of the business. I certainly knew who he was, but I didn't think he knew me. So I was surprised when he walked over to me in the field office, one of the old hotel offices on the top floor. He was holding a thick contract in hand. "Read this," he said, handing it to me. "Memorize it. Write down *everything* that happens on this job and make sure it is covered in the contract and that you have put in a price for it. Cover your ass. The son of a bitch"—meaning Trump—"is going to sue us for sure." This was my introduction to Donald Trump: the guy who was going to sue his own contractor.

Fischer had worked before with Fred Trump, who was known for slicing as thin as possible and fighting like hell—fairly and unfairly—for every cent. He was notoriously cheap, rumored to have picked up loose nails from the floors of his sites. While I don't believe that story, I can attest that he was a penny-pincher and a cheat, traits his son would raise to an art form. Fischer was also well aware that the Trumps almost *enjoyed* suing people. Everyone knew the power of their infamous lawyer, the detested Roy Cohn, whose goblin eyes haunted the dreams of anyone on his radar. Just the threat of a phone call from Cohn was enough to shut down most problems. That's why Fischer drilled into me that I had to keep absolutely perfect records: Mistrust of the Trumps was baked into the project.

I remember the first time I saw Donald and Ivana. I'd only been on the job a few days, and they were walking around the site together, which they would do from time to time. She had on a designer blue suit and an unusual hat in a nautical style, a rectangle that came to a point at both ends. Ivana was stylish and beautiful, with a small, delicate face and her blond hair in an updo. Donald was quite attractive, his hair longer and shaggier in the style of the times, covering most of his ears, a swoosh over the right eye. He was dressed in a tailored dark pinstripe suit and a red tie with a thick Windsor knot. I learned later that he bought his suits at Barney's and had them shipped to his assistant's home in New Jersey to avoid paying sales tax. Back then, the Trumps seemed like the epitome of glamour and glitz, especially to a working-class girl from Queens.

Up close, Donald was a little less impressive. Handsome, but also like an unfinished drawing. With wispy eyebrows over light blue eyes, he had this distant gaze that seemed to both size you up and look straight through you. His voice was nasal and high-pitched, slightly effeminate, with a much heavier outer-borough accent than he has now. Donald often behaved in a friendly manner with the tradesmen on the job, stopping to say hello, seeking praise on the building. But it didn't take me long to learn what he really thought of his workers; he just knew enough to hide his contempt. Trump was well aware of the public relations benefit of being liked by "the common man," and he exploited it, a behavior he continues to this day.

Even then Donald had this specific mix of confidence and insecurity, which fed each other in a continuous loop. Both he and Ivana were hardworking but inexperienced, often making poor judgments and then compounding them with even worse ones. They were used to hearing "Yes" or acting with impunity, another thing that would become a recurring theme, especially with Donald. Trump didn't know much about construction (he once said only a masochist could enjoy it) and even less about renovation. What he did know, which he had learned from his father, was how to run a real estate operation, building low- and mid-rise apartment complexes, collecting rent, and cultivating powerful politicians—the skills that had made Fred's fortune. He also learned from his father how to cut corners, cheat contractors, and mistreat workers—skills that Donald would perfect.

Fred was said to have been very hard on his son, and some of Donald's character flaws no doubt were influenced by his father. But Fred, a German immigrant who grew up poor, also had this idealized version of Donald, revering him like he was the Second Coming. He viewed Donald as the Trump who would break through the barriers that he himself never could overcome. The irony in all this is that Fred actually *was* the self-made man who Donald always pretends to be. Fred really did start with nothing and become a very wealthy man on his own. As for Donald, without his father's money and connections, he could never have gotten anywhere near Manhattan real estate. I think some of his insecurity, his need to create fictions about his success, is the result of him knowing in his heart this is true.

THE GRAND HYATT was Donald's first job as a developer. In his ignorance, Trump thought that by keeping as many of the existing elements in the building as possible, he could save a lot of money. But that's not how renovation works. Selecting what can and should be saved takes thought, experience, and skill. Trying to save things that should be removed results in *increasing* the overall costs.

The Commodore was a dilapidated hotel fitted with out-of-date equipment and piping, ductwork, and fittings that could not be reused in their current condition. The rerouting and special fittings required to make them operative would exceed the cost of simple removal and replacement. Keeping the old equipment, and having to work and reroute around them, was a pain in the ass and cost a fortune. Despite Trump's demands, we tried to avoid this because the end result would be rebuilt crap squeezed into spaces where maintenance would be extremely difficult. In the instances where we kept fans and other machinery, such as on the roof, it cost so much money to work around them that it would have been cheaper to just demolish everything.

We were constantly wasting time and money trying to adhere to Trump's insistence on saving everything: sandblasting the paint off the old doors and frames, which cost more than replacing them, and protecting the old wood floors in the ballroom, which we later had to replace anyway. The Grand Hyatt construction work ended up costing more than twice the original budget, and I'd estimate around 30 percent of those cost overruns were directly related to Trump's not knowing what he was doing. No one would explain that a complete gut of the building would have been cheaper and faster. The architects were afraid to challenge him, and the general contractor, HRH, mostly went along, spending its energy on making sure HRH got paid, one of the tasks for which I was responsible.

The Commodore was still occupied when Trump bought it, with residents who dated back to the single-room-occupancy (SRO) days. Donald's people got rid of all of them, along with a handful of prostitutes, who came back later to service the construction workers. There were also retail stores that Trump had to force out. He did this through cutting services, intimidating, and (through his attack dog, Roy Cohn) threatening to sue. This was a regular pattern for Trump, as I would learn—behavior that grew more vicious in later years and would eventually extend to things outside real estate. He would wipe out what was there to put in what he wanted, something that could serve him financially or publicity-wise, and he didn't care much how it got done.

I began on the Grand Hyatt as an assistant project manager, in charge of the requisitions (requests for payment) and change orders, which were critical to the progress of the job. I was given an office in the Commodore's old money-counting room on the top floor near the hotel offices. It was a tiny space tucked into a corner with a concrete shelf behind the desk. The door was steel and the walls were thick concrete, like Fort Knox.

Several months into the Hyatt job, HRH president Artie Nusbaum came to see me. Artie played a dual role in my life, both mentor and tormentor. He made so many inappropriate remarks to me that it was sometimes hard to take him seriously, but he taught me the business. I had previously worked as an estimator for Artie on Citicorp Center, the distinctive Midtown skyscraper with the forty-five-degree slant, at the time one of the tallest buildings in the world. On Citicorp, Artie taught me everything about the mechanical trades. He brought me over to the Grand Hyatt and made me assistant project manager. A heavy guy in his fifties with a large round head, Artie contained a universe of knowledge about construction, but he looked like an unmade bed. He was the kind of man who wore a short-sleeved shirt under his suit even in the winter.

The morning Artie wandered into my office, he seemed distracted. I could tell something was on his mind. "How're things coming?"

"Good," I said. Obviously he wasn't there to chitchat. "What's up?"

Artie took a seat across from me. "This fucking mechanical superintendent," he said in his heavy New York accent and clipped cadence. "What do you think of him?"

"Yeah," I said, laughing slightly. "He's getting steamrolled."

"Yeah, he's a fucking disaster," Artie said. The mechanical super has to handle coordination between the electrician, the plumber, the steamfitter, the tin knocker, and the sprinkler guy— what are known as the mechanical trades. (HRH was the general contractor, running the show; all the skilled trades on a job are known as subcontractors, or "subs.") Coordinating all the mechanical subs' work to fit into sometimes very tight spaces often required subs to change their designs at their own cost. The mechanical super's job is to organize all this and make the decision about who has to move or alter things. It is not a role for the fainthearted, and a weak mechanical superintendent causes chaos. Coordination took someone who could sniff out bullshit and keep control over tough personalities.

"Yeah, I'm gonna replace him," Artie said matter-of-factly.

"Good idea," I said.

He scrunched his brow, like he'd just thought of something. "Why don't you take over? You know all the trades." Artie had known me for years and also seen I had steel nerves and wouldn't take any shit.

I shrugged. "I can't do any worse than this guy," I said.

"Okay, so you're mechanical super now," he said. Then he peeled himself out of my chair and walked out.

I like to think I would've risen anyway, but with Artie's choice to put me on as mechanical superintendent (in addition to my assistant project manager duties), I'd soon land on Trump's radar. This promotion would affect much more than my work and my salary: It changed my life.

It took someone with steel nerves just to be on-site, because the Commodore jobsite was so disgusting. There were gigantic rats living in the hotel basements that were so fierce, they killed the cats we brought in to get rid of them. But that wasn't even the most repulsive thing. Rather than hiking to the Port-A-Johns, workers would regularly piss on the columns, something I saw many times.* They didn't mind the walk; they just liked doing it.

All the shanties, the temporary plywood offices built for the subs, were papered with pictures of naked women on every conceivable flat surface. As the only woman in the field, I'd get harassed anytime the doors closed on the elevator, asked out during lunch by

---

* This was common on all work sites. When we turned on the heat at Trump Tower, the smell of piss was unbearable. We had to fumigate around the columns by the fan coil units.

men who knew I was married, accused of sleeping with the boss to get my position, and forced to listen to open discussions about my body. I can't say I was ever able to entirely look the other way—it was too painful—but, in my own way, I got used to it.

When I first started in construction, I was called every variation of "bitch," "ballbuster," "man-hater," "dyke," and "cunt." Each job was the very essence of a hostile work environment, but in the 1970s you'd have been laughed off a site for suggesting something like that. Only a few years earlier, the same Artie Nusbaum was then working for another company building an addition to Mount Sinai Hospital. I was an engineer on that job, doing some drafting for a subcontractor. When Artie learned that I had toured the site, he was furious. He wrote a memo that banned women from visiting jobsites for any reason. It wasn't the first time I'd heard this on a job. The rationale shifted from how their hairdos wouldn't fit under hard hats to their footwear was too dangerous to walk in to their skirts and dresses would get in the way. And if none of those objections were convincing, there was always the argument that women's presence would be too distracting to the men. It was all a thin cover for the obvious goal: keeping women in their place.

Seven years later, I was working on-site for the Grand Hyatt, but the hostility toward women persisted. Knowing that complaining would get me nowhere—or worse, just reinforce what the men already thought about women's backbones—I internalized a lot of the abuse. It took many years for me to realize that none of it was my fault, that I had done nothing to bring it upon myself. To this day I speak to women, primarily in the construction industry, about how to navigate the kind of sexism that was rampant way back when and still exists today.

* * *

Doing coordination on the Hyatt did garner me a level of respect. One dispute in particular earned me my stripes. The restaurant's kitchens required extensive black iron ductwork for the kitchen exhaust system, and the tin knocker's layout for it took up the entire ceiling space; nothing else could fit up there. When the electrician had to locate a pull box in the same space, the two of them clashed until I stepped in. The only solution would have been to reconfigure the duct, which is exactly what I told the tin knocker to do. He was six feet four, maybe 270 pounds, a small head on a massive frame with a voice that bellowed through the floors. When I told him the duct wasn't going to work, he got in my face, stared me down, and started cursing at me. We went back and forth and I wouldn't give an inch. "Lady," he said. "it's already fabricated, so tough shit."

I didn't blink. "Then throw the fucking thing out and do it again the right way!" I said, raising my voice to a level that matched his. The electrician's eyes popped out, clearly impressed. I had caught the tin knocker by surprise; he paused for a few seconds before telling me to go fuck myself. Then he walked out of the meeting.

Before I could even report the incident, the president of the sheet metal company called Artie, telling him I was incompetent and demanding that I be removed. But Nusbaum backed me up, and standing up to the ogre won me points with everyone. Presumably word got back to Trump. Proving myself by taking it and dishing it out was a daily occurrence, as much a part of my job as the actual coordination. The incident cemented me as Artie's protégé; it convinced him that I was a true leader and that he was right to have put me in charge of coordination.

Besides coordinating, one of my duties as mechanical super was to attend the owner's meetings. These would take place in one of the old conference rooms on the top floor of the Commodore, and we'd all sit around a large wood table—HRH executive Artie Nusbaum, the HRH project manager (Ed) and superintendent (Ronnie), the architect (Ralph), the structural and mechanical engineers, usually Ivana, and always Donald and his representatives.

The purpose of these weekly meetings was to have the professionals sit with the owner and report on where everyone was in their timelines, what was happening or about to happen, if new drawings were coming out, if there were changes to be made, and if there was a problem that needed to be solved. On a construction project, an architect's drawings go out and there are always questions that arise from it—things that were missed, were not altered according to new information, or needed updating. The general contractor showed up every week at the owner's meeting with a list of questions from his subs that had to be answered by the architect within a week. Essentially, the meetings were about the two biggest things on any construction project—money and time, which everything ends up translating into anyway. Delays and extra costs were the primary thing the owner would focus on, and Donald was no different.

On the Hyatt, Trump had only a staff of three. His representative, Ernie, was an older man who may have been a holdover from Fred's team. He was a competent and knowledgeable guy, but Trump was merciless with him. If there was a change Trump had to pay for, he would blame Ernie or his assistant for not telling him, even though they almost always had. "Just call me directly," he'd tell Ralph, the architect. "Don't talk to these jerks," he'd say, referring to his own people.

Poor Ernie would just take it, quietly nodding or mumbling apologies while Trump raged. Throughout the project, I observed Donald whack away at Ernie's confidence, cutting him off in meetings, making him so hesitant to speak that he would hardly speak at all. Ernie became terrified of making a move on his own, which defeats the whole purpose of having an owner's rep. These meetings were my first exposure to Donald's way of exploiting people's weaknesses. Like a dog who could sense fear, Trump looked for weakness; and if he caught a whiff of it, he would pounce.

In one meeting, a change order came up for additional steel for the existing framework, which would cost ten thousand dollars; this predictably sent Trump raging. Ed Sullivan was our project manager, a thin and pale Irishman, more gentle than your average construction guy. He was my direct boss, and he understood how to keep an even keel in these meetings. Before he was even done going over the change, Trump was on top of Ralph. "You should've seen that coming before you made the plans, Ralph! This is your fault. I'm deducting it from your fee." Ralph was a tall, handsome guy with wavy, thick black hair, genteel and well-spoken. Though he was a competent architect and amiable, when he was cornered by Trump, I saw him shrivel and then lash out at the contractor. "Hang on, Donald," Ralph said, "You should talk to Artie. He was the one who—"

Donald turned to Artie and slapped the table, a pop that echoed in the room. "C'mon, Artie. What are you doing to me?" As Artie calmly explained, Trump stopped listening. He shifted to Ernie, his favorite target. Donald shook his head. "Jesus, Ernie!"

he said, exasperated. "This is ridiculous. You're letting these subs make a fool of me!"

Even back then, I could tell this behavior was all a charade. Trump knew (or should have known) it was nobody's fault; these kinds of things happen on renovations all the time. He just took advantage of the opportunity to beat up on people, especially his own crew. "You approved this, Ernie? Did you know about this?" I could see Ernie's face drop, his aching to disappear. Ernie didn't say a word, so Ed, the HRH project manager, continued.

"Well, I talked to Ernie, but he said—" Ed tried to say.

"Do me a favor, Ed. Don't ask Ernie," Trump said. "He doesn't know a fucking thing."

Seemingly satisfied that Ernie was cowed, Trump shifted back to Artie: "You got him to approve it because you know my people are pushovers. Ernie doesn't know shit. He doesn't care about spending my money." The pattern was reproduced pretty regularly; Trump would lash out first at the source (the architect), then the messenger (HRH), and finally his own people (Ernie.) Despite all of Trump's theatrics, the changes were legit and Trump would end up paying.

I would watch Trump closely at these meetings, and I could see he had a habit of intimidating people. Of course, he didn't want to spend extra money, but he usually just sniffed out the weakest player so he could attack with impunity. He was more interested in the personalities, the dynamics at play, than the details of the work itself. Just as he attacked weak people, he was drawn to those who didn't take shit. And I didn't take any shit. He noticed how I freely spoke to people—below me, at my level, above me. To me, showing respect didn't necessarily mean being quiet.

Donald may have seen me in the field—maybe someone told him I was an engineer—but he didn't see me in action until those owner's meetings. At another meeting, Ed was presenting a change order on walls that had been moved. "Wait, wait," Trump interrupted. "I'm not paying for that. No fucking way. Whose fault is that?"

Silence filled the hotel office. Then the architect dipped his toe in. "Well, they weren't using the right drawings," Ralph said. "If they—"

"Hold it! That is total bullshit!" I jumped in. "When the walls went up, the contractor's guys were using your current drawings. You changed the drawings later, which meant the contractors had to take the walls down and relocate them. They have to be paid for that. It's extra work." Trump took me at my word and threatened to back charge the architect, who hemmed and hawed in a half-assed attempt to get the heat off himself. Before he was even finished, Trump would again yell at Ernie, this time for not giving proper directions. Ultimately, Donald would pay.

Ivana was at those meetings too, and she and Donald seemed to be very close. She hung on his every word, and back then he was relatively nice to her. These meetings could run all day, so we would take a break at lunch and have sandwiches brought in. Donald and Ivana were in excellent shape, she on the very thin side, and they both watched what they ate. He'd get something like a turkey on rye, take the meat out of one half and put it on the other half, then throw the extra bread away. Ivana went a step further. On the second half, where she had put all the meat, she also threw the top piece of bread away and ate it as an open-face sandwich. I had never seen anyone do that, but I assumed those tricks kept them fit. Their silent lunch ritual always struck me; it was like a peek into their lives.

Ivana didn't say much in those meetings, but Donald went out of his way to defer to her, or at least to appear to. If there was anything that would affect the design, he would lean over or put his hand on her leg and say, "What do you think, honeybunch?" I learned that this was a ruse. Donald did this knowing she would agree with him. Trump was able to win two ways: He got the support he needed while making it look as though he was giving her some say. The time would come when Ivana too got blamed for things that were not her fault. But that was some years into the future.

In the end, all the delays and change orders did not matter, because the hotel, glamorous and sleek, with its glass-enclosed bar cantilevered over the 42nd Street sidewalk, was a huge success. The room rates were substantially higher than predicted, and Trump scored an incredible tax break for the hotel, an unprecedented forty-year abatement that relieved the property of any real estate taxes for that period of time. This made the profits skyrocket. As usually was the case with developers, Trump and Hyatt most likely slapped a loan on it that was far greater than what they spent on the hotel, allowing them to use the remaining millions for themselves.

To Trump's credit, no one could have predicted the success of the Grand Hyatt, which he would later sell for at least triple the investment. In the late 1970s, when he bought, the Commodore Hotel and the surrounding area were in serious decay. New York City was in economic distress, and no one knew if it would bounce back. By the time the Grand Hyatt opened, the city would be on the rise again and Donald caught the wave. Through a mix of fortune and foresight, his first foray into Manhattan was a success. But it was his next project that would really put him on the map.

IN THE SUMMER of 1980, as the Hyatt project was winding down after two years, my husband, Pete, and I were at a black-tie party at the Hilton, where we spotted the Trumps. After so many meetings, I felt comfortable talking to them. So I brought Pete across the room to meet them. As Donald shook his hand, he said, "Pete, let me tell you something: Your wife is great."

"Thanks," Pete said, smiling, "I can—"

"She's gonna work for me," Trump interrupted before Pete could get three words in. "And you know what? I'm gonna double her salary. How about that?" This silenced both of us. Then Trump turned to me and said, "Set up an appointment with Ivana tomorrow. Let's make this happen. Okay?" Before I could answer or even process what he'd said, the Trumps sort of danced away. I don't know if the offer was planned or impulsive, but I was struck dumb. For one thing, he was trying to steal me from his own contractor, HRH, who had been hired to be the general contractor on the job. I knew Artie was grooming me for bigger things there, but I didn't feel I owed HRH anything. It was a no-brainer; I called Ivana the next morning and set up a time to see them.

Riding the elevator to the top floor of their apartment building on Fifth Avenue, I was a little nervous. This was not my world, and I knew Donald would come on strong. I wanted to be prepared and had already spoken to my husband about how I wouldn't agree to anything on the spot. But I admit that the location—with its atmosphere of luxury and excess, which seemed to emanate from Donald and Ivana like perfume—threw me off balance.

Ivana took me into the living room, where Donald sat on the couch, framed by a wide set of picture windows that opened onto a panoramic view of the lush green Central Park. The park is for use by every New Yorker, but most of us see it only in pieces. If you have enough money, however, you get to wake up to the whole thing every morning, like it's yours. I think that does a number on the rich people of New York; they tend to feel they possess the city. The Trumps' apartment was immaculate—it was hard to believe anyone lived there—and everything was some shade of white: the carpeting, the couches, the tables, and the draperies. There was a bar in the corner, and even that was white. I wondered at the time how their toddler, two-and-a-half-year-old Donald Jr., could live in a place so white.

Ivana came over to me. "Wonderful to see you, Barbara," she said in her thick Czech accent. "Can I get you anything? Some orange juice?"

"No, thank you," I said. *No way*. I could just imagine spilling orange juice on that white carpet. Their standard poodle, Chappy, barged in, and Ivana shooed him away. Trump didn't seem to like the dog at all; he had been Ivana's before they got married.

"Let's talk," Donald said. From Donald, this meant "I want to talk," so I let him.

"You've heard about Trump Tower?" he said, more statement than question.

"A little, yeah." This was an understatement. Everyone around HRH knew about it by that point, because Donald made sure we did. Trump Tower was to be his next project, and the demolition of

Bonwit Teller, the famed luxury department store that had stood on the site, had already started on 56th Street and Fifth Avenue. He launched into his pitch, describing it to me in his inimitable style. "It's going to be the greatest building in Manhattan. The most luxurious, the most important building ever built in New York, maybe the country. It's gonna be seventy stories with the highest high-end retail shops from all over the world. Then a dozen stories of offices. And then"—he was using his hands to mime rising floors—"super-expensive, high high-end condominium apartments. It's gonna be like Olympic Tower, only better, more luxurious." I had been to Olympic Tower, built by Aristotle Onassis's company, which was one of most luxurious and expensive apartment buildings in New York at the time. "It's gonna be the most talked about building in the world."

"Wow. Sounds really great," I said, trying to match his enthusiasm.

"The best apartments anywhere"—he was counting on his fingers—"the best stores, and the best office space," he said. "Trump Tower is going to be a very, very famous building. The biggest, most famous building in the world. And the best location in the world. It's called the Tiffany Location and it's actually right next to Tiffany's. Trump Tower will be the center of the city." He kept saying the building's name, which he clearly enjoyed. "And I want you to build it."

It's good I hadn't taken the orange juice, because I would've done a spit take. "I'm sorry?" I said. I was sure I had misheard him.

"I want you to head up construction," he said with a little laugh, clearly enjoying my reaction. "I want you to build Trump Tower for me. What do you think?" Donald had a penchant for the theatrical, and just like the initial offer he'd made at the Hilton party, he knew this was supposed to blow me away. Which it did.

"You're gonna head up construction on what's going to be the most famous building in the world," he continued. "It was Ivana's suggestion, initially," he said, gesturing to his wife. "When I said I had to replace the people I had on the Hyatt. But I knew all along she was right. You're a killer."

"Thanks," I said, well aware by that point that this was the ultimate compliment he could give. If Donald saw you as a "killer," that was like being anointed by him. He used the term often to put down his own people by saying they were *not* killers. Or he'd brag about how a new lawyer he hired or wanted to hire was a killer. This was one of the many things he got from his father.

"I want you to be me on the project," he said. "I'm gonna be busy, I have a lot of other amazing things going on, and I want someone I can trust, someone who can answer for me. You'll be like a 'Donna' Trump," he said, smiling at his own cleverness. Everything was coming at me so fast, it was hard to know what to say. Fortunately, Donald kept talking.

"Listen," he said, leaning forward, elbows on his knees. "I know you're a woman in a man's world. And men are better than women. *But,*" he said, "but, but—one good woman is better than ten good men."

I just nodded, not wanting to argue, correct him, or change the course of the conversation. I figured anything I said could only spoil his impression of me. I assumed he meant I was that good woman. It was such a strange mix of a compliment and insult that I wasn't sure how I felt about it.

"A woman will work harder, better, and smarter than a man," he continued. "They have to prove themselves." It was true. I was at the jobsite the earliest, left the latest, took almost no breaks, and was the most outspoken person at HRH, including my supervisors. We were also paid less to do the same job. A woman who had achieved something had to be far superior to the men because she had to stand out just to make it. Artie once told me that if I weren't so outstanding, he would not have let me do much of anything.

Donald actually liked surrounding himself with strong women. On Trump Tower, besides me, the leasing agent, the condo sales manager, and the head of the advertising company would all be very assertive women. He was comfortable with that, because he was confident that no matter how accomplished or intelligent they were, they could never be a threat. He was superior just because he was a man.

"So I want you to be me," Donald said. "Make the decisions I would make. Donna Trump. You know, direct the work—the day-to-day things. I'm just gonna be too busy. We have"—here he gestured to Ivana again—"just too much going on right now. You wouldn't believe it."

Although I realized, then and now, that he would never be hands-off, I could see he was offering me a vast amount of power and a very important and demanding job. It was something I had never even thought of doing, not at that time; I was only a month shy of thirty-one. Donald assumed it was a done deal, but for my part, I was in total shock.

"What do you make now, twenty-five thousand dollars?"

"Thirty," I said.

"How's fifty-five sound?"

"Better," I said, smiling.

"Great," he said, "And we'll make you vice president, too." Donald pulled back, his arms stretched over his whiter-than-white couch. His relaxed body language told me that he thought he had closed the deal. I took a few days to think about it, talked it over with Pete, but there was no way I was going to say no. Donald got his "killer."

So in October 1980, I left the world of construction contracting to join Trump on his glorious venture. As a vice president, I was respected by the people in the contractor's office, though the men in the field didn't know or care about my title. They either resented me or were amused by me. But I made sure they knew I was in charge.

The Trump Organization's offices were located in the Crown Building, directly across Fifth Avenue from the future site of Trump Tower. The waiting area outside Donald's office on the second floor overlooked the work site, which was only a gigantic pile of rubble when I started. Trump's office was very large and full of windows looking onto 57th Street, with these enormous vertical blinds. His new desk was of Brazilian rosewood, which had been custom made in Italy. It was beautiful, so shiny that it was as though a hundred coats of lacquer had been laid down on it.

I set up in the larger of the empty offices, alongside two other executives and an open office that would later be taken by Donald's younger brother, Robert. Whether I was mechanical super or vice president, work for me started at seven a.m., so that's when I showed up. At first Donald was usually there when I got in, and he would answer the phone. Thinking he shouldn't be the one doing that, I started to handle the phones until his assistant arrived. Once Donald saw me on the phones and turning on the lights, he stopped coming in so early. As the project progressed, he would come in later and later. When I needed to speak with him, which was all the time, I started calling him at home, maybe too often. One day, he asked me to stop calling so early, because I was disturbing Ivana.

While it was not the tallest reinforced concrete building in the world, as Donald claimed, Trump Tower was still a very complicated, ambitious project. It had a small floor plate, the lower floors were different shapes, and we were using high-strength concrete and additives that had not been widely used before. The decision was made early that the building would be all concrete. Office and retail buildings are usually built with steel, which has to be designed, detailed, approved, and fabricated, all of which takes time. With concrete you just pour. It allowed us to start months earlier. But concrete is not easy—it's just fast. While structural steel doesn't change, concrete changes all the time. The way concrete is made strong is through the use of steel reinforcing rods, the placement of which is essential to the integrity of the structure. Changes to the number and location of the rebar are made on the spot, and such changes are frequent. It is both an art and a science.

We worked six days a week; once we finished the atrium and retail levels, we started building the tower on a two-day cycle, so every other day a new floor was poured. It was a fast-track job, which meant work started before the plans were complete. Just like our choice for concrete over steel, the reason was simple: money. Interest rates in 1980 were the highest they had ever been in the United States. The faster Trump Tower could get built and occupied, the quicker Trump and his partner, Equitable, could start to make a fortune. One-bedroom apartments started at $500K (about $1.3 million in today's dollars), and that didn't include any of the changes to the basic design and fittings, which nearly every single buyer made, and Donald also got a piece of that, too.

Trump Tower's exterior design was conceived by famed architect Der Scutt, the design partner for Swanke Hayden Connell Architects. Early on, Der sat down with Donald and asked, "What do you want to build?" and the two of them worked it out on scraps of paper. What they came up with was this cutting-edge sawtooth shape that gave every apartment two different views.

Though Donald claims it's a sixty-eight-story building, Trump Tower is fifty-eight stories tall. The first five floors, for retail, are each about sixteen feet high, then eleven stories of office space at thirteen feet. There were three mechanical floors, and then thirty-nine stories of apartments at about nine and a half feet. That makes the building 664 feet tall. He called the five retail floors and the basement "concourses" and relabeled the first office floor, which was actually the sixth floor, the fourteenth. The three mechanical floors brought it up to twenty-nine, the first apartment level was the thirtieth floor, and the last, the sixty-eighth, was the top floor of Donald's triplex apartment.

Trump had involved Ivana in his business from the early years of their marriage, allowing her to interfere with the construction of both the Grand Hyatt Hotel and Trump Tower. She was way out of her depth, but she did her best. I grew to be somewhat fond of her, but her only real qualification was that Donald trusted her. At least she was smart—smarter than Donald, I always thought— and we usually got along well.

Sometime during the construction of Trump Tower, Ivana got the idea that she should be a vice president (I may have even suggested it) and made up cards with the title: Vice President for Interior Design. Her meddling—mostly regarding materials and quality of work—made my job difficult. She didn't really understand construction and had an idealized picture of how things were supposed to look that was just not based in reality. We were working with union contractors, who were good but not perfect. For perfect, you needed finishing contractors, who cost three or four times as much. I complained to Donald about Ivana, and I recall Louise Sunshine, who sold the apartments, also doing so. But it was pointless. Ivana was Donald's eyes and ears on-site; he trusted her at a level he was incapable of trusting others.

I tried to turn my connection to Ivana to advantage and use her as a means to get through to Donald. (Reports are that people in his presidential administration do this same thing through Donald and Ivana's daughter, Ivanka.) Sometimes I'd go to Ivana and ask her to bring up to him something that I needed. Other times I would soften Donald up by complimenting her beauty. Then I would raise my difficult situation, especially if I was going to complain about her interference. "I was just talking to Ivana," I'd say. "By the way, she looks stunning today, and she said . . ."

Though a grown man, Trump was still somewhat afraid of his father, who continued to have a major influence on him when we started work on Trump Tower. Fred supplied financing for Trump Tower and, more important, the connections he had accrued from forty years in the construction business. Fred Trump was a character out of a Damon Runyon story, a guy who tooled around in a brown Cadillac limousine with vanity plates (FCT), sported a brown logo on his business card, and used brown ink in his type-writers and plenty of brown dye in his gray hair. He was seventy-five when I met him and not active in building anymore, but he was as full of piss and vinegar as his son. Fred was a man holding on for dear life to the world of the past, even as everything was passing him by.

Fred hated me. It wasn't personal; I was a woman with power in a field where women had had none. When Donald hired me to run construction on Trump Tower, Fred was beside himself. During his brief stint on the project, Trump's father did everything he could to make my life hell. I would complain to Donald and he would tell me to "suck it up," in a tone that let me know he understood but wasn't going to intervene. "Just go with it," he'd say, shaking his head. Donald had offered me $55,000 a year, but he told me he was going to pay me $49,000 in salary and $6,000 for expenses. The reason for this complicated arrangement was Fred. The highest-paid person at the Trump Organization, the comptroller, made $50,000, and Donald knew his father would not stand for a woman making more than him.

Fred called me constantly on the phone, usually to complain about something he knew nothing about and to suggest a terrible solution. I didn't care how successful he had been in the low-rise residential world twenty years earlier; the construction of Trump Tower was many orders of magnitude beyond his scope. Yet he forced his way into negotiations with the concrete contractors, against HRH's and my objections, and even insisted we use one of his 1950s contracts. I politely told him that HRH's lawyers had a boilerplate contract that they adapted individually to each subcontractor. "You don't know what you're doing!" he screamed.

"You don't know what you're talking about!" Though it got on my nerves, I grew used to this kind of outburst and disrespect from him. In an effort to look like he was still in charge, Fred also insisted on being at the contract award meeting. To put forth the image of a big shot, he liked to walk around and pass out silver dollars to people. Years earlier he had bought a few thousand silver dollars from the 1880s, an investment that didn't pan out, and he liked to give them out as gifts. The aged pied piper with silver dollars; it was sad to watch.

Fred left soon after that, although he continued to insert himself every so often. I can still hear the loud, grating sound of his voice: "Nah, nah, nah, you don't know what you're doing!" Fighting me was really his way of battling his own irrelevance. On rare occasions after Trump Tower was built, I would see the senior Trumps and I would talk to Mary, Donald's mother, who always liked me. I'd tell her how great Donald was, how Trump Tower was coming along, and what celebrities were buying apartments there. I also worked with her on the decoration of their apartment in Trump Tower, which Donald claimed to have given them as a gift. We got along, and she seemed tickled that I was a woman in a "man's job"; I'd heard that in the old days she used to drive around in the Cadillac and collect coins from the machines at Fred's Laundromats.

At Donald's wedding to Marla Maples in 1993, I went over to Mary and Fred to congratulate them. Mary was very sweet, and happy to see me. Fred, still with the brown hair at eighty-eight, said, "I know I gave you a very hard time." I couldn't really protest—we both knew it was true. Then he continued, "I didn't give you a chance. But you did a very good job. Donald said you were great." I was gracious; there was no reason not to be. But it felt more like he was acknowledging his son's wisdom in choosing me rather than the skill I brought to the job.

I think that neither father nor son really understood what being an effective leader entailed. Once I complained about a man Trump had hired to manage the retail part of the building, telling him that the man was strongly disliked. "There you go again, Barbara," Donald said. "That's your problem: You care too much about being liked." If being a "killer," as his father had taught him, was the ultimate praise from Donald, then this was the ultimate criticism.

"You know what's wrong with you, Barbara?" Trump said to me close to the completion of Trump Tower. "You want people to like you."

"Yeah," I said to him, "I do. You know why? How the hell do you think we got this place opened in time?"

Through the years, we would have this argument many times.

Trump Tower would never have been finished as quickly as it was if the workers had hated me. You cannot get that kind of dedication and sacrifice from people who don't like and respect their leader. We had planned to have Trump Tower's grand opening party on Valentine's Day, 1983. Three days earlier, the building was not even close to being ready and we got hit with one of the worst snowstorms to ever hit New York. It seemed impossible, but we got it done.

"How did that happen, Donald?" I asked. "You think it was magic? No, it was because people liked me and respected me." They were willing to work around the clock, make runs to New Jersey to buy carpeting, carry racks of clothing through the streets, do each other's work without union shutdowns, stay in the city and work through the weekend. Everyone on the job pulled together. That's how far "like" goes on a job, but Trump never got it. He still doesn't get it. He thinks it's all about fear.

The grand opening that February—which was actually just the opening of the first three floors of Trump Tower—was really a reveal of the atrium. When finished, it would be six stories of polished bronze escalators with glass railings and mirrored balustrades, an eighty-foot waterfall, and fifteen thousand square feet of Breccia Pernice marble we found from northern Italy. The architects wanted granite, which is more practical, but Trump wanted the drama of marble. The marble we chose had this gorgeous coral-and-pink hue, and I traveled with Ivana and the design architect, John Barie, to Italy to approve it. They had big slabs of our marble ready to view at the fabrication facility in Carrera. Ivana walked up to the marble slab and pointed to a small portion of it, saying, "I want it all to be like this."

Barie and I exchanged a look, letting the Italian factory owner politely correct her. "Oh no, sorry, Mrs. Trump, marble is not like granite," he said. "The beauty of marble is the variation of color and the size of the streaks and stones that move through it. What we have here is one of the most beautiful and elegant marbles anywhere in the world." I think Ivana got the point. When we were doing the floors and waterwall in the atrium, I got nervous because the marble came out so inconsistent—veins in one place and blocks in another—that it started to look visibly different, but Trump loved it.

The landscaping in the atrium was gorgeous as well, though it was far less than originally intended. Almost two years before we would need them, the landscape architect selected five young ficus trees for the atrium and three for the entry that were nurtured in a nursery in Florida. A few months prior to the opening, when it came time to bring the trees to Trump Tower, it was a big ordeal. We had to transport the trees in heated trucks and then get them into the building through heated tunnels we constructed from the street. We worked through the weekend, and then on Monday, Donald came to look. He was apoplectic. Standing on the balcony overlooking the atrium, he could see nothing but millions of leaves. "I can't see a fucking thing!" he said, his voice echoing through the atrium. "Cut them down!"

Everyone was stunned. Two of the architects were there, as well as the landscape architect, the project manager and the superintendent from HRH, me, and my assistant. We all looked at each other's blank faces, stunned by the reaction. "Cut them down!" he repeated. The superintendent sent his labor foreman to get a chainsaw. One by one, we watched those magnificent trees come down. After each one met its demise, the architects would beg and plead with Donald to save the rest. Trump just ignored them. Finally, there was only one tree left. You could see most of the atrium now, and we were all begging him to leave it. "Donald, it's one tree," I said. "Just leave the last one."

"No, no, no," Trump said. "Take it down. Get rid of it!" It was hard to watch that last one go—we had nurtured and invested in those trees. But he was right. People were supposed to be able to look down from the railings on all the retail floors and see the activity below. We had to kill the trees to save the atrium.

The atrium looked fantastic for the party, and the *New York Times* would write it "may well be the most pleasant interior public space to be completed in New York in some years." But in order to open in time, that atrium had to be put together with spit and glue. We turned on the waterfall for the first time only while Trump was speaking, because we were worried about the temporary fixes keeping the stones in place. I had two guys with walkie-talkies preparing to shut it off the second Donald stopped speaking. During Trump's speech, he feted me and other figures who had helped to construct his crown jewel. "Don't I have the best people?" he said, which is Donald's way of complimenting while still keeping the spotlight on himself. It was a short speech, and I don't think anyone else got a chance to talk, but we were relieved since we didn't know how long the waterfall could run without a stone or two falling down.

The party was a catered affair with important guests—celebrities and political figures. Donald introduced me to plenty of people that day—it was a rush of names and faces that didn't really stick. A chocolatier, one of our new retail tenants, made chocolate hearts wrapped in red and gold foil; there were bowls of them all over the atrium. My personal assistant, Roberta Bryant (Kalan), helped to oversee the execution—everything from the balloons to the invitations to the coordination of the retailers and the workers—and was indispensable to the whole project. Even though we had a few months until we opened the whole tower, I basked in the moment, taking it all in.

The Trump Tower atrium would go on to be a public space because Donald secured a zoning bonus for it. A zoning bonus gives a developer the ability to build more square footage than the law allows by providing amenities such as a plaza, a through-block arcade (a path through the building that connects two streets), improvements to subways and theaters, public art, and/ or, most significant, affordable housing. The amenity is often a one-time cost, but the extra buildable area can produce income for the life of the building. A concession Trump made to the city to get the zoning bonus was to create a path from Fifth Avenue to Madison Avenue and keep it open. He put a marble bench in the atrium across from the elevators alongside a musician at a grand piano, so people could sit and listen to the music. But in 1980s New York, guess who sat there? All this glass and marble in the ultimate tower of opulence, a tuxedoed musician playing show tunes on this $50,000 piano, and the city's homeless passing the day on the bench. So Trump covered the bench with potted plants. The city would make us remove the plants, and we had a standing direction from Trump to put them back as soon as the inspectors were gone. To get his zoning bonus, the city required him to leave the atrium open to the public until ten p.m., but he would close it and rent it out for private parties. Donald eventually ditched the piano player, which was costing a small fortune anyway, and ultimately the piano itself.

For a short time, Donald did manage to make Trump Tower the most important building in the world. It was on the cover of Paris *Vogue*, was featured in countless U.S. and European newspapers and magazines, and immediately became a tourist attraction. Trump Tower made Donald a celebrity. It was the big bang that led to everything else, his first real taste of publicity and fame, and he absolutely became obsessed with it. I honestly believe it was the beginning of the end of the person I once knew.

But I still mourn that man, the one who had his moments. Back when we were still in the Crown Building, in the wintertime, one of the women who worked in our office wore a beautiful dark brown mink coat, which we all admired. Around Christmas one year she told us she was selling it. The walk from the reception area to Donald's office was a corridor created by two parallel rows of desks occupied by secretaries and assistants. That day it became a runway for mink models. Donald was not in the office at the time, and all the women in the office were trying on the coat, just for fun, and so I did as well. And while I was strutting down the corridor in the mink, Trump walked in. The minute he appeared, everyone quickly scurried back to their desks—except me.

"What's going on here?" he asked.

I was standing alone. "Myrna is selling her mink coat," I said. "What do you think?"

He took a beat and looked at it. "Do you like it?"

"Sure," I said.

He thought about it. "How much?" he asked.

"A thousand dollars."

"Buy it," Donald said. "I'll pay for it."

And sure enough, he did. I wore that coat for years and loved it. Then I remodeled it into a shorter jacket I paired with jeans until everyone stopped wearing furs. Though I never wore it again, I still have the jacket squirreled away in a corner of my closet, not wanting to get rid of it. Maybe for sentimental reasons.

In the old days Donald would have these moments of humanity, which stand out now because they seem so rare. He always welcomed visitors I brought to meet him: my father, my high school chemistry teacher, my cousin. He'd give them his time and attention, if briefly, and it meant a lot to them and me. Most touchingly, Donald actually came to the funeral home when my brother died.

I had only been working for him for less than a year, and it was a gesture he didn't have to make at all. My relatives still talk about his doing that.

———————————

ONCE EVERYTHING BUT the office space was completed on Trump Tower, I left Trump for two years to work on another project, an office building that became the New York headquarters for Hartz Mountain. When I returned to the Trump Organization as an executive vice president in 1987, Donald was a very different man. The celebrity that began with Trump Tower grew like weeds in an untended garden. He "saved" Wollman Rink, the ice-skating rink in Central Park, launched his Atlantic City empire, and began creating and selling the Trump brand. In my mind, one of the turning points in Donald's persona was the enormous party he had to launch his first book, *The Art of the Deal*, around Christmas 1987. I marveled at the two thousand people who packed into the atrium. They paraded about in their tuxedos and haute couture gowns, while I tried to blend in with my black two-piece Dior knockoff. As they walked by the violin players and beneath the champagne flutes held high, everyone paid their respects to Donald and Ivana as though they were king and queen.

I never saw so much finery in one place, so many designer gowns, such exotic fur, so many jewels sparkling in the lights. Among the crowd were big names like Michael Douglas and Norman Mailer and Barbara Walters. Hanging from the rafters was a ten-foot blowup of the book's cover, Donald posing in front of that familiar office window, his name bigger than the title, his face the largest thing in that room. I remember Donald walking, almost prancing, arm in arm with Don King (who arrived in a long mink coat) from the front entrance of Trump Tower to the back and again to the front, as though they were parading themselves, Trump's blond swoop and King's gray explosion of hair popping up amid the sea of guests.

When Donald spoke to the crowd, the voices stopped, heads turned to look down over the second-floor railing, all eyes on him. That evening validated Trump's opinion about himself—a man worthy of such feting, an ultimately superior person. Then the book became a bestseller, which launched Trump into a new level of celebrity, a place where the air was different, where breathing it changed him.

Soon thereafter, he bought the Plaza Hotel, the Eastern Air Lines Shuttle (briefly the Trump Shuttle), and the enormous yacht. Then a very public affair with Marla Maples and a divorce from Ivana, which was front-page news. During this period, Trump didn't seem focused on work at all. He bragged about women, was unnecessarily cruel to people, and acted as though he was more important than the rest of us.

Looking back, I can see the buds so clearly, the signs of the person he'd one day become. In the years since, through bankruptcies, rising and falling celebrity, years as a punch line and parody, television shows, the birther conspiracy, his candidacy, and his presidency, he's only become more so. There's a clear line from the man back then to the man today. Trump's behavior over this time can be reduced to a simple set of rules, guiding principles, that enable us to understand how and why he is what he is.

TWO

A PARADE OF YES-MEN (AND WOMEN)

Rule: Donald Trump has created a world around himself populated by people who agree with him, will do what he says, and constantly reinforce and validate him.

This is the first rule because it is the one that allows for all the others. If no one ever says no to you, and you get rid of those who will, then you never learn anything and you never change. Your understanding of reality is slanted toward a version that makes you look good, popular, and correct. Donald J. Trump is the very embodiment of this rule. The characteristics we see in him today were there back when I first started, but they were counterbalanced by competent people with dignity and integrity who reined him in. I know because I was one of them. While his power and celebrity grew, those tempering influences slowly dissipated as these people were terminated by Donald or just quit. After thirty plus years of this, Trumpworld is now a place that has been completely eradicated—almost fumigated—of any tempering influences, a place that does little but serve his worst impulses. It is a kingdom designed to protect arguably the world's oldest, most narcissistic child.

The process happened gradually, but I know when I first noticed it. After two years away from the Trump Organization, I returned in 1987 to a new Donald and a new power dynamic in the office. I learned quickly that people didn't talk back to him anymore. Though I still did it, I got the feeling that my outspokenness had been grandfathered in. He had always been the boss, but now there was an unmistakable distance between him and the rest of us. He had Norma Foerderer, his executive assistant and gatekeeper, and then she brought in her own gatekeepers. Over time the number of yes-men just grew from there, like weeds.

In the years since, he has continually built and perfected this environment that rewards the worst and punishes the best, a kind of reverse natural selection that has left him with the dregs. Those who remain—in business and in government—aren't strong enough to challenge him, smart enough to correct him, or self-respecting enough to quit. They have one nonnegotiable quality: They say yes to the boss.

Donald used to hire the best, listen to their advice (even if he didn't always follow it), and let them do their thing. It was an integral part of his early success. Those days are long gone, and I think the change happened for two reasons. The first is obvious: It's just easier for him. He gets his way more often and, as with a child, this is ultimately his goal. The second reason is more complicated, but it basically boils down to this: The charade of "Donald Trump" became so elaborate that he fell for it himself. In selling the idea that he was a brilliant and self-made man, he consumed his own hype, gorged himself on it so completely that he has forgotten it wasn't true.

What actually got him to the top? Quality people.

Donald's contributions were mostly in the public relations department, and he indeed has a gift for that. But selling something and making something are not the same thing. For all his "I alone can fix it" bluster, there's not a single positive thing he's ever done on his own. From his father to HRH, from *Apprentice* creator Mark Burnett to chief strategist Steve Bannon, to plenty of less-famous names in between (including Louise Sunshine and me on Trump Tower, Harvey Freeman and Steve Hyde in Atlantic City), there were always more competent or experienced people around.

If you follow the progression of his early ups and his later downs (casino failures, multiple bankruptcies, Trump Ice, Trump Steaks, Trump Shuttle, Trump Vodka, etc.), the pattern becomes clear. His failures came out of his penchant for "following his gut," insisting and believing that he knew better than anyone. His past successes were ultimately tied to listening to people who knew what they were doing.

When we first moved into Trump Tower in 1983, there were eight or nine of us with offices on the twenty-sixth floor. Sometimes Donald would wander the halls to see what people were up to and pop his head into their offices. As a boss, he was totally approachable and accessible, with an office door that was often open. Even when it was closed, you could just knock and walk in. He had a speakerphone on his desk; he'd press the button, a voice would come over, and he'd just start talking immediately. Whoever was in the room would hear the conversation, and it went on like that all day.

For meetings in Donald's office we'd be arranged around his giant rosewood desk, some sitting in these tacky silver-toned bucket chairs upholstered in maroon, some people standing. Norma would enter and drop items in his inbox, which he would peek at, often rip up, and then drop on the floor. There were sticky notes attached to various stacks of paper, some sketches, and an array of newspapers and magazines, usually with items about himself that he wanted everyone to see. In eighteen years I never once saw a book in his office that didn't have his name on the cover.

A Yale-educated lawyer, Susan Heilbron, would walk into his office every hour or so, without a word, and hand him little yellow slips of paper with stock quotes. I thought he had turned this savvy and intelligent woman into his errand girl, but I soon realized it was the opposite. Susan, a financial wizard, was on top of his investments and knew exactly what to look for and what to bring him. Importantly, she also understood how to handle him without constantly acquiescing, and it was obvious he valued her. Again, the best people.

What he began to assemble at the Trump Organization, beginning in the late 1980s, was a meek staff afraid to anger the beast, lest they get thrown overboard and lose their cushy perches. Though there had been plenty of smart, competent people in the early days of his business, just as there were in the early days of his presidency, those people disappeared once they spoke their minds. "Everybody is too scared of their own shadow to speak the truth," a senior official recently told the *Washington Post*. The line referred to the coronavirus pandemic, but it really could apply to anything in Trump's universe.

Of course, there are far more people in Trump's orbit now than there were back then, but it doesn't follow that he's getting better feedback. Quantity isn't quality. Sometimes it's its opposite. Having more gatekeepers doesn't provide more protection from Trump's worst instincts; it just makes it easier for everyone to hide. No one wants to play the gatekeeper role or tell him what they really think. Anyone who tries to corral him—like Chiefs of Staff Reince Priebus or John Kelly, National Security Adviser John Bolton, or Defense Secretary James Mattis—gets eaten alive. So to survive, people give in. The number of people who have traded in basic principles of decency and honesty to please Trump is simply astounding.

When his poll numbers against Biden were looking bleak, Trump threw a tantrum and berated his polling people and his campaign manager, Brad Parscale. Guess what happened: They came back with "better" polls that told him what he wanted to hear. Not more accurate polls, just polls that pleased Trump and saved the pollsters' jobs. He would eventually replace the pollsters altogether with those who regularly brought him "better" polls. This dynamic runs up and down Donald's business, his administration, and his family. One can imagine the damage caused by any institution geared this way.

The culture of yes-men is so embedded in Donald's world that it even infects his doctors, who are supposed to be answerable to a higher ethic. Both his personal physicians and White House doctors seem to be there just to serve him. Trump's former personal physician, the wild-eyed Harold Bornstein, declared Trump would be "the healthiest individual ever elected to the presidency," in a statement that he later admitted Trump had dictated. In 2018 rear admiral and physician to the president Ronny Jackson gave a fawning report on the then seventy-one-year-old obese, nonexercising, junk-food-eating president's health. Dr. Jackson spoke repeatedly of how "excellent" Trump's health was, how if he had eaten better over the last twenty years he could have hoped to live to two hundred because "he has incredibly good genes, and it's just the way God made him."

In my opinion, Jackson's assessment has Trump's fingerprints all over it, with the reference to living to two hundred and his genes. That Aryan-style language is pure Donald: What does his doctor know about his ancestors' health? But physicians, like everyone else, seem to have fallen prey to his demands, because they know that without yessing Trump, they, too, will be cast out. Jackson clearly understood the game. Soon after, he got nominated to a high position in the Veterans Affairs department for which he was totally unqualified, but he had to withdraw due to substantive allegations of personal misconduct as White House physician (some of which he has denied). Now he is the Republican nominee for a seat in Congress.

There was a time when it was possible to speak a semblance of truth to Donald. Though he usually thought he was right, if you were skillful enough, you could side door your advice and backdoor your suggestions in a way that would get through to him. One particularly effective tactic to get him to accept your ideas was to trick him into thinking they were his own. If I had to reject one of Trump's ridiculous proposals, I would reframe what he suggested in such a way that it actually said what I wanted it to. Then I would thank him for being so creative or helping me understand the situation. He didn't have a grasp of details, so I could easily switch around who said what and he would fall for it. Or I would just nod at his ridiculous ideas and then let them wither and die. I would say I was going to follow through on something, then just hope he'd forget all about it.* Fortunately, he forgot quite frequently. But it was a constant dance. Sometimes I relished the challenge; other days I got home and collapsed from the exhaustion.

I remember a blowup he had over the atrium's columns in Trump Tower. When we started cladding the columns with marble, you could tell that the stone was only three-quarters of an inch thick. Where the slabs met at the corners, it was obvious, and when Trump saw them, he turned bright red. "They ruin the whole atrium!" he screamed at John Barie, the design architect. Barie was a handsome man in his late thirties, balding, who came to work so elegantly dressed, his overcoat slung over his shoulders like a cape, that I called him "the gentleman architect." Toward the end of the job, it looked like the power had gone to Barie's head, but he still didn't want to talk back to Donald.

"They look like shit!" Donald yelled. "They ruin the atrium and they make me look cheap!"

Since I was there, in the line of fire, and Barie had gone mute, I spoke up. "Wait, wait, Donald, that's bullshit," I said. "You knew all about the thickness of the marble. We had a bunch of conversations with the architect and the contractor about it."

---

* Bob Woodward, as well as Philip Rucker and Carol Leonnig, reported that National Economic Council Director Gary Cohn and White House Staff Secretary Rob Porter both would do this at the White House. Each lasted about a year.

He waved me off with one hand, reminding me of Fred. "No, no, no, Barbara," he said. "I never would've—"

"Yes, you did," I said, talking over him, not angry but firm. "Now that you're seeing it, you're changing your mind. But anyway, it actually looks beautiful."

Trump wouldn't budge and insisted on changing the columns. "No, no. It makes me look cheap and it's your fault," he said. It was unclear if he was talking to Barie or me. It didn't really matter as long as it wasn't his own fault. Donald regularly rewrote history, pretending he hadn't agreed to something he had or vice versa.

"Wait, wait, I got it," he said. "It's brilliant. Listen to this: We cover the corners in bronze!" Silence. Even someone who hadn't spent a day in construction or design would know this was dumb. Barie and I yessed him, hoping to just move on. I was assigned the task, so I pretended to go along, giving a sketch of what Donald wanted to the bronze guy to price. Then I let the subject drift into the ether, until eventually he just dropped it, never mentioning it again. Ironically, the *New York Times* architectural critic would specifically praise the rounded marble corners, calling them "absolutely sensuous."

There were a number of us on staff back then who would regularly engage in what I called "civil disobedience," yessing Donald's harebrained ideas or outrageous demands but not following through on them. In the late 1980s, on the renovation of the Plaza, which I oversaw, the architects designed the two bathrooms off the main ballrooms with one handicapped stall each. It was not the law yet, but we knew it would be soon in New York City, and it would've been a pain to retrofit later. When Trump saw the design plans, he freaked out, ranting and raving and refusing to do it. "No handicapped stalls, period!" he said. We just ignored him. Later, we figured out how to convert a nearby unused closet space into a single unisex handicapped toilet. Then we sold it to Donald as his idea and he was on board.

Things like that happened all the time. I remember a meeting with Donald, me, and one of the architects to talk about the elevators in Trump Tower. We were looking at the sketches, and when Trump noticed that there were little dots under the numbers on the drawing of the control panel, he pointed to them and asked, "What's that?"

"That's Braille," the architect said.

"What? *Braille*?" he said like it was obscene. "We don't need that. Get rid of it."

The architect took a breath and then looked over at me, trying to catch my eyes. "Uh, we have to do that," he said, scared to poke the beast.

"It's the law, Donald," I said. "We have to." I'd been through this enough times. I knew he wouldn't care, as they were just details to him.

"Forget it," Trump said. "No blind people are going to live in this building." He would say outrageous things like this as fact, and I knew to ignore him. So we dropped the subject, Trump walked away, and I told the architect to just disregard him.

The strange thing is that I think Donald knew we had to put Braille in the elevator cabs, just like he knew we'd eventually need handicapped stalls. He would just say whatever came into his head, ordering an underling to do something that was unlawful, wrong, or impossible. I think it gave him another opportunity to belittle or blame. These mental games, throwing out legal or illegal suggestions, practical or impractical ideas, were just one of the many ways for Trump to exert his power or amuse himself. Sometimes I just did what he asked, planning for the necessary fix or damage control later. But many times the easiest path was for me to play along with him and just not carry out his order, trusting he would forget about it entirely.

The problem at the Trump Organization was that it reached a point where there were many people around who *would* do anything Donald said. Sal was a handsome guy Trump had hired from Bonwit Teller, the luxury department store that was demolished to make room for Trump Tower. He was one of the many people Trump accumulated along the way, because of either their look or their ass-kissing potential. Though I was probably protected from Trump's worst schemes because he knew I wouldn't do them, Sal said yes to Trump on just about anything.

Sal started as my assistant, but that lasted maybe two weeks because I couldn't really stand him. I was a professional engineer who had high expectations of anyone under me, and he was a high school graduate with no training who seemed to resent working for a woman. I soon shoved him off, and he ended up working on a job on the Upper East Side, an apartment building to be called Trump Plaza.* My new assistant, who was involved in the project, came to tell me that Trump had been pushing Sal to start demolition on the old brownstones without a permit. When Sal tried to explain what they were waiting for, Trump pushed back. "You don't need a permit, Sal. The buildings are empty, right? Just do it."

---

* Not to be confused with the one in Atlantic City. For all of Trump's confidence in his naming abilities, his choices were pretty narrow.

Just to emphasize, demolishing without a permit is as dangerous as it is illegal. The buildings were empty of tenants though there was still a cat there. When I talked to my assistant later that day, he said he thought Sal was going to go ahead with the demo, more scared of Trump's wrath than of any real-world consequences. I was ready to step in when, fortunately, they discovered a gas line that had not been properly disconnected; even Trump knew not to disturb an active gas line. It was a close call but just shows how much damage Trump could do with nothing but the will and the requisite yes-men.

By the late 1980s, the organization was filled with obsequious Sals, people desperate to please him. His people would be willing to skirt the law,* hurt others, and do whatever needed to be done to get or stay in Trump's good graces. His security team was filled with guys like this. I remember an organized protester once set up a display on Fifth Avenue in front of the Trump Tower to distribute pamphlets. He had a microphone, a speaker, and clearly a permit to be there. He wasn't even protesting Trump or the building. When Trump spotted the protester outside one morning, he came upstairs and went right for his security guy. (I heard later about their exchange.)

"That guy out front with the table?" Trump said. "Get rid of him."

"Yes, sir."

"Just do what you have to do," Trump said, as though he were a mob boss.

The security guy and his partner went down to the street and moved the protester's tables over to Sixth Avenue. When the

---

* As documented in multiple legal complaints and lawsuits.

protester came back the next day, there were words between him and security, who again moved the tables one avenue over. After returning for a third day, the protester was "spoken to" and he never came back.

Trump's in-house leasing agent, a competent but relatively meek guy in his late forties named Daniel, got browbeaten by Trump constantly. "Okay, Donald," he'd say, after Trump lashed out at him. "Yes, Donald. Thank you, Donald." I had nothing against the guy—we were friends—but his acceptance of Trump's treatment made it hard to respect him. Donald harped on Daniel—mostly about an outside broker Daniel worked with, Joan, who was a superstar. While Daniel finalized all the leases for the stores in Trump Tower, Joan was the one who got out there, set up the interviews, and did the legwork to get these high-end retailers into Trump Tower: Cartier, Harry Winston, Charles Jourdan. Like an obnoxious coach, Trump would constantly berate Daniel about how Joan was outshining him, doing all the work, making him look bad. Daniel would never argue, never explain that he did plenty finalizing all the leases. He just took it: "Okay, Donald," he'd say. "You're right, Donald." Trump loved the fact that Daniel was getting bested by a woman, which gave him so much fodder for his emasculating remarks.

There was also Mike, a lawyer who was in charge of protecting the Trump name. He was bright and nice enough; but as Trump expected, Mike took on the persona of those like Roy Cohn and Trump's future lackey, Michael Cohen. If anyone used Trump's name without permission, Mike would slap them with some kind of legal action. There were plenty of places on the roadway to Atlantic City that got caught doing this. People tried to use

Trump's name for everything, from pawnbrokers to gas stations, and Mike's job was to sniff them out. Even though he did a job that Trump absolutely required—especially since the name would become his most valuable asset—Trump walked all over Mike. If he called or came by the office, Trump treated him like an annoying pest. I watched him insult or berate Mike for any reason. Trump acted like he had no respect or time for Mike, who just took it.

The changeover in the type of people Trump hired was like a slowly gathering storm. I watched while his need to be agreed with, coddled, and praised kept growing. As the balance of power shifted from those of us who would temper Trump to those who did whatever he asked or said whatever he wanted to hear, the organization started to suffer. Enough people like that can take down a company. If the boss is not a details person—and Donald is not—it can happen without him even noticing.

To understand the kind of ass-kissing interactions that Trump eventually required, just look at his first U.S. cabinet meeting in June 2017. It was absurd; it was like a comedy sketch. In front of the press, each cabinet member around the large conference table had to fawn over Trump, pledge their undying gratitude to him, talk about how honorable it was to serve him. Each successive person was trying to outdo the last. A few, like James Mattis, took a pass, opting to praise his troops.* These were the most powerful people in the country, but their behavior reminded me of those Trump Organization flunkies: Ernie, Sal, Mike, Daniel,

---

* Anonymous notes in *A Warning* that those who did not explicitly praise Trump (opting to compliment their staffs instead) are gone now.

the security guys. Just much, much worse. I'd seen people kiss up to Trump for decades, but nothing like that cabinet meeting. I was stunned.

Later cabinet meetings and public sessions with Republican governors have followed this pattern, with leaders competing against each other to brownnose themselves into Trump's good graces. Everyone understands that our president responds to this kind of flattery and that their standing depends on their ability to practice it. Thirty years later Trump demands from people a level of sycophancy that even Sal would find unseemly.

Then there are Trump's rallies, which represent his desire for adulation in its purest form. It's why he turned rallies into a regular feature of his presidency, even when there was no campaign or election going on, even during the pandemic, when it risked people's health.* Trump's yes-men no doubt laid the groundwork for this as well. Even if some members of his circle tried to carefully discourage him from holding the rally in Tulsa this past June, at the height of the pandemic, there were plenty who agreed with him that it was a great idea. Those are the ones he listened to. It's a contest, and the most obsequious always wins. And nowadays, no one dares tell him he's wrong.

In the early days the staff included me; Louise Sunshine, a dynamo saleswoman with incredible connections; Norma, his executive assistant; and a few others who weren't afraid to stand up to him. Donald valued our opinions, and none of us were beholden to

---

* Former presidential candidate Herman Cain attended Trump's June 2020 Tulsa rally without a mask and passed away from COVID-19 a few weeks later.

him in such a blind way. Over time, those people either left when he became too much or became supplicants. By the time I left the Trump Organization in 1998, many of the people I once knew were unrecognizable, and the new ones were even worse. They had all drunk the Kool-Aid.

Trump's presidency has followed the same ass-backward Darwinism that I saw at the Trump Organization, just on a much shorter timeline. He began that first year in office, which seems like decades ago, with military generals like Secretary of Defense James Mattis, Secretary of Homeland Security John Kelly, and National Security Adviser H. R. McMaster; a Wall Street titan (economic adviser Gary Cohn); a Republican establishment guy (Chief of Staff Reince Priebus); a business giant in his own right (Secretary of State Rex Tillerson); and a media Svengali (Senior Adviser Steve Bannon). Whatever you think of them or their politics, they at least were professional and qualified. These men agreed to serve their country but didn't understand that they'd be serving Donald. I'm sure they assumed they could round Trump's rough edges and ensure that his wackiest thoughts would never get past the idea stage. They probably had no idea what they were in for.

In his first year in the White House, Trump admitted he battled with nearly all of them. "I argue with everyone," he once told a reporter. "Except Pompeo." At the time, Mike Pompeo was the CIA director who, among other things, forcefully agreed with Trump's decision to pull out of the Iran nuclear accord. It's no coincidence that Pompeo, the one who wouldn't challenge Trump, ended up as secretary of state and the second most powerful person in the administration. As for Bannon, who probably did the most in getting Trump elected, he committed the cardinal sin: getting too much credit. After Bannon landed a *Time* magazine cover, which is one of Trump's obsessions, his days were numbered.

As all of them made their way through the revolving door, it was the same pattern: The people Trump had hailed as "the best" on the way in, he called "the worst" on the way out. The only thing about them that had changed was their allegiance. That first batch didn't provide the oxygen that Trump needed—constant praise, unending reassurance, and always, always, always an exclusive place in the spotlight—so they had to go.

One of the most disconcerting examples of Trump's obsession with praise came during the first coronavirus spike in the spring of 2020. During the worst pandemic in a hundred years, in charge of a confused and scared nation, Trump admitted that he was playing favorites with the states. He said—aloud, to the public, on camera—that he wouldn't talk to governors who didn't express their appreciation of him. "I tell Mike [Pence], don't call the governor of Washington," though the state was one of the virus's epicenters at the time. "If they don't treat you right, I don't call," he said, sounding frighteningly like a mob boss. The fact that Trump said this to the American people, and didn't see anything wrong with it, proves how long he's been operating this way. Did it even occur to him that refusing to talk to or help governors of states whose citizens were dying was inhuman? According to the *New York Times*, Trump did the same thing with Governor Gavin Newsom in California, "who was told that if he wanted the federal government to help obtain the swabs needed to test for the virus, he would have to ask Mr. Trump himself—and thank him." It's what would happen if a petulant child became king.

Yes-men have to offer Trump constant praise but also share information about adulation from others. Trump has long had an obsession for collecting media about himself, so much that you could almost mistake it for his primary job. On his desk at Trump Tower he kept a stack of articles, magazine profiles, or quotes to show anyone who came through. In 1990, when his personal life and affair with Marla Maples put him on the cover of the *New York Post*, when a regular person would be horrified, Donald was elated. I had never seen him happier. The world cared about him, and that's all he really wanted.

Now that he's in the White House, Trump often carries printouts around with him, reading them aloud to people, once even hijacking a Coronavirus Task Force briefing to do so. Cliff Sims, a White House communications adviser, wrote about how he stayed in Trump's good graces by regularly passing articles to the president that praised him. The apparatus has grown substantially since his days in the tabloids. Now there are journalists—at Fox News and the *Wall Street Journal*, not to mention One America News Network (OANN), an entire network seemingly dedicated to pleasing Trump and serving the same yes-men role from the outside.

When I describe Donald's appetite for publicity as an addiction, I don't just mean it's voracious. I also mean that, like with an addict, the effects dissipate quickly so he always needs more. Donald can never get enough—hence his obsession with "ratings," which he sees as hard evidence of who is paying attention to him. This was to be expected while he was hosting and producing a television show, but for a president the obsession is just unseemly. Even during the pandemic, he latched onto the ratings of the coronavirus briefings as evidence of his popularity. These were emergency press conferences that were supposed to offer expert, informative advice, but all we got was more Donald talking about Donald. Again, I'm sure his circle of yes-men told him how great they were going, until one day, with his approval rating at rock bottom, there could be no denying what a disaster they were and they ended. Lately, in an effort to raise his poll numbers, he has started them up again.

Another effect of living within the bubble of yes-men is that Trump never gets corrected. Long-held gaps in his understanding persist because no one tells him any different. He still keeps claiming that that the flu epidemic of 1918 happened in 1917 or that he won Michigan's Man of the Year Award, which doesn't exist. This past August, when he finally got busted by CBS's Paula Reid for his oft-repeated lie that he passed a health care bill called "Veterans Choice," which Obama passed in 2014, he walked out of the press conference. Though CNN reports that he told it 150 times, I'm not even sure he knew it was a lie. Trump knows so little about his own policies that maybe he thought he passed that bill, and no one on his staff would dare correct him.

Trump's refusal to hear anything negative about himself is not just a character flaw; it has gone so far that it has serious national security implications. An August 2020 investigation in the *New York Times Magazine* by Robert Draper uncovered how America's entire intelligence apparatus has been cowed into not bringing him information about Russia's meddling efforts. This is the ultimate sore spot in his ego, because he sees any discussion of 2016 interference as "assuming you were calling his election into question," a senior adviser told Draper. Draper reports that both John Bolton, his national security adviser, and Mick Mulvaney, his acting chief of staff, did everything they could to keep information about Russian interference, both past and ongoing, away from Trump. (Both declined to comment in the article.)

This was a serious issue when it was just about understanding the past: Russia's role in the 2016 election. But with the 2020 election looming and, according to U.S. intelligence agencies and the Republican-led Senate, Russia doing it again, Trump's denial—and his insistence on others' denial—became a vastly bigger problem. Last time he was just a candidate; now he's the president, with all the power that bestows on him. Trump's previous two directors of national intelligence were relieved of their duties after saying the truth about 2016:* Russia helped Trump. It's a world of skinny mirrors where only the most flattering reflections are allowed.

Trump built his business and made his name by hiring the best and letting them do their work. When he hired "killers," he didn't punish them for going toe-to-toe with him. I truly think, though he might not have admitted it to himself, that there was a time when he wanted honest feedback, because he knew it would create the best result. Though his ego didn't love it, he understood that pressure is what makes diamonds.

Donald and I would have these epic fights over the years. He would give me a hard time, but not in front of people and never to embarrass me. I was able to put up with everything he threw at me, especially on the construction of Trump Tower. We would call each other names, but I was always a bit deferential to him. I

---

* The Republican-led Senate Intelligence Committee released a report in August 2020 confirming Russia's involvement on Trump's behalf and offering even more details on how involved Trump's campaign was in the meddling.

had to be, but not so much that I wouldn't talk back. Our disputes were often over changes he didn't want to pay for, changes he had already approved.

"No fucking way I'm paying for this," he'd say.

"You *wanted* the change," I'd say. "Ivana wanted the change. They did it and now you have to pay them."

"I'm not—"

"I negotiated these numbers in good faith," I'd explain. "There's no way in hell I'm going back there and telling them you're not paying for something you ordered and I got them to cut their price for. I gave my word and I am not going back on it." I always got my way in the end. I may have been a killer, but I was always fair and honest; no subs got screwed on any of my jobs.[*]

On Trump Tower, one of our main points of contention was Verina Hixon, an eccentric friend of Ivana's from Texas. Verina was a character, a stylish blonde with a bright smile and piercing eyes. She stood out from other Trump Tower residents, coming across as something of a huckster. She bought three apartments underneath Trump's triplex and combined them, even putting a swimming pool in one. At first, Trump told me to give Verina "anything she wants." When I argued with her over additions or changes, Donald would always take her side. Her close friend John Cody was very high up in the Teamsters Union. Cody was extremely connected and could stop a construction job cold if he wanted. So he (and Verina) had sway with Trump, but Trump was conflicted: He hated anyone who had power over him. Later, she wouldn't pay for alterations we

---

[*] As much as I like to think it was solely my influence that kept Trump honest, on Trump Tower he had Equitable as a partner, and they would not have taken kindly to screwing people.

made, and I got caught in the middle.* Her demands and changes got to be too much, even for Donald, and the two started to go at it. She flooded her bathrooms and would call him "Donald Duck," which got under his skin. Eventually Donald reached his breaking point and said no to Verina. The next thing you know, Cody stopped all the concrete on HRH's projects. Once we made a deal with Verina, things went back to normal.

Late one afternoon Trump and I were having a dispute about work he owed Verina that he was refusing to do. I dug in to take him on. Out of nowhere, he asked flatly, like he was asking the time, "What's she paying you for this, Barbara?" Donald knew full well that I would never take anything, but he also knew that the accusation would make me crazy. He was just angry and needed to take it out on someone.

"What the hell is that supposed to mean?" I asked. I was incensed and lit into him. "You're the one who made the deal with her, and now you want to get out of it. You made a shit deal, Donald, and now you're stuck. Don't blame your fuckups on me."

"Bullshit," he said, waving me off. "It's not only Hixon, it's everything. You are costing me millions of dollars because you are letting the subs shit all over you!"

"That's bullshit and you know it. You've been changing your mind and moving things around constantly. You're driving the architects and everyone crazy with your stupid ideas. If I didn't control you and your wife, this building would be a year behind." I could see he was turning red. "We have all been breaking our

---

* Trump sued Verina for nonpayment on alterations and maintenance items, and Hixon countersued. The claims were eventually settled by the parties.

asses for you, especially me, and this is what I get? I don't need this shit. Fuck it!"

I turned around to leave, shaking. Donald was saying something as I stormed out, but I didn't hear him. I just wanted to get my car and go home.

Driving home on the East River Drive, I couldn't think straight. In my life, I never took a cent from anyone, though I had plenty of opportunity. To be accused of being dishonest, by Donald, cut me deep. He knew better than to question my honesty. The combination of that and being blamed for Trump's choices and mistakes had me horribly riled up. All of a sudden, I smashed into a granite curb, blowing out two tires. I was stranded on the shoulder of the East River Drive until my husband arrived and a Good Samaritan helped us replace the tires.

The next morning, I was ashamed of the way I had acted; I'd just gotten carried away and totally lost it on my boss. When my head was clearer and I realized what I'd said to my boss, I thought I should speak to him. I went into Trump's office. "Donald, I'm sorry," I said. "I was out of line."

"I was too," he said.

Though he rarely apologizes, if ever, that day—to me—he did. The American people have never once seen him do it. I seriously doubt he apologizes to anyone anymore, even in private; he doesn't respect anyone enough to do so.

Today, whether it's his West Wing staff, his cabinet (especially Attorney General Bill Barr), his administration, the Republican leadership, they all just do his bidding. Everyone tells him what he wants to hear and keeps silent about what he doesn't. With very few exceptions, they have turned into an army of Ernies, the meek owner's rep from the Hyatt days, cowering in the corner, afraid to hurt Donald's fragile ego or trigger his wrath.

Yes-men will never betray him. They will remain loyal, no matter how disloyal Trump himself proves to be. Donald's cousin John Walter told me that Fred said if an employee isn't trying to steal from you, he's stupid. I have no doubt Donald took that advice to heart. But this creates a strange conundrum for him. The only people he can trust—by his own criteria—are dumb. So he doesn't respect them.

Another way he keeps control over his people is by keeping them powerless. Trump likes putting people into positions for which they are not suited so they will not advocate too strongly or stand up against him. In his cabinet he has Betsy DeVos as secretary of education, who worked in charter schools and didn't even know what IDEA* was; Rick Perry, who advocated for the abolishment of the energy department as secretary of energy; and Ben Carson, a surgeon with no experience in housing, to run Housing and Urban Development. There were rumors he was going to pick Newt Gingrich or Chris Christie for VP, but they clearly had too much independence for him. So he ended up with Mike Pence, the most servile and spineless pick he could find. This is someone whose poll numbers were in the toilet, who was on the verge of being voted out as governor of Indiana, who would owe Trump everything and ask for nothing. Trump knows never to put someone second in command who would benefit from his fall. He never had to worry about Pence, but for insurance, he made his VP head of the wholly

---

* Individuals with Disabilities Education Act

ineffective Coronavirus Task Force. The very fact that he put a politician, and the vice president no less, at the head of it tells you how effective it was supposed to be. Now Pence has no choice but to go down with the ship.

He also controls his people by installing them in their positions on an "acting" basis. This is not just a few middle managers in the government but top people like the secretaries of defense, labor, interior, and homeland security, and dozens of others who were all at one point on an acting basis. He's on record saying "I like 'acting' because I can move so quickly. It gives me more flexibility." But in what way? In being able to fire people? It's a psychological tactic. It gives him more power over them, keeps them on their toes, and makes them less likely to challenge him. He hires people based on their potential to be yes-men and then cultivates an environment to make sure they stay that way.

During my days with him, Trump benefited from independent-minded people, but he couldn't bring himself to fully trust them. Harvey Freeman, an attorney out of Columbia Law School who worked on acquisitions and gaming permits, was the executive vice president who ran most of Trump's casino empire. Harvey was Donald's eyes and ears in Atlantic City, but he was over a hundred miles away and thus given a degree of freedom. Attractive and smart, Harvey had the education Donald didn't have and an even temper that made him impossible to needle. He was clearly a threat to Trump, so Donald installed his brother Robert in Atlantic City, and it seemed to me his only role was to keep a check on Harvey.*

---

* Later, he did the same thing for Steve Hyde, a professional casino manager Trump brought in from Vegas.

Placing Robert out there backfired when he and Harvey became like two peas in a pod. Trump could not divide as he loves to do, so he would just beat up on Robert.

When you look at Trump's campaign hires, his cabinet appointments, and his West Wing staff, the pattern becomes undeniable: He values loyalty over talent, sycophancy over independence. Family members are the ultimate yes-men because they're loyal by blood. That is the source of the power of Ivanka and her husband, Jared Kushner. The thirty-nine-year-old son of a real estate scion and convicted felon, who is not particularly bright or charismatic, Kushner has the thickest portfolio in the White House, from criminal justice reform to Middle East peace to PPE distribution during the pandemic. Though he is too dumb to know that he doesn't have the power to postpone an election, he is useful because his loyalty will always be to Trump.

I don't see any mystery behind Trump's fondness for dictators like Russia's Vladimir Putin, Kim Jong Un of North Korea, Recep Erdogan in Turkey, and Rodrigo Duterte in the Philippines, while he remains disdainful of the leaders of democratic countries, such as Germany's Angela Merkel, France's Emmanuel Macron, and Canada's Justin Trudeau. For starters, he simply admires the dictators, especially Putin, with whom he seems to have some kind of secret pact. Trump is impressed by—and envious of—the power totalitarians have over their people. In all his talk about "twelve more years," he acts like he wants to achieve that here in the U.S. With that kind of power, he could have an entire country of yes-men.

I see a clear parallel between Donald's choice of hires over the years and his choice of wives. Early on, Ivana was in the mix on all the projects; she was deferential to Donald but he was to her as well. She was not presented as a mere "trophy wife" and had real duties in his business, even an office on the twenty-sixth floor of Trump Tower. It was small, floor to ceiling pink, and right next to his. The thought of Marla or Melania having a high-ranking position in the Trump Organization, as Ivana did, is almost laughable. Ivana told Trump her opinion and, occasionally, even dared to disagree with him. Marla was a model, seventeen years Trump's junior, who made Trump feel and look virile as he was moving into midlife. She was a souvenir of his celebrity who was seemingly afraid to stand up to him. I know this because Marla once got a parking ticket in Beverly Hills and called someone in my California office in a panic, asking him to fight it on her behalf. She was afraid to put it through Trump's accountants and have Donald find out. I told my assistant to pay it, and it went away. If a wife can't share a parking ticket with her husband, there's an obvious power imbalance in the marriage. As for Melania, he used to refer to her in public as "my supermodel," which tells you everything you need to know.

Without deference Trump cannot function. Reports from inside the White House are that his staff is now tasked with bringing him any positive news or sound bite about the coronavirus and his response to it. This strategy explains a great deal about how the battle against the pandemic is playing out in the White House. In August, Dr. Stephen Hahn, the FDA commissioner, got grilled on CNN for not refuting Trump's claim that COVID-19 is "99 percent harmless," a factually untrue statement that he certainly should have known to be untrue. "I'm not going to get into who is right and who is wrong," Hahn said. No doubt people will listen to him and go about their normal lives, falsely believing COVID-19 is not a threat, which is behavior that spreads the virus. This is what Donald's need for yes-men has come to: Better that Americans die than contradict Donald.

A few months ago Donald claimed that even the doctors were in awe of his intelligence about diseases and health science. "Every one of these doctors said, 'How do you know so much about this?' Maybe I have a natural ability. Maybe I should have done that instead of running for president." This from a man who openly suggested that we inject disinfectant into our bodies to cure the virus, while no one on the podium contradicted him. Only someone surrounded by grovelers could be so mistaken about his own intelligence. Which leads us to the next rule.

THREE

THE BEST WORDS

**Rule: Trump's intelligence is limited and
he is very insecure about it.**

*It would take an hour-and-a-half to learn everything there is to
learn about missiles. . . . I think I know most of it anyway.*
—DONALD TRUMP, 1984

Sound familiar? That's thirty-eight-year-old Donald
Trump, New York City real estate developer, bragging to
the *Washington Post* that President Reagan should hire him to
negotiate an arms deal with Russia. He is not joking. This is
the same man who said that the moon is part of Mars, that the
Continental Army took over the airports in the Revolutionary
War, that nineteenth-century abolitionist Frederick Douglass
has "done an amazing job and is being recognized more and
more," who didn't know England was a nuclear power, thought
Finland was part of Russia, believed "clean coal" meant coal that
you "cleaned" after taking it from the mines, said that windmills

cause cancer, suggested we nuke hurricanes, and recommended injecting disinfectant as a cure for coronavirus. It would be funny if it weren't so horrifying. No one expected Trump to be a scholar, but there have been many reports from the White House about people who were shocked at how little he knew—or cared to know. "This job is a lot harder than I thought it'd be," an adviser heard him say about two weeks into his presidency. This is a man who admits that he doesn't read books, just "passages, I read areas, chapters, I don't have the time." Not surprisingly, but still somehow surprising, Trump gets information about his own administration's actions by watching Fox News and takes regular advice from its personalities, especially Sean Hannity.

I'm not an elitist. There are different kinds of intelligence, and you don't need to be a scholar to be a good leader. There is no denying that Trump has certain smarts; he did get himself elected president. But the confidence with which he speaks about most things out of his wheelhouse is breathtaking. John Bolton said he was "stunningly uninformed," Rex Tillerson called him "a fucking moron," and John Kelly would privately rage about what an idiot he was.* It's the mix of ignorance and brashness that makes him uniquely unqualified and uniquely dangerous. There are plenty of people less informed than Trump and others who are more arrogant and ignorant, but I can't imagine anyone on this Earth who possesses such a toxic mix of both qualities.

On election night 2016, after Trump was declared the winner, former New Jersey governor Chris Christie, one of a series of mini-Trump wannabes, went over to the president-elect to express some

---

* Kelly denied it, though tellingly, Tillerson never did.

alarm. Christie was in charge of the transition, and he knew they were nowhere near ready to take office on January 20. "Chris," Trump said, "you and I are so smart that we can leave the victory party two hours early and do the transition ourselves." The next day, he would get rid of the entire transition team altogether, including Christie.

Trump was obviously in over his head. His solution: Get to work? Learn about the world's most complex job? Not quite. Anyone who was surprised that Trump didn't insist on a crash course in civics, in policy, in international affairs, in even the basics of the Constitution or government, clearly doesn't know the guy. I do know him, and I know that he simply doesn't have the patience to learn about anything this complex. This is not even a slight; it's just a fact. Rather than learning, he just says what he thinks will fly, fully expecting to be believed. When he isn't, he has developed an alternative method to get by. It's called denigrate and pretend. Denigrate the opposition and pretend that he knows what they don't, that he has a better idea, that things are going well when they're not.

This is Trump's approach to just about everything, and depending on how you keep score, it's worked out pretty well for him. Rather than fill or admit gaps, he *leans* into them—refuses to learn, almost willfully so, then lies about what he knows or what is true. I know one major reason he hasn't bothered to learn is that—from my experience—he has the attention span of an overly distracted child. Perhaps the most chilling example of this is how Trump has lost interest in saving the lives of the people from the ravages of COVID-19. According to David Carney, a Republican adviser to Texas governor Greg Abbott, a full-throated Trump supporter,

"The president got bored with it." *Bored* with the pandemic that has already killed more than 200,000 Americans.

In a recent CNN interview about whether or not the government should institute a national mask requirement, Dr. Jonathan Reiner, a DC cardiologist, reiterated what anyone who understands basic science knows: There is no dispute that masks offer protection against the virus. If people wore masks, the virus numbers would go down. Yet Trump continues to equivocate, falsely claiming there's a debate about the effectiveness of masks and testing. Dr. Reiner hit the nail on the head when he called Trump "unteachable" and said "the fact that the president of the United States can't get [masks] straight raises serious doubts about his competence now." Then Reiner pointedly tried to explain it in "terms President Trump would understand" by saying his poll numbers would go up and the economy could reopen if Trump mandated masks. He reframed the issue directly toward Trump's self-interest. This leads us to a subrule.

Subrule: It's impossible to get Trump to concentrate on something, unless it's about him—and even then . . .

The Trump I knew was a quick study about things that interested him, but he never wanted to know the details, even when they were essential. He was convinced he could get what he needed in just a few sentences. If you were explaining something, he would never let you get too many sentences in without interrupting and allowing others to interrupt you. Then he would get angry if you repeated yourself, even if it was clear he hadn't caught it the first time. Later, if missing something caused a problem, he would inevitably blame you for it. It was a tiring cycle, but I almost got used to it, the way you would adjust to a boss who was hard of hearing or nearsighted.

Memos, even on complicated issues, had to be less than a page in discrete, separated paragraphs with short sentences. Even those would not always be read. If you had ten important things to go over with him, you picked two, simplified them, and hoped for the best. You just knew that if you had to get him to pay attention, especially to something complicated involving a legal case, real estate deal, or construction issue, it would be an uphill battle.

Since I communicated in writing to Donald every single day, it was easy for me to tell if he had read even an extremely simplified memo. For the most part, he just skimmed things, an essential skill for someone with such a short attention span. Those of us in the office knew how to write things in a way that would give him the gist. Anyone who didn't know how to communicate with Trump would find later, in trying to talk to him, that he had no idea what they were talking about.

The issue of whether or not Trump reads what is put in front of him has come to a head a few times during his presidency. In the summer of 2020, U.S. intelligence agencies determined that Russia had been paying a bounty to Taliban-linked fighters for every American soldier they killed. Trump's excuse—though he also labeled it "fake news"—was that he didn't know about it. He continued to offer this excuse even when his own intelligence people insisted they had included it in his briefings. From what I know about how Donald operates and how his people are forced to adjust, I think the Russian bounty scandal was never *supposed* to get to him. Everyone knows he doesn't read, so his people likely figured they'd hide it from him in plain sight. Either they couldn't trust him not to leak something to Putin or they knew he would blow up at them, as he does when confronted with any negative Russia story. But they still had to cover their asses. It's equal parts hysterical and terrifying that to hide something from the president they just had to put it in writing. Famously, before a call with Russian President Vladimir Putin, who had just won a crooked election, Trump was warned in his notes, in all caps: DO NOT CONGRATULATE. Congratulate Putin was the first thing he did. Besides showing his deference to Putin, this shows that either he can't be bothered to look at what's put in front of him or he actively chooses to ignore important warnings. I don't know which is worse.

During his term in office, the public has been bombarded with stories of how Trump's intelligence briefers cannot get him to pay attention. He regularly skips the written President's Daily Brief (PDB), a collection of intelligence about the most serious issues facing the U.S. from around the world. It is a compendium of the single most important things a president needs to know, yet Trump can't be bothered to read them or even listen. So, just as we at the Trump Organization did, Trump's intelligence briefers have learned how to adapt: They cut back from ten pages to three and then to one, or sometimes just bullet points and visuals, and then resort to *putting his name into the document* in order to grab his attention. Even with all that adapting, they still can't get through.

According to Anonymous, the administration insider who claimed in an op-ed he/she was part of a resistance inside the administration: "You cannot focus the commander in chief's attention on more than one goddamned thing over the course of a meeting."

John Bolton: "I didn't think these briefings were terribly useful, and neither did the intelligence community, since much of the time was spent listening to Trump, rather than Trump listening to the briefer."

Unnamed White House official: "He just rants and raves. It's mostly about what was on Fox News. He really does believe that he knows more than the generals, more than the intelligence professionals."

Trump consumes hours of cable news every morning and night, but he has no room for the most significant threats to our country. I wonder how his enablers, especially those in his party who are supposedly responsible and intelligent, find this acceptable. I wonder how his supporters justify voting for him again after knowing this is how he operates.

I do not envy those who have to get Trump to focus on complex geopolitics that don't make him money or get him publicity. I had enough trouble getting him to focus on construction, real estate, and legal matters that did. In the 1990s the Trump Organization was involved in a lawsuit in Los Angeles over developing the famed Ambassador Hotel. Donald was the developer partner of a group that had bought the site in 1989. We wanted to tear down the hotel itself, which was where Robert Kennedy was assassinated, and build a project to be called Trump City West. The plan called for a base of retail, including restaurants and stores, a movie theater, a large venue for concerts, a hotel, class A offices, and superluxury condos. Years before any New York City developers even dreamed of it, we were planning apartments on the hundredth floor of what would have been the world's tallest building (125 stories) at the time. It was an ambitious plan, though in the city of earthquakes, I wasn't so sure this would work. Our 6-million-square-foot project would actually have been a great boon for the area and the city at large, but we were in a legal battle with the local school district. The Los Angeles Unified School District (LAUSD) attorney was going to come to New York to take Trump's deposition, and we had to get him ready.

Deposition preparation is essential in a lawsuit. Cases have been lost over what gets said in depositions long before the case makes it to court. There is an art to taking a deposition, an art to being deposed, and an art to being the attorney representing the person being deposed. It's not just about knowing the questions and answers, which most do already. It is essential to educate people *how* to answer so they can still be honest without giving the other side information it wants or doesn't have. Our position was detailed and complicated, and we needed to prepare Trump, who hadn't really done anything on the project and knew very little about it.

I told Donald we needed two days to prepare. He would not even consider it. "I don't need preparation," he told me. We asked for a day. *No.* We asked for a half a day. *No.* Though the opposition got a full day to take the deposition, we got only two hours to prep him. The lawyer flew in from Los Angeles to lead the prep, which was painstakingly byzantine. The prep session was held in Donald's office with the lawyer, me, and my assistant. Donald was constantly getting distracted, taking phone calls, and allowing people to walk in and out. Worse, when he didn't know something, he would deflect and get upset with our lawyer, rendering the process virtually useless.

The deposition took place the next day in the conference room on the twenty-sixth floor of Trump Tower. I sat next to Donald as the LAUSD lawyer questioned him across the table. When he asked Trump a question about our lead condemnation lawyer, whose last name was Bitting, Trump replied angrily, "There was no bidding. We never even got to do a design." His statement hung in the air; Trump clearly did not have a clue and wasn't even following the questions. He didn't know Bitting was the name of our lawyer, although we'd told him many times, including the previous day. Besides, from the context of the question, it was clear the question was about a person. He heard one word, "bidding," and went off. Trump came out looking terrible and did nothing to help our case. In fact, some of his totally inappropriate answers were used against us in court.

Trump's lawyers, whom he still collects like trophies, are just another example of his insecurity about his own intelligence. He always had plenty of attorneys, both in-house and outside, some of whom he liked to push around and treat as personal assistants. In many ways they were also possessions that served to buttress Trump's image. He bragged about his lawyers but also resented them for their superior education. He felt intimidated by them, inferior next to them; and he overcame this by having so many, some of whom I saw him openly mistreat. It was like the school bully getting the nerds to do his homework. They knew more than he did, so he had to push them around.

There is nothing wrong with being slow or ignorant, but Trump can be arrogantly stupid, almost vengefully so. It's why he thought just meeting with North Korean dictator Kim Jong Un, without even preparing for it, would result in an agreement that would land him a Nobel Peace Prize. Trump is deluded about his own abilities and, thus, incapable of improving himself. Trump claimed victory and said there were agreements with North Korea, which never materialized. In fact, the nuclear weapons situation got *worse*. Kim rubbed Donald's face in his failure by doing testing he promised not to do, making a mockery of Trump and the United States in the process. But Trump continued to claim victory and got away with it because, as Steve Bannon explained, his strategy is "flood the zone with shit." He just keeps doing new outrageous things to hide from his lies, failures, and gaps; he simply cannot be called on everything.

Carl Bernstein recently wrote that Trump is so unprepared for calls with foreign leaders that everyone around him believes it is a national security risk. For these calls, Trump makes meager efforts to understand who the leader is, what the country's relationship with the United States is about, or the call's significance. "He continued to believe that he could either charm, jawbone or bully almost any foreign leader into capitulating to his will," Bernstein wrote, "and often pursued goals more attuned to his own agenda than what many of his senior advisers considered the national interest." This comes as no surprise. Why spend the time and energy learning when he's spent his whole life faking his way through and relying on others to get the job done? This has long been a Trump tactic. It's obvious from his stilted tone and mispronunciation of words off the teleprompter that the first time he looks at his speeches is when he is delivering them.

"I'm highly educated. I know words," Trump bragged during the 2016 campaign. "I have the best words." The heart of the problem with Trump's intelligence is self-delusion. Trump seems to believe that he's some kind of genius, though the inarticulateness of that sentence should've put the issue to bed. What articulate person says, "I know words. I have the best words"? It's practically parody. I have been asked my thoughts on whether Donald is suffering from cognitive decline, and though I have no expertise, I can tell his vocabulary has clearly diminished in recent years. Though he was never an eloquent speaker, he at least used variety in his descriptions. Now he uses the same words over and over again. Adjectives like "weak," "strong," and "powerful" were always popular with him, but now he repeats them constantly, even using them in ways that don't make sense, as in "We put it in very powerfully that [China] should not have advantages over other countries," and "We're monitoring regions with increasing cases, including Boston, Chicago, and the Midwest. And we're monitoring them very, very strongly and very, very hard."* And of course, there was "big-league," which people heard as "bigly," though he seems to have retired it after using it constantly during the 2016 campaign.

An important point: A lot of Trump's most outrageous statements are just a consequence of him speaking without thinking. He has such faith in his instincts that he thinks he can just talk his way out of anything. However, especially in the last few years, we've seen that he has talked his way *into* so much more trouble. Then he doubles down rather than backtrack, multiplying the problem.

Trump's speaking without thinking habit is everywhere. Years ago it was saying he'd perhaps date Ivanka if she weren't his daughter, or commenting on baby Tiffany's future breasts. As a candidate

---

* I chose these two examples randomly from the same August 10 speech.

he made the comment about punishing women for having abortions. As president he took an impulsive decision to abandon our Kurdish allies by pulling out of Syria, confessed to Lester Holt that he fired Comey over the Russia investigation, revealed sensitive intelligence matters to the Russian ambassador about Syria. He just talks—and then, because he can't admit wrongdoing, ever—he has to lie or backtrack to clean it up. It's a feedback loop that is so automatic it practically runs by itself. All he has to do is open his mouth.

Trump's scary lack of knowledge has long been a problem, but never so glaringly. When I worked with him, Trump got by because he was a quick study who was able to fake understanding or get his people to make the decisions, especially when it concerned a certain level of detail. The engineer would explain the steps that needed to be taken, and I'd bring it to Trump. "Don't bother me with that, Barbara," he'd say. "Just figure it out." The buck often stopped with me and other executives. When he did shift his decision, it was often done in order to protect himself from getting blamed for something.

The "great deals" Trump has claimed to have negotiated in his business career were not because he was some great dealmaker. Most of them happened because he had leverage, power over the other party. This came in two forms: He had something they desperately needed, or he had something over them. When the leverage was weak or absent, Donald made either a bad deal or no deal at all. Because he's so used to having this uneven playing field, he rarely sees how dependent he is on it. It's like oxygen; it's just there.

But it's easy for us to see. I watched with amusement when he was forced to back down in his 2018 dispute with Speaker of the House Nancy Pelosi over the budget and government shutdown. He did not have his usual edge, but thinking he did, he went on record saying he wanted to own the shutdown. Because he was president, he thought he had the greatest leverage in the world, but he doesn't understand even the basics of government: how the three coequal branches work, or the extent and limits of their powers. With little experience negotiating on an equal footing, he caved. On the international stage, he makes the same mistakes. He thought he was allowed to hold up Ukraine's security money until Ukraine started investigating the Bidens because he is the president. But he has no concept of what presidential power actually is; he confuses it with being king or one of the various dictators he cozies up to.

Those same dictators play him like a fiddle. Leaders like Putin know Trump needs them as much as they need him, and they are not afraid of him. Trump's taunts to dangerous people like Kim Jong Un, promising bigger missiles and threatening "fire and fury," all land with a thud. One of Trump's big selling points during the 2016 campaign was that he knew how things really got done, was a great negotiator, and would put this to work for America. Almost four years later, has anything Trump has said been more thoroughly disproven?

Sometimes Trump is consumed by his insecurity, so he over-compensates, claiming to know everything about something he doesn't know the first thing about. It's why he's claimed to know more than the generals about the military, more than anybody about Korea, renewable energy, taxes, banks, even the U.S.

government itself. He claims his opinion on the pandemic is more important than experts like National Institute for Allergy and Infectious Diseases (NIAID) director Dr. Anthony Fauci, and Trump's own coronavirus response coordinator, Dr. Deborah Birx, which is pure overcompensation. I don't believe for a second he really thinks this. Other times, Trump really does believe he knows everything, which is even more dangerous. He is incapable of understanding his limitations and therefore thinks he knows a lot about issues when he knows virtually nothing. Not only does he think he knows it, he believes he knows it *better* than anyone else. It's an upside-down version of reality.

When I worked closely with Donald, he always claimed to be smarter than the person he was going up against, whether it was a contractor, architect, or city commissioner. He once wrote that the most important thing he learned in college was not to be impressed by academic credentials, but this is just the opposite of how he behaves. Trump claimed he graduated at the top of his class, when he was apparently an average student. He also brags about going to Wharton, which is among the country's most esteemed graduate business schools, but Trump was in their less prestigious under-graduate program, and at a time when they accepted nearly half of the applicants. He had a connection through his brother and transferred there after two years at Fordham. Because he points to his Ivy League education as proof of his intellect, we know he cares about its value. His former fixer Michael Cohen testified to Congress that Trump told him to threaten all his schools to prevent them from releasing any of his grades or transcripts. Once again, his actions betray his statements. This fact tells us two things: He was an unimpressive student *and* he doesn't want anyone to know.

MY EXPERIENCES WITH Donald were a constant battle against his ignorance and apathy about learning. After my two years away from the Trump Organization, I returned in 1987 serving as the executive vice president of construction and development. Among other things, I was put in charge of developing the properties of Alexander's Inc., a publicly traded retail company that had malls and stores in New York and New Jersey. Donald, along with his partner, Steven Roth of Vornado REIT,* owned a controlling interest in the stock and basically ran the company.

In addition to two shopping malls and eleven operating stores, Alexander's owned the land under almost all of them. The stores were on their way out, but as a real estate play, they were pure gold. Donald and Roth's plan was to close the stores and develop the real estate. Trump was the official developer and was paid a 4 percent fee on all the expenditures he made in connection with the development. This included all the work that I did—negotiating deals, selling property, hiring architects, engineers, and attorneys and overseeing their work—as well as my salary. So Trump made money not only on my work but on my salary as well.

One time I was working on getting approvals to demolish the Alexander's building in Paramus, New Jersey, which was garnering a lot of opposition from local citizens. While we were discussing the approval process in his office, Trump shared what he thought was a brilliant idea.

"Barbara, wait, wait. I got it," he said. "Listen. Just drop the X and the R in the Alexander's sign."

* Real Estate Investment Trust

"Why?" I asked. "What will that do?"

"Then they will *want* us to tear it down," he said with a little gleam in eye.

In his ignorance, Donald thought it would make the building look like an eyesore and therefore make the local population *want* to see it demolished. First of all, it couldn't even be done: It was obvious that the R was attached to all the other letters in the sign. But it was also a terrible idea, reminiscent of when he told me not to clear the weeds or wash the windows of one of the other Alexander's buildings we were trying to demolish. He thought these actions would persuade the locals to drop their objection to his tearing it down. But I understood what he didn't: The people in Paramus wouldn't hate the building if we did these things—they'd hate *us*. It was such a transparent gambit that I didn't even bother to argue with him; I just nodded and then didn't do it. The only thing it would've accomplished was make him look like a slumlord and solidify opposition against him. There were other ways to accomplish what he wanted without angering the residents or hurting the Trump name.

While I was concentrating on getting the designs done and approved for the malls, Trump would bombard me with his juvenile ideas about clearing tenants and share his thoughts on what to name the properties. He insisted on the two malls being called Trump Centre, with the "elegant" British spelling. The Queens location was in a section called Rego Park, which Trump said had no pizzazz; he insisted we say the mall was in the ritzier neighboring community of Forest Hills, though it was not. This was in line with what Trump usually focused on: how to promote things and what to name them. Trump was the titular head of the project, but he really didn't do much work on it. He had a very surface view of what we did and never bothered to learn anything beyond the basics.

As for Trump's knowledge of finance, which he treats as a given, his bankruptcies have been covered in detail in many places. Although Trump claims going bankrupt showed how good he was at gaming the system, in truth it reflected the failure of his enterprises. He ran his casinos and plenty of businesses straight into the ground. The banks bailed him out only because Trump was worth more alive than dead, as it were. If the banks were to take over undeveloped properties, they'd have nothing but open land, which they'd have to liquidate for pennies on the dollar. Whereas with Donald involved, he could get approvals for development projects, greatly improving their value, maybe even repaying the banks everything they were owed.*

Asked many times whom he takes advice from, Trump has offered up himself. "I'm speaking with myself . . . because I have a good brain," he said on the campaign trail when pressed to name his foreign policy advisers. "My primary consultant is myself." How does he have the temerity to come out with this? Trump has zero experience in government and knows nothing about foreign policy. Even the world's foremost experts seek outside counsel. "I don't want to talk to anyone," Trump repeatedly complained to his first chief of staff, John Kelly. "I know more than they do. I know better than anybody else."

Trump believes he's his own best counselor—partly out of arrogance and partly to deflect from the fact that he knows so little.

---

* This is eventually what happened to us on the West Side Yards project, discussed in Chapter 4.

I don't know when or how this became debatable, but the president of the United States should know more than the average person and be well above average intelligence. He should have the patience to read, the ability to understand experts' reports, and the good sense and humility to follow their advice.

Trump is clueless, and it is against his constitution to admit it and seek help. Gary Cohn, Trump's first National Economic Council director, talked about how Trump literally thought the U.S. could just print money to get the country out of debt. He *still* doesn't understand tariffs or trade deficits, though he claims to know more than anybody about it. He can't seem to grasp that it's not China paying for the tariffs, as he keeps saying; it's American consumers who bear the cost.

Trump says he trusts his instincts, but that's because they are all he has, not the background, the knowledge, or the willingness to learn. He either lacks the ability to learn or is just too lazy. It's likely a mix of both. His failure to meet these basic requirements has damaged the United States, endangered its citizens, and destroyed our reputation around the world. Going back to when I worked for him, Trump never invested himself in learning, or paying attention, because he has never had to. He has put all his effort into the show, which leads to the next rule.

FOUR

A TALE OF TWO TOWERS

**Rule: Trump's focus on appearance over
substance is a way of life.**

Appearances have always been extremely important to Donald Trump. When I worked with Donald, he detested what he called "fat" people, disrespecting and insulting them, and regularly chided employees and consultants with comments like "You like your Snickers, huh?" I first heard him say this to our land use attorney for a project in Los Angeles. The lawyer, a very large man, was the absolute best in the business. When I brought him in to see Donald, one of the first things Trump commented on was his weight. When he made that Snickers crack, I was shocked and embarrassed, but the guy was a pro and just ignored it. I was insulted but not surprised when Donald made the same comment to me a few years later after I had gained some weight. He also used to make fun of the woman who was perhaps the most important member of his staff on Trump Tower because she was overweight. In meetings, after she would walk out, he would mock her with cracks like "She must be going to get more doughnuts."

Attractiveness is certainly a Trump obsession, and he regularly hired people based on whether or not they had a certain look. But his focus on appearance is not just about looks. He is consumed with putting on a show that always puts him in the best light. Trump's buildings are made of concrete and steel and glass, but I watched as many were sold to the public through smoke and mirrors, from how involved he was in their construction to his ownership of them to what they contained to how big they were to what they were made of to who lived there to what they were worth. He even said that the apartments in Trump Tower were sold before we were actually allowed to take deposits, and he inflated the amount of money people were paying for them. He spread rumors about the king of Saudi Arabia or Sophia Loren looking to buy there, about talk from Washington about making the presidential suite (where the U.S. president stays when in New York) in the Plaza instead of the Waldorf Astoria. He comes from a world where hype, exaggeration, and lies are an accepted part of the game and a lucrative tool. Trump is a salesman, a P. T. Barnum type taken to twenty-first-century extremes.

Pretending he has a strong work ethic is another key part of the Trump show. His father, Fred, was tireless and hardworking ("Sleeping is a waste of time," he once said), traits that his son saw impressed people. Donald doesn't have to work hard and he has no desire to, but he does work on the *appearance* of working hard. He used to brag to us that he slept only four hours a night, though I never believed it. Even if it were true, it wouldn't prove anything, because we know how little he works during daylight hours. (Twitter's time stamps also helpfully reveal what he's really doing with morning and evening time.) Donald knows what people expect of him—as a businessman and now as president—so he presents the image of a man who works nonstop and expects people under him to do the same. He continues to go back to this sleep barometer as proof of something, bragging about his Coronavirus Task Force working around the clock and about how Mike Pence "doesn't sleep anymore."

During the government shutdown of 2018, the White House released photos of President Trump "in the White House, working hard," including one of him in the Oval Office. In a white MAGA hat with the brim pulled low, Trump sat at the Resolute Desk, body slightly turned to the camera, phone to his ear. The only problem was that the desk was entirely empty, and it was pretty obvious that the phone was a prop he'd picked up right before the photograph was snapped. Donald was posing, pretending to be a man at work.

He's almost always just posing. Trump is aware of what a president is *supposed* to be doing, but he only does what he likes, and he doesn't care for his presidential duties. As many of us at the Trump Organization knew years ago, he doesn't have the patience, interest, or attention span for the presidency. He pretends he's working hard over weekends, even when there are pictures of him golfing. Though he hounded President Obama about it—and claimed that he wouldn't have time to play golf as president—Trump has been on the golf course 278 days in three and a half years, two and a half times as often as Obama had been at the same point in his presidency.* Of course, Obama also wasn't dealing with the worst recession in nearly a century and a national epidemic.

---

* Compared to Trump's 278 by Labor Day 2020, Obama spent 333 days playing golf in *eight years*. Minus the pandemic and shutdown, Trump might've reached that in four.

It has been widely reported that Trump comes down to the Oval Office around eleven a.m. (and doesn't stay particularly late) and demands even more "executive time" during the course of his shortened workday. His schedule is sometimes so barren that it may show only a single meeting or lunch on a given day. The one thing Trump is always working on and thinking about every waking hour is his singular project in life: to become richer, more powerful, and more famous. This is what his time is dedicated to.

Trump made a big show of his meetings with Kim Jong Un, as though these were the greatest foreign policy achievements of the century. Of course, nothing ever came of the two leaders' supposed love affair. According to National Security Adviser John Bolton, Trump never bothered to learn any details of what was negotiated but zeroed in on one thing: He wanted to be able to say he ended the Korean War.* Trump was so enamored of the idea that he didn't even ask for any concessions in return. According to Bolton, Trump saw it as "a huge media score, and didn't see any international consequences." So our president gave North Korea, a pariah nation, a huge win by meeting with the most powerful world leader, and the United States got nothing in return. Trump, however, took our leverage, which the U.S. had held on to for decades, and flushed it down the toilet, trading it for his own publicity. The one thing that came of the summit that never was: a series of commemorative coins. I have no doubt who came up with that one. The single tangible product of an agreement that never happened: a celebratory souvenir. I can't think of anything more Trumpian.

---

* There was an armistice in 1953, but the war never officially ended.

Trump is a showman by nature, but his focus on appearance over substance has become much worse. He once worked to sell what he built, which is an important part of the business. But gradually the selling came to matter more than what he was selling.

I'm reminded of the apartments in Trump Tower, which to me serve as a metaphor for Trump's entire brand: fancy surface, mediocre to shoddy underneath. The condominiums, which started on the thirtieth (actually twentieth) floor, were quite large by today's standards, with one-bedrooms averaging around a thousand square feet. The apartments had nice views, some spectacular, through a glass exterior. Trump touted the building, especially the condos, as superluxury, with the finest fittings. While he did spend a lot of money on the atrium and retail floors, and the residential lobby had very expensive finishes—Vermont and Italian marbles, gold leaf, designer furniture—the apartments themselves were far from luxurious. They were being sold for fortunes to some of the world's richest people, yet beneath the glitzy, flashy exterior, the apartments themselves could be considered ordinary. Trump got away with it in part because many of the buyers had them redone, while most of the rest were pieds-à-terre for owners who didn't care that much. The places weren't even lived in, so what did they care about the floors and cabinets?

In an effort to save, save, save, many things in the Trump Tower residences were medium quality at best, from the cabinets and counters to the marble and appliances.* The flooring was not the three-quarter-inch pecan planks that the Museum Tower, a

---

* Trump's "restoration" of the Plaza a few years later—discussed in Chapter 9—had the same pattern.

nearby luxury building, used or the high-quality parquet that Trump initially talked about. It was the far cheaper quarter-inch glue-down oak, literally a thin veneer of wood glued directly to the concrete. For plumbing fixtures, we used American Standard, a middle-market brand. The air-conditioning and heating systems were top-notch, but everything else was run-of-the-mill, mediocre material you'd likely find in subsidized housing. Trump claimed the marble in the bathrooms was Paradiso, a highly coveted Italian marble that Olympic Tower had in its bathrooms. Trump had used it extensively in the lobby of the Grand Hyatt. But for the Trump Tower apartments, what we actually used was Paradiso Marble 96, which was not marble at all. It's an amalgamation of pieces of marble, held together with a matrix (glue). It looked nothing like real marble, and it wasn't hard to tell the difference; it looked like what it was, cheap tile.

The biggest insult was the kitchens. High-end buildings were using imported European cabinetry made by companies like Poggenpohl or Smallbone, which offered beautiful materials, exacting craftsmanship, and hand-finished details. We ended up with cabinets and countertops made of Formica, which would have been fine in a lower-end apartment where the use of plastic laminate was common. But in a high-end apartment, let alone one in "the greatest building in the world," this was preposterous. A luxury condo at the time would have used Thermidor or Viking refrigerators, stoves, and dishwashers, but Donald bought General Electric, the kind of appliances you'd find in a middle-class home. Ivana did her best to spruce up the design of the cabinets, with curved edges and touch latches so the cabinets would open with a push, but they were just substandard for a luxury building.

I took a lot of poetic license in writing up the condo offering plan when I described the finishes, but people didn't buy Trump Tower apartments for the finishes; they bought them for the location, the spacious layouts, the views, and the Trump name. Trump created the illusion that his name meant luxury, quality, and high style, which was buoyed by the high-end retail shops below. But the reality of the apartments was far from luxurious. In Trump Tower, he made an investment in the public spaces and it paid off. He carried over this version of luxury—high-end finishes and flourishes like pianos and beautiful plantings in huge public spaces with only mediocre finishes and fixtures in the apartments—to other buildings, eventually parlaying it into a franchising business of buildings bearing his name that he had virtually nothing to do with.

For the apartments in Trump Tower, Ivana selected three of the top interior decorators at the time, each to design and fit out a model apartment that could be used to sell the others.

After working on the apartments for weeks, she brought Donald and me up to one of the residential floors to see the finished products. I could tell on the walk there that he was in one of his moods and wasn't going to like anything he saw that day. Trump walked into the first apartment, which was very sedate and manly, and looked around for a few minutes. "It looks like shit, Ivana," he said. We walked into the next model apartment, which was all glitz, with lots of mirrors. "How am I going to sell this?" he asked, shaking his head. The third was ladylike, with chintz and floral upholstery. He shook his head again, almost laughing to himself. "I must've been a fucking idiot to let you do this. You don't know what you're doing." I thought all three were well done, well conceived and clever. They were also so different that it was impossible for him to not like at least one. But it was almost like he was trying to humiliate her. Part of it was his mood and part of it was that he was primed to dislike anything that came from Ivana. However, the salespeople were more than happy to show fully decorated apartments rather than the empty ones, where the cheap finishes were glaringly obvious.

The look of the Trumps' original triplex apartment on the top floors, which I also built, was subtle and tasteful. It was designed by the late Angelo Donghia, a proponent of "less is more" who decorated the apartments of a number of entertainment figures and fellow designers and who also designed the Metropolitan Opera Club as well as the headquarters for many major corporations. There were some gaudy plastic panels installed on a fascia in the living room (Trump told people they were ivory), but overall it was pretty classy and sedate for the Trumps.

Trump's kitchen remained like those in the other apartments, though he changed the countertops to granite, and he might have replaced the linoleum-like vinyl flooring with tile. I don't think there was much cooking going on there, as they were out almost every night, so maybe it didn't matter to them. A nanny prepared the children's dinner in a kitchen on the third floor, which also had the kids' bedrooms, a beautiful family room, and a room for Ivana's mother.

Years later, Trump went to Russia and visited the Hermitage, the Winter Palace where the czar once lived. The Hermitage is like Versailles, extremely over-the-top and gaudy, gold leaf everywhere. It is perhaps the most ostentatious building on Earth, and Trump loved it. He came back and had his apartment completely redone in that style, and that's how it is today, lots of gold leaf and cherubs, wildly excessive, like a child's version of how a rich person lives. I believe he used a designer who did the high-roller suites at his casinos, which are purposely garish. Donald invited me to his apartment to see it after the remodel was done.

"What do you think?" he asked, his arms wide. I think he was expecting me to fawn. The Hermitage-meets-casino vibe was thick in there. It was so visually loud that I wanted to turn the volume down the second I stepped in. My mind went searching for something to say.

"It's beautiful," I said. "But to be honest, I couldn't sleep here." As soon as it came out of my mouth, I knew it was a mistake.

"What do you mean?" he asked, a blank look on his face. Tripping over my words a little, I managed to cover myself. "Oh, I mean, it's just that it's so ornate and alive," I added. "I would be distracted." That seemed to satisfy him.

Trump's focus on façade extended to his office as well. As mentioned earlier, Donald's office had a beautiful and very expensive rosewood desk, but it was surrounded by cabinetry that looked like burl wood but wasn't wood at all. To save money he used Formica. If he went for knockoffs in his own office, you can guess how much he cheaped out anywhere else he thought he could get away with it. It didn't matter if things were well made and expensive, only that people thought they were.

ANOTHER IMPRESSION THAT Trump works hard to put across is that of being a strong leader, a decider, the one who makes the big call. From my experience, this reputation, like so much else about him, is basically contrived. Though he would weigh in on some things like colors and other design elements on Trump Tower and the Plaza, Trump left most of the major decisions to his executives, which was actually an effective way to do things.

At Trump Tower, most of the condo purchasers wanted to make changes to their apartments while the building was still being built. A lot of times this involved swapping out fixtures or switching finishes, changes that had very little effect on the overall project and would not cause delays. But other changes were more substantial, and Trump had to approve these. I wanted to get the building finished so he could start collecting his money— and I explained to Donald why making certain changes was a bad idea. Steven Spielberg used an architect who wanted to relocate important elements of the kitchen, including walls, which would force us to redo all the waste plumbing. I explained to Trump how destructive this would be and reminded him that we had agreed not to make "structural" changes to the building, which the apartment buyers knew. Trump went along with my advice, not permitting the changes Spielberg's architect wanted. But the architect went over my head directly to Donald, who, not really understanding the ramifications, said okay. I lost that fight; Spielberg was a big name and Donald felt he had to please him. Plus Donald knew I could make it work. "Just do it, Barbara," he said. "Find a way to do it," and I did.

Other times things actually couldn't be done, and I had to sit with Trump and explain: enough to convince him but not so much that he lashed out. He only had so much patience to listen to people. Sometimes he would get extremely agitated and even throw you out of his office, which absolutely happened to me on more than one occasion. Sometimes you won, sometimes you didn't, but you had to put up the fight because his decisions were often just not informed ones. In my mind I didn't work for him, I worked for the project, and I refused to let him screw up the building.

Subrule: Appearing to be successful is far easier than attaining success.

When I first started working for Trump, he was very involved in the actual work. What he built was not always what he claimed, and he used substitutes where he could get away with it, and he exaggerated how much things were selling for and the notoriety of the buyers, but he was heavily involved in the design and construction of these buildings.

But that was a long time ago. Trump made his name, much of his fortune, and his entire political career on presenting something that is not real. There is no longer anything underneath because *there doesn't have to be.* In the world of real estate and business, some amount of hyperbole is to be expected, though Donald pushed this to its limits as well. He would take what was built and sell it as something grander, more luxurious than it actually was. That was his skill, and he ultimately fooled himself.

Over the years, Trump grew accustomed to selling an idea, a style, a persona, a brand. You can make money like this, but as we are all learning the hard way, you cannot run a country in this manner. He could claim Princess Di was looking to buy an apartment in Trump Tower or Elton John was going to stay in the Presidential Suite at the Plaza, and there was no real harm done. He could ignore building and zoning regulations, and no international alliances would be endangered, no disease would ravage the nation. His coronavirus response has been so catastrophic because, even after unabated suffering, sickness, and death, he still sees it as a public relations matter. Knowing he can't defeat the virus, he puts his energy into downplaying it or lying and getting others to lie about treatments and vaccines and comebacks that are just around the corner. The reality is too difficult to manage, and it makes him look terrible, so he has constructed façades that hide this reality.

Before he became president, Trump's wealth and influence constituted a triumph of appearance over reality. He didn't have the empire he claimed to have, didn't own what he claimed to own, and didn't even have control over the things he did own. In the 2004 contract for one of his Atlantic City casinos, which had been taken over by the banks, he was stripped of his ownership interest but kept on as manager for a yearly fee. But the banks made sure there was no confusion about the degree of his involvement. The contract actually stated: "Mr. Trump shall not be required to devote any fixed amount of time to the performance of his duties." This should go on his tombstone.

Because Trump has given himself over entirely to the spectacle, he is incapable of following through or achieving what he says he will. While he was a candidate, his talk of draining the swamp (he's filled it past capacity), of building a wall on Mexico's dime (which even he knew was a fantasy), of replacing Obamacare with something better (his people couldn't come up with anything) was all just empty slogans.

Even the campaign's beginnings were an illusion. The Trump Tower atrium wasn't really filled with an adoring crowd that June

2015 day he announced his run for the presidency. Trump hired a company that took out a casting notice and paid actors fifty bucks to be there and act excited. It's a big atrium, sure, but in a city of 8 million people, they couldn't find enough people who wanted to be there? The choreographed escalator entrance, the rapturous crowd, it was all for show. It laid the groundwork for what his campaign and eventually his presidency would become. From day one, he would try to present a fake reality, claiming he had a bigger crowd at his inauguration than President Obama, though the pictures said otherwise. He sells the myth, not the reality.

The perfect distillation of this rule is *The Apprentice.* In the 2000s, in the years before NBC and Mark Burnett saved Trump from oblivion, he was a walking parody of himself, a minor celebrity doing McDonald's and Pizza Hut commercials, a relic of another era. *The Apprentice* was not just a successful reality show, it was a successful *reality*. It reframed and resurrected the 1980s image of Donald, adding this veneer of the successful CEO. But it was fake. Trump had faltered on so many of his businesses at that point, been rescued out of personal bankruptcy, that many of his "deals" by then were really just to license his name. *The Apprentice* would cover Donald with a new coat of paint, presenting an illusion of the man, the business, even the location. The boardroom and the reception area on the show didn't actually resemble a single place in Trump Tower. It was a set they built in the tower's basement, with Donald's chair intentionally made higher than everyone else's.

As for his catchphrase, that too was an illusion. Over the nearly twenty years I worked with Trump, he really didn't like firing people; he was reluctant to do it and wavered when the time came. If he wanted to get rid of someone, he would pawn the job off on an underling. Firing takes courage, which he doesn't have. For all his tough-guy persona, Donald is a coward. It's not easy to fire people—I don't like it either. It humanizes them; you have to look them in the eye, hear them plead for their family, their livelihoods. You have to sit there and deal with their personal story, and that's the last thing Donald wants. You have to see them as a person, and he doesn't. All these factors behoove him to have someone else do the firing. In his mind, this leaves his own reputation intact. I have seen it work—fired employees retained their affection for Trump and reserved the anger for the messenger who was saddled with the job.

In the Trump Organization we always joked that if you were close enough to Donald that he had to be the one who would fire you, you were set for life. We've seen this cowardice during his presidency as well: berating and humiliating Jeff Sessions in the hopes that he'd quit, firing off tweets at Robert Mueller, tweeting out firings or passing them off to minions. It is just who he is. The brash and confrontational Trump, the man who made a brand of himself by saying "You're fired," simply cannot do it in person. I've seen him set up people and then throw them under the bus, but direct firing is not for him.

Pretending Trump will fire people creates this tough façade. He is clearly impressed with strength, likes to surround himself with it, and pretends that he possesses it. His favorite adjective is "strong," whether it's about decision-making, warnings, or physical prowess. At his 2016 rallies, Trump engaged in a lot of talk about beating people up and throwing them out, but he is a wimp. He thinks acting this way will throw people off the scent. In October 2018, Greg Gianforte, a Montana Republican running for Congress, body-slammed a journalist, and of course Trump was effusive in his approval. At a rally soon after, Trump lauded the man: "Anybody that can do a body slam, that's my kind of guy," he said to a cheering crowd, then pantomimed the flipping motion. I have never seen, read, or heard about Donald ever actually engaging in physical contact. It's all about the illusion of toughness. We're seeing this on a mass scale in the summer of 2020: While bellowing about "law and order," Trump sent unidentified federal agents to go after protesters in Portland, Oregon, and threatened to do so in other cities like Chicago. It's his way of saying: "Nobody fucks with Trump," as long as he doesn't have to take part in any of it.

A great example of Trump's fixation on both toughness and appearances was the hiring of Matthew Calamari. I was in my office at Trump Tower one day when I was summoned across the street to the Crown Building to see Donald. It was the fall of 1981, and the U.S. Open tennis tournament was going on out in Queens. I knew Donald had been there that day, so I asked him how it was. A big smile flashed on his face. "You gotta hear this," he said, and launched into the story: Donald was in his seat watching the tennis match when some rowdy young guys nearby started causing problems. They were sitting in reserved seats, and when the patrons who belonged there showed up, it led to a ruckus. Donald said he saw this big guy (linebacker frame, mustache) come running from across the stands, grab the two troublemakers—one in each hand—and pull them out of the arena. "It was incredible," he said, still marveling at the manhandling performance hours later.

Afterward, Donald approached the big guy and got his name, Matthew, and his number. He was a recent college graduate without a full-time job who was working security at the U.S. Open.

"Barbara," he said, "call this guy and get him over here, I want to put him in charge of security at Trump Tower. You should've seen him—he was great. He'll be fantastic."

This was not uncommon: Trump is impulsive and tends to make hires based on looks or maybe a single impressive act, not experience. I pushed back a little; Donald had a bodyguard for himself, and we had already discussed hiring a security company for Trump Tower, which Donald had dismissed out of hand. The Matthew hiring wasn't a fight worth having, so I tracked him down and brought him up to meet with Trump. Matthew was soft-spoken and clearly impressed with Donald and his surroundings. After a few minutes, I took him over to the jobsite at Trump Tower. Because Fred was still watching over my expenses and I already had several people working for me, I put Matthew on HRH's payroll, but he reported to me.

Everybody liked Matthew personally, though some resented him because he had no security credentials or experience other than the legend of the U.S. Open. I can vouch that he was hardworking and watched people like a hawk. After performing well doing security for construction, he was hired as part of the team for Trump Tower when it opened. Ironically, the more experience Matt got, the less people liked him. Soon he was head bodyguard, then head of security for all the New York properties, then all the properties. Now he is COO of the Trump Organization and an executive vice president. How Matthew's background and skills have prepared him for this level of responsibility is hard to imagine. But he is invaluable because he knows where all the bodies are buried,* and

---

* I mean this metaphorically.

more important, he worships Trump.* In fact, according to Harry Hurt III's biography of Trump, when Donald once asked Calamari, "Would you kill for me, Matty?" he answered, "Yes sir."

Maintaining the false tough exterior still matters a great deal to Trump. During the first weekend of protests following the Minneapolis police's murder of George Floyd, there was a considerable crowd in Lafayette Square across from the White House. As a precaution, the Secret Service shut the building's lights off and escorted Trump down to the basement bunker. He would later deny it, claiming that he had just coincidentally gone down there earlier that day for an inspection, which was proven to be a lie. He later would put extra fencing around the White House, and everyone saw what those of us who knew Donald understood: He is governed by fear.

The bunker story was all over television and the internet, and he was mocked relentlessly. The ridicule clearly drove him nuts. A few days later, he put on a show to upend the image of "Hiding Donald." On a Monday evening, he came out of the White House surrounded by his minions to walk through Lafayette Square—but only after riot officers tear-gassed and pushed back peaceful protesters to clear the way—so he could pose for a photo holding a Bible in front of St. John's Church. That was the whole thing. Then he walked back to the White House. He thought it would demonstrate his courage and his faith in God. The entire performance backfired and made him look worse. Even his own

---

* Trump did a similar thing with Johnny McEntee, a handsome college football quarterback whom he hired as "body man" (the president's aide), a job from which he was fired. Trump then promoted him to a campaign position. McEntee had made a viral video (of himself throwing footballs) and later worked at Fox, the perfect Trump combination.

people—including Defense Secretary Mark Esper and the chairman of the Joint Chiefs of Staff, Mark (Mike) Milley, disavowed it. I heard it was Hope Hicks's idea, and if it was, I think she should've been fired. But the hollowness of the whole thing felt like a Donald production: Hide and then make a show of how tough you are.

Whether it's pretending to be hardworking or to be tough, Trump understands the world of showmanship, and he looks for it in just about everything. I remember once, during our legal battles fighting the Ambassador Hotel condemnation case, he had me hire a famous entertainment lawyer, Bert Fields. I was against it because he had zero experience in this specialized field of law, but Trump insisted. Trump's entire reason for hiring Fields was a *Vanity Fair* article in which Fields claimed he had never lost a case and was billed as "the most feared lawyer in Hollywood." Donald had to have the best lawyer, to add to his collection, and good press is the ultimate credential. The fact that Fields worked in show business, which Trump had long wanted to be a part of, didn't hurt either. "He's the guy," Trump said. "That's who we gotta hire. Bert's the guy." This was one of Trump's favorite expressions. When he found someone who was "hot," Donald would declare "He's the guy," as though he were anointing him.

Fields was actually the second lawyer Trump made me hire for the LA project. The first one had been a politician who had a relationship with the mayor but also no condemnation experience whatsoever. I tried to explain to Trump that his connection to the mayor was irrelevant (we were up against the school district, which is autonomous), but to him, that friendship was a golden ticket. "He's the guy," Trump instructed, so I hired him. It was a disastrous choice, and Trump fired him, or rather had *me* fire him, pretty quickly.

Bert Fields was brilliant. Though he hadn't done condemnation cases, he knew the law inside and out and was a great reader of people. He also brought an impressive firm with him who did their homework on the case. But the problem was Trump. When we were well along developing the case, Fields set up a meeting with Trump and an important client, knowing that both were interested in acquiring a piece of the Miss Universe Pageant. Trump was able to use the information he got from this meeting to his own benefit and, at the same time, screw Fields's client. In one of Trump's books, he claims to have fired Fields, but that is the opposite of the truth. Fields not only quit, he ultimately volunteered to surrender the fees he had earned because he was so disgusted by Trump's actions.

As payback, Trump insisted on firing Fields's entire firm, although they were millions of dollars deep in our case, and it would be catastrophic for us. Trump then made me interview and spend time with another lawyer, Harvey Myerson, whom I had to convince Donald not to hire. Myerson had represented the United States Football League's suit against the NFL and later went to jail for overbilling clients. After that I got Trump to stay with Fields's firm. Everything was going smoothly for a while—we had it all set up, operating 100 percent and getting the case in order—when all of a sudden Trump had another brilliant idea.

Sometime around February 1996, I was in Donald's office discussing the case when he brought up Johnnie Cochran. It was a few months after the O. J. Simpson case had ended, and Cochran, Simpson's most visible lawyer, was everywhere. He seemed to be leaning into his newfound celebrity, and Donald no doubt noticed. "Johnnie's the guy," Trump said. "He's in California, he knows everybody. We gotta get Johnnie. He's the guy." Never mind Cochran was a criminal defense lawyer who also had no history with condemnation cases. In fact, all three of the lawyers Trump forced me to hire lacked any kind of experience in condemnation cases. As usual, Trump's ignorance—his failure to understand that lawyers are not interchangeable in their areas of expertise—played a big role in his decision-making. As did his obsession with fame. Cochran was another celebrity and coveted lawyer Trump could add to his collection. Donald was also convinced that Johnnie had his finger on the pulse of the people, which would be helpful if we had to go to trial.

So we put Johnnie on the team, though we ended up working mostly with one of the other lawyers from his firm, Carl Douglas. I met with Johnnie a few times, and he suggested that we needed to conduct a mock trial, so we brought in a jury consultant, the same one he used in the O.J. trial. This was a fun experience but a total waste of money. We did confirm that a potential jury composed of LA citizens would instinctively dislike Trump, which we would've known anyway.

Overall, Trump gave very little of his attention to the Ambassador case, but whenever he did focus on it, he made impulsive decisions that contributed little and only caused problems. He has never had patience for the work, and he thinks everything is about press and public opinion, which oversimplifies things beyond recognition. No matter how hard I tried, I couldn't convince Donald that it wasn't just about putting on a show.

THIS PAST MARCH, I watched with a mix of familiarity and horror as the president talked about the coronavirus pandemic as if it were a TV special he was hosting. He said in a Fox interview that he wanted to open the country on Easter, and he treated it like it would be a big reveal, like a movie premiere. "Wouldn't it be great to have all those churches full?" he asked, thinking it would prove how successfully he'd handled the pandemic.

In reality, packing people into rooms where they all sing and speak in close quarters would have been catastrophic, as has been proven by the frequency of superspreading events in U.S. churches. This is at the root of all his failures on the pandemic: He spends far more time and energy, and has his people spend more time and energy, on the appearance of beating the virus than on actually beating it. They are working on building the illusion of a successful reopening rather than an actually successful reopening.

Over and over, he has declared that we have defeated the virus, that it is going to disappear, and that we have the lowest mortality rates, the lowest rates of infection, the highest rate of testing, of all countries—when not one word of this is true. There are so many quotes on record of him dismissing the coronavirus through February and into March, but all of a sudden, there he was on TV, claiming "I've felt it was a pandemic long before it was called a pandemic." The virus was a particularly difficult challenge for Trump because it was everywhere and people were getting sick and dying. He couldn't get himself out of it with wild claims on Twitter or invented facts at press conferences and in interviews, or even rely on Fox and others to make him look good. The numbers are the numbers and the virus is real. No Trump spin can change that. But that doesn't mean, as we get closer to the election, that he's not trying his damnedest.

Building a buzz around something helps sell it; that's the nature of business, and it's not inherently a problem. But the stakes of misleading and distorting by a president during a deadly pandemic are obviously different. It can put people in mortal danger and ruin lives. While Trump's staff works to make sure that he's not responsible for anything, he puts on his leader costume. His daily virus briefings were proof of his preference for show over substance. What were they but minirallies for him to meander and riff? Anytime reporters asked less-than-unctuous questions, he struck back at them. He didn't even pretend he cared about informing the public: He talked mainly about himself for the bulk of the time, while the experts stood silently behind him, visibly wincing. Then he would tweet about his ratings. This could have been a dark comedy skit a few years ago; now it's a haunting reality.

To Trump, running the country is just another show: poll numbers, TV ratings, crowd sizes. No amount of salesmanship can change the fact that Americans have suffered and died because of his refusal to face facts, help the country face them, and act accordingly. Trump acts like statistics are just numbers that reflect either positively or negatively on *him*. That's why he keeps saying, "If we stopped testing right now, we'd have very few cases, if any," and why he asked to "slow down the testing, please." The cases are not people, just a set of numbers to him.

There's evidence that the Trump administration meddled with the Centers for Disease Control and Prevention (CDC) guidelines so that fewer people would get tested. The cases and deaths are just tallies on a debit sheet, not lives. If the tally reflects badly on him, then he has to change it—though that only makes it worse. Even his long refusal to wear a mask was based on appearance: He thought it made it him look weak, like he was capitulating. He also literally didn't like how he looked in one. So millions of people followed their president and refused to wear masks, continue to refuse to wear masks. Trump pretends that he is beating the virus instead of working to actually do it, and he values his own vanity over public health. All the while people continue to die.*

Donald told me that Roy Cohn advised him to "never, never, never admit to anything." There is no looking back, just a relentless push forward and the rewriting of what happened. Whether that's the government shutdown that he caused, his administration's catastrophic pandemic response, or the slew of executive orders he signs (on the economic crisis, on Muslim and transgender military bans) that end up meaning nothing, Trump is not looking for a win, just *the appearance of the win*. He never learned the game because he was always able to work the referees. That used to be zoning boards and politicians, but now it's the public and the American media. The scope of the destructiveness is not comparable, but the strategy is the same.

Projecting himself as a winner—something Trump's obsessed with—is just a smokescreen for all the times he has lost, caved, or walked away. The fact that he bankrupted all three of his casinos,

---

* In July 2020, Trump posted a picture on Twitter of himself in a mask, saying masks were patriotic, but that didn't last long. He's almost never seen wearing one and has done nothing to encourage them. At his rallies, he's also far up on stage and protected, while the audience is not.

along with a handful of hotels; wildly overpaid for the Plaza and
the Eastern Air Lines Shuttle (both sold at huge losses), drove the
short-lived United States Football League into the ground; and
failed at selling his own brands of wine, water, vodka, and steak
(among other things) doesn't seem to hurt his reputation as a
business genius. Trump lost so much money in some years that he
paid no taxes at all, but he has spun even this into another example of his acumen. Some of his followers continue to buy the story
because they have so much invested in it. Trump the success story,
Trump the dealmaker, and Trump the billionaire are all products
of the triumph of appearance over reality, of his ability to spin a
loss into a win. Perhaps no project better exemplifies this than the
story of the West Side Yards.

Trump had long had his eyes on a tremendous piece of property in
New York City that ran along the Hudson River from 59th Street
to 72nd Street. This was a great site, but it had been used as a dump
for Hudson River dredging spoils, which affected its value. It had
changed hands several times over the years until Trump eventually
bought it. In November of 1985, during my hiatus from the Trump
Organization, Donald called a press conference to announce plans
for a multibillion-dollar development of the West Side Yards to be
called Television City. The centerpiece of the project would be yet
another "world's tallest building," a 150-story skyscraper. Trump
would use this tactic again on the Los Angeles project. I know he
never intended to build the world's tallest building; it was a way
to get leverage because it scared municipalities into making concessions. Television City would also include eight thousand apartments, forty acres of parks, retail space, along with television and

I met Donald Trump on his first construction project in Manhattan, which was to transform the aging Commodore Hotel into the Grand Hyatt. 1976. (Photo by John Pedin/NY Daily News via Getty Images)

Donald's next project was to build Trump Tower, for which he hired me as vice president and head of construction. Here I am working on the site. 1980–82. (Photos by Sy Rubin)

Above: Donald in his apartment just after he heard he would have no real estate taxes for the Grand Hyatt project for forty years. 1976. (Photo by Bettmann Archive/Getty Images) *Below:* Even back then, Donald seemed to love the cameras. Here he is being interviewed during the construction of Trump Tower. Circa 1982. (Photo by Sy Rubin)

Above: (left to right) Donald, me, Evangeline Carey (the New York governor's wife), and Louise Sunshine at the Trump Tower topping-out ceremony to mark the completion of the structure. 1982. (Photo by Sy Rubin) *Below:* Donald with his parents, Mary and Fred. 1994. (RTalensick/MediaPunch)

When GOD
Created
Man,
SHE Was Only
Joking

SOMETIMES
THE BEST MAN
FOR THE JOB
IS A WOMAN

Above: Me in my field office at Trump Tower while it was under construction. Circa 1982. (Photo by Sy Rubin) *Right:* My business card. (Res Personal Collection)

BARBARA A. RES
EXECUTIVE VICE-PRESIDENT

THE TRUMP ORGANIZATION
725 FIFTH AVENUE
NEW YORK, N.Y. 10022

TELEPHONE
(212) 832-2000
TELEX•427715

Opposite: Donald standing in front of Trump Tower. 1983. (Photo by Arnold Newman Properties/ Getty Images) ***Above:*** After Trump Tower was completed, I left the company. Donald threw me a big going-away party and gave me this gold-and-diamond bracelet from Cartier to thank me. The inscription says: "Towers of Thanks" Love, Donald. (Photos by Res) ***Right:*** This is one of two 1880s silver dollars that Fred Trump gave me. He handed them out when contracts were awarded to the subcontractors. (Res Personal Collection)

	CORRECTED	Form **1099-MISC** Approved I.R.S. Department of the Treasury—Internal Revenue Service 13-2678063		
PAYER'S name, street address, city, state, and ZIP code		1 Rents	OMB No.1545-0115	
Donald J. Trump 2611 West 2nd Street Brooklyn, N.Y. 11223		2 Royalties	19**85** Statement for Recipients of	**Miscellaneous Income**
PAYER'S Federal identification number	RECIPIENT'S identification number	3 Prizes and awards	4 Federal income tax withheld	**Copy B For Recipient**
RECIPIENT'S name, address, and ZIP code Barbara Res		5 Fishing boat proceeds	6 Medical and health care payments	This information is being furnished to the Internal Revenue Service.
		7 Nonemployee compensation 15,000.00	8 Substitute payments in lieu of dividends or interest	
		9 Payer made direct sales of $5,000 or more of consumer products to a buyer (recipient) for resale . . . . ▶ ☐		
Account number (optional)				

Opposite top: The atrium at Trump Tower. (Photo by Keute/ullstein bild via Getty Images) *Opposite bottom:* The 1099 tax form for one of my Christmas bonuses. (Res Personal Collection) *Right:* Donald with a model of Television City, which would eventually become Riverside South. 1985. (Bettmann/ Contributor) *Below:* Donald in his new office at Trump Tower with his executive assistant, Norma Foerderer. If he was on the phone, it was almost always on speaker. 1983. (Photo by John Iacono/Sports Illustrated via Getty Images/Getty Images)

Above left: Louise Sunshine, the outstanding head of condo sales for Trump Tower, was there in the early days along with me and Norma. 2015. (Photo by Angel Valentin for the Washington Post via Getty Images) *Above right:* Verina Hixon (left) and me. Verina bought three apartments in Trump Tower, and we installed a pool in one of them for her. Circa 1982. (Res Personal Collection) *Below left:* Donald kept a similar photo of Roy Cohn in his desk drawer and would pull it out to threaten a lawsuit against subcontractors when they couldn't settle their differences. 1977. (Photo by Getty Images) *Below right:* Robert Trump (Donald's brother), and his wife, Blaine. 1987. (Photo by Ron Galella/Ron Galella Collection via Getty Images)

10 August, 1984

*Wishing you
the best of luck
and warmly hoping, too,
You'll find success
and happiness
in everything you do.*

*and you'll always
have a home right
here —

love Donald*

BEST WISHES TO YOU
In Your New Venture

The card Donald gave me when I
left the Trump Organization the
first time. 1984. (Res Personal Collection)

Opposite: Ivana Trump outside the Plaza Hotel. 1988. (Photo by Ari Mintz/Newsday RM via Getty Images) *Above:* Donald with Marla Maples, who would become his second wife. I went to their wedding at the Plaza Hotel in December 1990. (Photo by the LIFE Picture Collection via Getty Images) *Below:* Donald with Melania Knauss, who would become his third model wife. 1999. (Photo by Evan Agostini/Getty Images)

Above: Donald and Ivana at their home in Florida, Mar-a-Lago, with their household staff behind them. (Photo by Ted Thai/The LIFE Picture Collection via Getty Images) *Below:* Donald at the opening of the ill-fated Trump Taj Mahal Casino in Atlantic City. 1990. (Photo by Yann Gamblin/Paris Match via Getty Images) *Opposite:* Donald gave me a copy of this recommendation letter he wrote for my personal use when I applied for a position on the American Arbitration Association's prestigious Construction Panel. 1998. (Res Personal Collection)

July 29, 1998

Ms. Agnes J. Wilson
Regional Vice President
American Arbitration Association
140 West 51st Street
New York, NY 10020-1203

Dear Agnes,

Barbara Res has asked me to prepare a letter recommending her appointment
as an arbitrator. I have known Barbara for over 20 years. She was in my direct
employ from 1980 to 1984, overseeing the construction of Trump Tower and again
from 1987 to 1991 on various projects, and then as a consultant until April 1998.
Barbara is extremely knowledgeable in all aspects of commercial and residential
construction and development. She also is experienced in leasing and sales
negotiations and has an exceptional grasp of the litigation aspects of the real estate
business. In her dealings with architects, contractors, tenants and bureaucrats,
Barbara has represented me with the utmost integrity and professionalism. She has
a strong reputation as a smart and tough but very fair person. She is well respected
throughout the industry.

What makes Barbara Res good is not only her intelligence and experience, but her
ability to cut through the excess and get things done. As an arbitrator, I am sure
that Barbara would be able to reach the right decision for the parties with a
minimum of time and cost. As someone who has used arbitration, I can tell you
that we need intelligent arbitrators and fast resolutions. I think Barbara would
be an excellent person to do that job. I hope you will consider her application
favorably.

Sincerely,

Donald J. Trump

Above: Donald being sworn in as the forty-fifth president of the United States. One of the saddest days of my life. January 20, 2017. (Photo by Chip Somodevilla/Getty Images) *Below:* I marched with hundreds of thousands of women and men at the Women's March in Washington the day after Trump's inauguration to say we will not allow him to decimate the rights women have earned. One of the happiest days of my life. January 21, 2017. (Photo by Res)

film production studios. Donald claimed he was in negotiations with NBC, which was considering moving out of its Rockefeller Center headquarters. The consensus was that NBC was just looking for leverage while it renegotiated its deal on rent and taxes with Rockefeller Center and the city. NBC never intended to move the studios, and certainly not to a purely hypothetical site with no start date. Trump ignored this reality and sold the fiction that NBC would move to Television City. Maybe he thought he could seduce them; maybe he was bluffing. All that mattered was getting everyone else to believe it.

Donald had feathered his political nest in preparation for the Television City announcement. He had given or raised hundreds of thousands for the reelection campaigns of Manhattan Borough President Andrew Stein, City Comptroller Jay Goldin, and Mayor Ed Koch. Even his father contributed $25,000 to Koch's 1985 reelection campaign. One thing Donald did not count on was NBC's reaction or that of local residents. Locals objected to both the density and the size of the buildings, which were completely out of character with the neighborhood adjoining the site.

Network officials promptly informed the media that they had made no commitments to Trump or anyone else. When it became clear NBC would not be in the picture, Trump changed gears and renamed the project, what else? Trump City. But the local resident problem only grew.

When I returned to the Trump Organization in 1987, I began work on several development projects, including the West Side Yards project/Trump City, for which I was in charge of any construction-related matters. In 1990, I was put in charge of the entire project, replacing Tony Gliedman. In the early 1980s, when

Tony was with the Department of Housing Preservation, he had held up the $20 million tax abatement for Trump Tower, thereby incurring Donald's wrath. Back then Trump referred to him as "the fat fuck," which was the only name I knew him by until I met him at the Trump Organization. Gliedman was indeed a heavyset man who dressed impeccably. He had real political connections, including a standing tennis match with Koch's successor, Mayor David Dinkins, every Sunday. For a man of his size, he was very spry. Trump was impressed that he couldn't steamroll Tony over the abatement, so he later hired him.

After taking over for Gliedman, I started organizing support for the Trump City project from the community and the labor unions. There was a real shortage of construction jobs at the time, and building Trump City would create thousands of union jobs. I was planning a march on City Hall in support of the development. I was also working with the Department of Environmental Protection, the last agency we had to clear and the one giving us the most trouble.

In 1990, while we were closing in on finally getting the project approved, Trump was approached by a trusted friend who told him in no uncertain terms that Trump City would never be built. There was a group of heavy hitters who had banded together to oppose him: the Natural Resources Defense Council (NRDC), the Municipal Arts Society, and other members of the political elite, along with local associations and some famous names like actor Christopher Reeve and author E. L. Doctorow. They had already had an architect design an alternative plan called Riverside South. It was to be a wall of buildings along the Hudson, about half the size of Trump City. I thought their project would be an eyesore, a lame imitation of the elegant buildings on Central Park West, like the Dakota, which they were supposed to emulate.

Savvy, organized, and well financed, this group—whom we referred to as the "civics"—complained that Trump City would dramatically increase traffic congestion in the area, overload the 72nd Street subway station, cast shadows on Riverside Park, and effectively destroy the quiet residential neighborhood. They also argued that the project would have unmitigable impact on the environment. According to Hurt's biography, while Trump was trying to buy his way through the process by making political contributions, these groups had real political clout, including the support of Congressman Jerrold Nadler and City Council President Ruth Messinger.

On a bone-cold December afternoon, Trump and I met with representatives of the civics in the boardroom in Trump Tower. It was a large space, but there were so many people that some had to stand. They were mostly upper-crust New Yorkers who were united in opposition against the project. There were members of various community organizations along with a contingent of people whose issue was that our project would block their views. As they filed in, Trump went into impress mode: He told me to get some of the "girls" to take drink orders from the attendees. I grabbed a few of the secretaries, including my own. When Trump saw that one of them was a little overweight, he waved me over. "What are you doing?" he asked, not loud, but not quiet either.

"What?" I asked, not realizing what he was referring to.

"Get rid of her." He gestured with his chin. "Bring in one of the other girls." Trump was proud of his trappings, such as the expansive table and the mirror and velvet walls in the conference room. To him, the "girls" in the office were just another part of the carefully cultivated image.

Despite all the back-and-forth maneuvering, it wasn't a contentious meeting. One of the civics, the man who represented the Natural Resources Defense Council, was quite handsome, distractingly so. "We don't believe that what you're doing is right for the city," he said. "We have an alternative that maybe you'd like, and if you do, we'll put our weight behind it and you will get approved." Donald was surprisingly quiet and polite, with no eruptions. When they had finished their pitch, Trump was even gracious. "Okay, let me take a closer look at this, talk to my people," he said. With talk of another meeting in the future, we finished and people began drifting out. Donald was uncharacteristically quiet that day, not taking a stand or giving any indication—even to us—what he would decide.

I felt pretty confident of our position and expected the final agency approval imminently. Donald scheduled another meeting with the civics, which I couldn't attend, When I saw Donald right afterward, he told me, "Yeah, we made a deal and we're gonna use their plan." He said it like it was no big deal. I couldn't believe he had caved so easily. He admitted they were stronger than we were and could stop him from doing anything. He didn't even try to negotiate. I was both shocked and furious.

Although Donald was in dire financial shape at the time, I have no doubt that he could have made a better deal. Even the civics' lawyer was shocked that he hadn't put up a fight. But under an amount of pressure he had never faced in his life, Trump panicked and choked. After a weak attempt at getting most of what he was planning, he didn't negotiate further. He ended up getting 7 million square feet, half of what he'd proposed. I'm sure he could've gotten 10 or maybe 11 million—minus the world's tallest building, of course—if he hadn't caved.

No matter the façade, the truth was that Trump was scared of anyone who had more power than he did, and while this was going down, he was in terror over the possibility of a personal bankruptcy. He was nearing bankruptcy and about to lose his casinos, massively in debt, hemorrhaging cash; and rumors about his spiral had already surfaced in public. At the insistence of the banks that had loaned him hundreds of millions, Trump hired a well-known "workout specialist" named Stephen Bollenbach to come up with a solution that would work for all the banks involved. As Trump himself admitted, if you added up the total value of what he owned at the time and subtracted his debt, his net worth was around negative $900 million.

The banks stood to lose a tremendous amount of money if Trump went belly-up. Steve would help them see that without Trump, the West Side Yards was just a massive piece of undeveloped property that they could only hope to sell for a small fraction of the money they'd lent to Trump to buy it. All the banks came to meet Trump, Steve, and me on neutral ground in an enormous hotel conference room in Midtown, with easels set up to hold our presentation boards. Representatives from what seemed like every bank in New York City sat in that room, including Citibank, Deutsche Bank, Chase, and NatWest, a British bank I had never even heard of. We explained to the anxious lenders and a roomful of lawyers how the proposed development was in their best interest. My job was to explain the project and demonstrate how Trump's involvement would infuse value into the properties, which would enable the banks to get some of their money back, even with the smaller civics' project, Riverside South. It was a gamble: If you stay in the game and keep betting, you have a chance to recoup losses, but if you leave the table, that's it. You'll never make your money back.

The banks agreed to a settlement plan in 1990, but the income Trump promised from the casinos did not materialize. That same year Donald's flagrant spending culminated in the outrageous purchase of a third casino—the Trump Taj Mahal—which added even more competition to his two operating casinos, already competing against each other. Inevitably, all three casinos would get into financial trouble. When Trump was saved, it was not because of business acumen but the banks' self-interest and his own PR skill. He had succeeded in associating the name with luxury—whatever the reality—and that impression gave the business actual value.

So the banks agreed to another plan in 1991. In the final workout, Donald was able to keep Trump Tower, which will always be his crowning jewel; Mar-a-Lago, his 126-room mansion in Palm Beach, Florida; and the Plaza (which still had debt). But his interests in the Grand Hyatt, the airline, his yacht, and Alexander's stock were given to specific banks. Trump held on to the casinos but gave up a 50 percent interest in the Taj Mahal. The banks gave Donald the amount of money necessary to run the empire, as well as a large personal allowance ($450,000 a month) and money to pay alimony to Ivana. The great businessman was now a kid with an allowance again, but this time, the role of Fred was played by the banks. They controlled his every move. With the Trump name involved, the West Side Yards was a site that could be worth a lot of money, which was the major reason Trump was saved. He lost basically everything, but he was able to shade the truth to the public and claim victory.

Trump then went to work doing what he does: spinning. "All you folks have persuaded me to really do what was right," he said publicly. In *The Art of the Comeback*, he tells a fabricated story of how this all went down. Donald even implies that he was the one who renamed the project Riverside South, as if he would voluntarily take his name off anything. Trump has to be the hero of every story, so it was he who had turned things around, done the right thing for the city, and made a lot of money. People say Trump ultimately won, and maybe he did, but what did he win? He was saved from bankruptcy and he got a small piece of a mediocre development with his name on some of the buildings.*

It's not just that Trump lost, it's that he lost because of his own shortsightedness. He could have submitted (and gotten approved) a proposal for a much less ambitious project than Trump City, but one that would still have been more impactful than Riverside South. But he insisted on the world's tallest building, a thing that enraged powerful people who would not have been bothered by something less grandiose. The great dealmaker clearly didn't understand the basics of dealmaking, because he first insisted on something he could never get and then ultimately gave up what he wanted to get much less.

A new entity would be formed to develop the property, headed up by Richard Kahan, whom the civics selected. He was extremely connected, well versed in government processes, and

---

* The name would be removed in 2019, when the residents, disgusted with Trump's actions as president, demanded it.

very experienced. I mistakenly thought I would have to report to him and reacted childishly.

One afternoon in late winter 1991, I knocked on Trump's door.

"Yes?" Donald said, looking up as I walked into the office.

"I just wanted to—do you have a second to talk?"

"Sure," he said. He was already annoyed because he knew it wasn't good news. Nobody ramps into good news like that. "Okay. What is it, Barbara? Spit it out," he said. Behind Donald was the vast expanse of Central Park and the Plaza, its copper gabled roof patinized over the years to a beautiful light green.

"Look, Donald," I said, "I think I'm going to quit." I watched as his expression went from agitation to just total shock, like a wave crossing over his face. Donald didn't often show surprise, but it was obvious I had taken him off guard, which I hadn't expected.

"Wait, wait. What do you mean?" he said, a little whine in his voice.

"The project has taken a turn," I said. "Kahan is in charge now, and you really don't need me. It's a good time for me to make a move."

"I don't understand, Barbara? Why?" I sensed some hurt in his voice, but I soon realized that it was about him. It didn't make sense to him: *Why would somebody in my position want to leave him? And what would it say about him that his highest-ranking development executive had resigned?*

Donald seemed genuinely confounded. "Well, what am I gonna tell people? What are we gonna say?"

I told him he could tell people whatever he wanted. In the course of the conversation—maybe to cushion the blow—I added, "You know, also, Donald, my kid is having some problems and I want to be around for him." His eyes lit up. Donald clapped his hands together and pointed at me, "That's it," he said, perking right up. "That's what we'll say." Trump seized upon the story about my kid. He knew I was leaving because of Kahan, but that version might reflect poorly on him, so he went with the one that cast him in the best light.

To my surprise, two of the civics' leaders, Richard Kahan and Kent Barwick of the Municipal Arts Society, learned I was quitting and asked me to lunch. We met at the historic Villard House, a treasure of nineteenth-century New York with baroque design and cathedral ceilings. I thought they were being magnanimous with a grand goodbye, though I hardly knew either of them. Barwick was a handsome man, quite tall and thin, slightly balding, with piercing blue eyes. He exuded a sophisticated and genteel manner. Kahan was on the short side, dark hair, and fast-talking in the New York style, but definitely a pro. My guard wasn't even up when I sat down, but before the water was poured, Kahan went right into it. "You can't leave," he said.

"I'm sorry?" I said.

"You have to stay, Barbara," he said. "You just have to."

I told them I was flattered, but I couldn't do it. Kahan and Barwick exchanged a fleeting glance. Then Barwick leaned forward and just told me straight out, "Look, we just don't want to deal with Donald on any kind of regular basis. We just can't—we can't deal with him."

"We'd love to deal with you," Kahan added, making it clear what they meant. They had no stomach for Donald's antics and needed me to run interference. "What can we do?" they asked. "Whatever you want us to do, you got it." But I demurred, explaining I was ready to move on. The very thing that made me valuable to them—my ability to act as a buffer with Donald—only reaffirmed why I had to go. It's ironic, but when I sat down with Kahan, I realized that it wouldn't be so bad with him in charge. But their pleading made me realize how much I wanted to leave: not because of Kahan, but because of Donald.

When Donald wasn't happy, I absorbed most of the blows. I liked working twelve-hour days and the whirlwind of excitement that came with Trump's projects, but he had changed. The financial woes and the divorce had taken a toll on him, and he was sullen and bitter. He was not the same man. The lunch made me more certain of my choice. From that point on, I would work for Donald in a consultant capacity, which gave me the freedom and necessary distance. The West Side Yards project had made it clear to me.

The West Side Yards story—which stretched on for years—is a perfect example of who and what Trump is. He has to control the narrative so he can present the version that makes him look the best, which is rarely the reality. His success comes directly from the fact that he is not beholden to the truth. And with that, we move on to the next rule, perhaps Trump's defining characteristic.

FIVE

LIE, CHEAT, AND SOMETIMES STEAL

Rule: Trump tells lies because they are infinitely easier than truth.

When I started with Donald, I believed everything he told me. I believed him when he said the Metropolitan Museum of Art didn't want the irreplaceable Bonwit Teller sculptures that he destroyed while making Trump Tower.* I believed him when he said he didn't know the demolition workers on the building were undocumented. I even believed him when he said that a steel beam that dropped out of the sky and fell on the street below was not from Trump Tower.

We were using magnesium beams to hoist the flue for the fireplace in Trump's apartment when one beam fell off the top of the

---

* The museum definitely did want the sculptures, and he had promised he would save them. (Louise Sunshine claimed in a 2016 *Frontline* interview that they weren't destroyed and one sits on her balcony, but I can't confirm this.)

664-foot building onto 57th Street, crashing through the roof of a truck parked on the street. No one was in it and no one was hurt, but reporters swarmed in an instant. Trump Tower was already getting a lot of media at the time, so this was a story they jumped on. I did not know what had happened, and I wasn't even told that HRH had erected a temporary hoist on the roof, but someone had to answer questions about it. Trump had found a kind of publicity he didn't like.

I handled the press on Trump Tower when Trump didn't want to do it, and he didn't want to go anywhere near this. So he needed me to deny that the beam was ours, but he knew I would not lie for him. Trump regularly complained to me that I was "too honest." He knew he couldn't always tell me the real story behind something, because if I talked to reporters, I would tell it the way it happened. Very early in the construction of Trump Tower, he asked me to sign off on the functional obsolescence of a building he had demolished, even though I hadn't even worked for him at the time of the demolition and had never been inside it. I just said "No," like I would to a regular question, so he got someone else to sign off on the building. Over time, this would become something of a pattern in our dealings.

But the incident of the beam was a problem for him: He couldn't refuse to talk to the press, which would make him look guilty, and he knew I would tell the truth—if I knew it. So he hatched a plan. The HRH project manager and superintendent, two people I trusted, joined Donald in his office. Then he called for me to join them. When I walked in, they were sitting around his desk, discussing the beam. I took a seat across from Donald, who greeted me with a nod as they kept talking.

"Hi Barbara. Yeah, it's strange," the project manager, said. He was very smart, with a careful, measured way of talking. "I don't know where it came from. We don't even have any beams like that, so it couldn't be us."

· "Okay, good. Good. Couldn't be us, then, right?" Trump said. His focus, as always, was the PR aspect, how the accident would reflect on him.

"Must've been from the AT&T building," the superintendent added. He was always quick to answer, more off the cuff than the project manager. "I know they're using that type of beam over there." Construction on the AT&T building was going on around the corner from where the beam had fallen.

"Okay," Trump seemed satisfied and looked at me. "Okay, we don't know where it came from, but we don't use those beams and they do at AT&T. Okay, Barbara. You know how to handle this. Do it." I wanted to do my due diligence, so the project manager took me over to the AT&T site a block away and showed me their magnesium beams piled on the concrete deck. I also called the structural engineer and asked if he thought it was possible the beam came from there, and he said yes.

So I went out with that story: The steel beam definitely did not come from Trump Tower, but maybe from the AT&T site. Every reporter said it was impossible for a beam to travel that far from another building, and I got ribbed a little. The *Daily News* put out a cartoon of a beam flying with angel wings. Since no one was hurt, the story just died. I'd witnessed Trump skirting the truth enough times, so I knew not to just take his word for things. But I believed the HRH guys, and they betrayed my trust. The conversation in

Trump's office must've been a setup, a fabrication to protect himself. I ended up looking a fool, and worse, a liar.

Some lies, like that, were to save himself. Other times they were to make himself look good—or the people around him, which was just another way of building himself up. He said Ivana had been an alternate on the Czechoslovakian ski team, that one of his attorneys graduated the top of his class at Yale Law (the school has no grades), even that there was an elevator to take him directly from his apartment at the top of the building to his office on the twenty-sixth floor. You can look it up. It's there in the *New York Times*, in *Travel + Leisure*, on Wikipedia. But it's not true. I know because I built the tower and it's not even possible.

The office and the residential parts have separate elevator banks. The elevators for the office floors stop at the twenty-ninth floor. The apartment elevators start at floor thirty and go to the very top, which is where Trump's apartment is. If there were to be an elevator from his office to his apartment, it would require destroying dozens of the most expensive apartments in the building. The notion is totally absurd. Trump must have seen it in a movie or something and liked how it sounded.

Lying seemed to come so naturally to Donald that if you didn't know the actual facts, he could slip something past you. It's a confidence trick, and it took a while for me to realize how often he did it. Things reached a point that when he said anything that seemed even remotely suspect, my crew and I would check it out before acting on it. If Donald claimed the project manager said an extra was included in the contract, we'd double-check. If Donald claimed the super said something would be completed earlier than I had told him, we'd ask the super. If Donald claimed that someone on my team had slighted me or someone else on the team, I'd ask them straight out. Usually I'd find that whatever Trump said was a fabrication or a stretching of the truth, a dishonesty that worsened through the years. As he lied, his yes-men would repeat the lies and reinforce Trump's version of events. I believe he actually came to believe the lies, especially the ones about himself. Truth is constraining, stubborn; it doesn't move at your will. That's exactly why Trump doesn't like it; it just gets in the way. It's so much easier to control things when truth is taken out of the equation. He has gone so far down his own rabbit hole that the lying isn't as intentional as it once was: He often doesn't know the truth anymore.

Back when he was a developer and publicity hound, talking up New York reporters and gossip columnists, Donald would spin them, telling any story they'd be willing to print. He wasn't alone in doing it, and he was gifted at it. Truth was just collateral damage on his way to the top.

I remember one night we were working late in his office after hours. I was sitting in one of those awful round silver-backed chairs, across from him at his desk, when he called *New York* magazine. "Watch this." Without even trying to disguise his voice, he identified himself as John Barron, a PR person for the Trump Organization. He was new there, he said, and then launched into the most obvious fabrications about Trump Tower (like Princess Di was buying an apartment there), and the business, and Donald Trump's exploits. He made faces to me like *Isn't this funny?* and every once in a while would put his hand over the receiver and make a comment and we'd laugh. He thought it was a game. After he hung up, he started explaining that John Barron was an alias he'd use on the phone sometimes. "What do you think?" he asked.

"It's great," I said, "I mean—great that you can get away with it." What I didn't say was that I actually thought it was nuts. It was a strange thing to do and an even stranger thing to brag about. Then he launched into how reporters print whatever he says, that he can spin reporters "like you wouldn't believe." That was the first time I "met" Barron, but it became something of a gag he would do in front of us around the office. It wasn't even a secret, and the lies I saw or heard him telling as Barron (and other aliases) weren't even necessary. They just allowed him to talk more about being better, bigger, the most, the best, like a compulsion. As far as I know, he never used aliases to get out of trouble; it was just to burnish his image and get people talking about him.

So much of Donald's fame and fortune was built on lies: His buildings were the largest, he was dating supermodels and stars or they wanted to date him, rivals' wives were hitting on him, he had never settled a lawsuit, he sold more copies of *The Art of the Deal* than he actually did, he belonged higher on the *Forbes* list, the Trump Organization owned more units than it did, his family was from Sweden, Trump Tower—which was sixty-eight stories— was worth more than it actually was. It was all noise, a sideshow to me. I was an engineer, dealing in concrete and steel and square footage, things you could measure. For me, as I'm sure happened for others, dealing with Donald followed a progression. First you fall for his lies, then you feel like you're in on it, then you sour, then you don't believe a word he says. Gradually, as the 1990s unfolded, Trump's need to invent things was no longer a sideshow; it became the main attraction.

Lying is the natural extension of Trump's focus on appearance, selling, hyping, exaggerating, and spinning. He reached a point where, to get out the version he wanted or needed, he could just lie. It was so much more efficient, literally a child's conclusion. *Wait,* a five-year-old figures out, *if I tell Mommy I didn't eat the cookie, I won't get in trouble.* That's Trump. The fastest and easiest way from point A to point B is always a lie.

———————

ON THE DAY Trump was sworn in as president, the American public saw that he and his administration were going to go all in on the big-lie theory, repeating something enough times that people will believe it. When photos comparing Trump's and Obama's inaugurations were put side by side, with Trump's crowd paling in comparison, the new president couldn't take it. He had Press Secretary Sean Spicer go out on his first day and lie that Trump had the bigger crowd. Trump and Spicer even got the National Park Service to deceptively edit the photos. Trump's followers wanted to believe him, so his people just argued that the real photographs were doctored by the "fake news," and his supporters bought it. Labeling the media "fake news" has been an absolutely essential part of Trump's lying. Though the term actually originates from the kind of Russian propaganda that helped him get elected, he has hijacked it to use on any reporting that he doesn't like.

Trump's lies were often so outrageous that he had to get others to go along, which can lead to all kinds of corruption: threatening, payoffs, quid pro quos, patronage, and cronyism. The inauguration lie is a perfect example of how Trump lies and then coerces others to protect that lie. It's an apparatus designed to rewrite the truth. In defending Trump's inaugural-crowd lie, Kellyanne Conway, his senior adviser, went on television and invented the term "alternative facts," an excuse for people to not believe what they were seeing.

The *Washington Post*, which has been tracking Trump's false claims in office, recently reported he passed twenty thousand. That averages out to twelve a day, more than one per working hour. The COVID crisis has been the apex—from how early he responded to how dangerous the virus is to "anyone who wants a test can get a test," to how we have the most tests and the lowest mortality, it's just been nonstop lies. At the same time, he has been pushing lies on other fronts: about voter fraud and mail-in ballots, riots and the breakdown of law and order in "Democratic" cities, Joe Biden's mental acuity and his "socialist" policies, lying (over a hundred times) about how he will always protect preexisting conditions in people's health care plans while his administration was in court trying to undo them. Before this batch, he lied about his high approval rating, that we defeated ISIS, that the caravan of migrants was going to invade our country (right before the midterm elections), that his Ukraine call was "perfect,"* that his tax returns couldn't be released because he was under audit, that he'd be entirely separated from his business while in office, that Russian election interference was a hoax, that any actual election interference was by Democrats and Ukraine, and countless other topics. The list is exhausting. I think now he's so caught in his own web

---

* This is just classic Trump. He has a phone call that gets him impeached. Whereas anyone on the planet would at least hedge, say *Maybe things got interpreted wrong but I didn't mean it that way*, Trump cannot stop calling it "perfect." How does that serve him? It's just his need to always go to the extreme—he can't help it.

of lies that he's lost. He has an inner circle, media apparatus, and followers, who all echo his falsehoods back to him, so where is he going to hear the truth? If he does see a fact check in the *New York Times* or on CNN, he treats it as an attack and goes on about how badly he's treated. The truth itself is an assault.

One of his most embarrassing and famous lies was the Hurricane Dorian scandal, branded "Sharpiegate." Trump made an error about Alabama being in the storm's path, a harmless mistake, easily corrected or just ignored. Yet he and his administration jumped through all kinds of hoops to get his gaffe confirmed as truth. He got the National Oceanic and Atmospheric Administration (NOAA) and the National Weather Service to lie in order to cover for his error. He even went so far as to draw, in visible black Sharpie, a larger circle around a weather map that had already marked the storm's path and then deny that he had done it. It was all absurd and will be mocked for a long time to come, but it offered a real look at how pathological his need to be right is and how he is willing to say and do anything to appear so. In my experience he did this frequently. If he was called out for saying something wrong, he would find someone to accuse or blame for his mistake, or he'd lie outright and claim that he'd said the opposite. He couldn't be wrong, ever, and he used lies to protect himself from ever appearing so.

Trump's lies act as a type of wish fulfillment. The way to understand him is to recognize that of all the lies he tells, *he himself is the biggest lie*. Trump was not the most successful businessman, the one who could fix the country; he was just the loudest and most famous, the one who played that guy on TV. What we see now in his failed presidency and the multiple crises it has triggered is like reality collapsing in on the lie that is Donald Trump. The more that Trump is forced to confront the truth of himself, his history, his abilities, and his failures, the more he goes to extremes to continue the farce.

Trump's wealth, the origin of the Trump brand, began as a lie. An extensive 2018 *New York Times* investigation revealed that from the day of his child's birth, Fred Trump worked to set Donald (and his siblings) up for life.* Donald's claim that he got nothing but a $1 million loan from Fred that he paid back with interest is just a flagrant lie. He actually got far more than that, and got it continuously throughout Fred's life and beyond.

The *Times* investigation determined that in total, Fred passed on to Trump $413 million in today's dollars. Financial experts have said that if Trump had done nothing but put the money he got from his father into the stock market, he'd be worth a hell of a lot more than he is today. And of course, Donald also broke into Manhattan real estate entirely on the back of his father's name, money, and connections. This is not shocking or even inherently wrong, but it's entirely divorced from the origin story on which Trump built his fame and fortune.

One example among many: When the casinos were tanking, Trump was so desperate that he called his father to come to the rescue. Fred sent his man down to Atlantic City one night to walk into Trump Castle, buy $3 million worth of chips, infusing cash into the business, and walk out. The stunt violated gaming laws, and Fred paid a hefty penalty. It wasn't even worth it; all it did was delay the inevitable: The same debt payment came up the next month, and all three casinos would eventually go bankrupt.

---

* Donald was a millionaire by age eight.

Donald also regularly lies about how much he is worth, going so far as to sue a biographer—Timothy O'Brien—for over $2 billion for claiming he was worth only around $200 million. A deposition Trump gave in the matter offered a brief look at how subjective his estimate of his wealth really is. He admitted his net worth changed depending on *his mood.* "My net worth fluctuates," he said to the lawyer, "and it goes up and down with markets and with attitudes and with feelings, even my own feelings." When pressed by the confused attorney, Donald reiterated: "So yeah, even my own feelings affect my value to myself." Asked the basis for his estimates, Trump replied, "I would say it's my general attitude at the time that the question may be asked. And as I say, it varies."

He's so attached to the lie about his wealth because he sees it as a reflection not just of his worth but of his *self*-worth. "I've earned billions," he told a 2011 crowd, "which is both a scorecard and acknowledgment of my abilities." Some argue he's not worth $1 billion, but even if he is, he certainly didn't earn most of it. His father made everything about him possible. In addition, what Donald created from what he was given is really not that impressive, from a construction and real estate point of view. In the 1980s he had a few high-profile projects, but he came nowhere near the accomplishments of famed New York real estate families like the Rudins, the Dursts, the Milsteins, and the Zeckendorfs, who had built tens of millions of square feet of office buildings and tens of thousands of apartments and hotels and retail spaces. Trump's total number of projects, his success rate, and his longevity cannot compare to what these New York City scions have achieved. Without Trump's oversized PR, Trump would be a footnote in the history of New York real estate.

Donald worked really hard to build his name—out of lies, his dad's money, and a good sense of PR—and it would be his name that saved him. By the 1990s, when he was in so much debt that he was toxic to the banks, he stayed alive because the biggest loans were for securing the West Side Yards and the banks had to keep him on life support. They knew that without Trump as a developer, and his self-created cachet, that property would maybe raise 10 percent of its debt at auction. Trump discovered that his name could make a property's value skyrocket.

As his fame ballooned, and he learned how to make money off his name, the name itself became the business. That's the Trump empire—the selling of a name. He neither developed nor owns many Trump-named properties—from Trump International at Columbus Circle (owned by General Electric) to the Trump SoHo (owned by the CIM group), which found business improved only after they dropped the Trump name. Overseas, the trend of slapping "Trump" on existing projects is essentially a business model. Trump is a licenser, not a developer anymore, and according to one investigation into his finances, "he doesn't own nearly 40 percent of the 62 buildings that bear his name." He puts his name on other people's work, charges them to use it, and takes a cut from what they earn. But he knows that's not as impressive sounding, so he tells a different story.

Subrule: Cheating is easier than playing fair.

Cheating is just dishonesty in action. I used to describe Donald's success to people like this:

"Have you ever played Monopoly?" I'd ask. "Well, imagine if you cheated. You took money from the bank, skipped spaces, put houses on your properties when no one was looking, and took everyone else's houses. Would you win?"

Trump cheats as "a way of life," as his niece, Mary, claimed. He does not think rules apply to him, and he gets away with it. When he's penalized for backing out of agreements or skirting zoning rules, the payment (even if he does pay) is never enough to matter. It all pales next to what he has gained by cheating.

A lot of times Trump would ask for something on a project that couldn't be done, and it was obvious that it couldn't be done and I would say no. "You can't do that," I'd say. "It's the law." Or "We can't. The plans are done." Or "Can't do it. The materials are already on-site."

"Oh, Barbara, you're so fucking negative," he'd say.

"No, I'm not," I'd say. "You just can't do things like that."

One time he replied, "Of course you can do them. *You* just can't do them."

Just like lying, cheating made Donald. The *New York Times* investigation into the Trumps' alleged decades-long tax scam broke down how cheating was part of the family legacy. I was astounded that when revealed, that level of cheating by our president caused barely a whimper from the general public. It's like he has placed the bar so low on what to expect of him that things that resemble outright criminality don't even make us blink. This holds true for the Trump Foundation, which was mostly a scam, and for Trump University, which was entirely one.

Not content to cheat taxpayers, the government, and gullible acolytes, Trump also created a fiction about his charitable donations. Trump barely, if ever, gave to charity, which I think is one of the many reasons he wants to keep his tax returns hidden. He used to get me to lean on various contractors to donate tens of thousands of dollars for various fundraisers, a tactic he used regularly. While Donald himself gave relatively little of his own money to the Donald J. Trump Foundation, it's been reported that he did get others, including his business associates, to donate millions of dollars to it. Those who have looked into the Trump Foundation have found an organization rampant with corruption. When he wasn't using the Foundation for "self-dealing and advancing the interests of its namesake rather than those of charity," he was just taking others' contributions out and giving them to charity under his own name, burnishing his image with other people's money. The Foundation was forced to disband in 2018, after investigations revealed, unsurprisingly, "unlawful coordination with the Trump presidential campaign, repeated and willful self-dealing, and much more."

As a candidate, Trump sold himself as the guy who knew the system and could make it work for the American people. The subtext was: *Yeah, I cheat, but now I'll cheat for America!* But that isn't what happened. He continued to cheat—but to enrich himself. David Fahrenthold at the *Washington Post* and others have painstakingly shown that through emoluments from other governments' currying favor with Trump by buying up blocks of his hotel rooms, and through his own steering of government services to his financial benefit, Trump acts as though the presidency is one big grift. He regularly uses the presidency to funnel publicity and money to his properties, like when he leaned on the U.S. ambassador to the U.K. to push England to move the British Open to one of his own courses. Then, of course, he lied about it.

The legislative actions he's taken in office have allowed him, his friends, and his corporate peers to pay even fewer taxes, cheat their own workers, swallow up loan money meant for small businesses, and pollute at will. A recent *Washington Post* investigation found that he has been bilking the U.S. government of money through exorbitant Secret Service charges that earn him money at his properties. It's no surprise that Trump sees the U.S. government as a tool for his own benefit; that's his background. It is how real estate and construction work. His first project in Manhattan, the Grand Hyatt, got off the ground because New York City gave him a forty-year abatement, which came out to be worth $160 million. (He got another abatement on Trump Tower, though he had to fight for that one.) That's considered a success in the business world, but the reality is that New Yorkers ultimately pay for that. It is not in his DNA to care about taxpayers footing his bill, even when he is their president.

I know stories of architects who got paid twenty-five cents on the dollar on Trump projects, and it's possible that Donald stiffed some subcontractors outside of my purview. But not a single subcontractor was screwed on Trump Tower, the Plaza, or the Grand Hyatt. I made sure Trump never got taken for a ride, but also that all the workers got paid what was agreed to. Trump hired me because I was a "killer," so I didn't let up once I worked directly for him. On Trump Tower, I was tough on the architects and particularly the engineers, showing up in their offices to look at where they were with the plans. This was outrageous of me to do, but I caught them lying about their progress. When I got on their backs, things came faster. So I didn't pussyfoot one day on that job, but I never cheated anybody.

However, working for Trump, you had to be careful. Whether it was a buildings department citation or politicians denying permission for something, he told us to ignore it. Trump's universal command was "Just do what we need to do." I know everyone had a line they wouldn't cross—I had mine—but I never got the impression that Trump did. His line was determined by what he thought he could get away with.

Donald would constantly try to cheat the contractors out of money for changes that were already agreed to: adding and deleting materials, moving walls, speeding up the work in certain areas, and clearing up errors. Changes are a normal part of any large construction project, and they occur in any trade. When subs get a changed drawing from the architect, and extra work needs to be done, they do it in good faith, and I would negotiate a fair price for it. (In most cases subs inflate the cost of their extra work, expecting the price to be negotiated down.)

Later, when Trump said he didn't want to pay or tried to negotiate the price down even more, I would have to explain to him. "No, no, no," I'd say. "That's not how it works. You don't get another bite at the apple. This is what we agreed to, and I gave him my word."

I repeatedly explained to him that changing these agreements would damage my credibility and reputation. He would still fight each one, and we'd go back and forth in a tango where we knew every step. If it was just the two of us, he would yell at me. In front of others, it would be more like complaining. I would not have stayed if Trump had refused to pay his contractors, his subs, and his consultants fairly. But there's more than enough evidence that on multiple projects, he didn't pay people for their work.

In the final stretch of Trump Tower, changes to the apartments were a daily thing, mostly for Trump's triplex. Sketches and new drawings were flooding in at a fast clip. The architecture firm did a lot of extras, which the design architect, John Barie, wanted to get paid for. I told Barie to wait, that I could get him a better deal after we opened, knowing that submitting extras at that time would enrage Trump. When I approached Donald with Barie's change orders, expecting the usual dance followed by a grudging approval, he went berserk. "What?! This is no fucking good, Barbara!" he screamed at me. "They're taking advantage of you!"

"That's not true, Donald. I already worked out—"

"What are you talking about? There were no material changes, and it was supposed to be included in the price!" This didn't make sense: Either there weren't any changes or there were and they were included. Trump regularly would throw out contradictions like this during arguments.

"You knew about all of this while it was happening," I said. "This is for changes to the work that you directed, all over the building. Mostly in your apartment."

"I didn't direct any changes!" Trump claimed. "If they had to do extra work, it was because they fucked up the first time."

"The architects did not include changing things after they were settled in their price," I tried to calmly explain to him. "Much less changing and changing the same thing over and over again. Their price was for *one* set of drawings. You know how much the job changed. You have to pay for this. The work was done."

I was able to settle with the structural engineer, but the architect's decision-making partner was intransigent. He believed correctly that he deserved every cent, but Trump doesn't need right on his side; he has the money and he doesn't play by the rules. Donald should have paid the architects and consultants—it was pennies compared to what the building was earning in rents—but Trump was Trump. I had left by then to work on the Hartz building, and meaningful discussions stopped. Knowing they had a legitimate claim, Trump made his usual preemptive strike; he filed a demand for arbitration, similar to a lawsuit. He basically sued his architects to get back at them for asking for extra money they deserved.

When I heard about it, I was not surprised at all. The way I see it, revenge was part of Trump's business model. Trump's claims against the architects contained allegations of improper design, which resulted in cost delays and other nonspecific evils. Donald's lawyers found an out-of-town expert who came up with an irrelevant design error in the mechanical work and delays relating to the foundations. (As far as I knew, there were no delays and no extras for structural changes.) Although in the end the arbitrators awarded the architect all their extras, they also found for Trump for the mechanical fault, resulting in a million-dollar windfall for him. It was a fitting coda for Trump's crowning achievement, to be suing the architects when the building they designed was a phenomenal success.

Back then, a controlling factor in Trump's propensity to cheat was that he had partners who wouldn't have stood for him screwing over everyone. But in later years, left to his own devices on the projects he owned, surrounded by people who feared him, Trump realized he could get away with not paying the subs, and reports are that he did. I think this really took off with the Taj Mahal casino in Atlantic City, where Trump did not have the money to pay his subs, at least at first. Trump knows when you have somebody's money, you hold them hostage and can make them do what you want.* So he would threaten to sue, which meant tying up the party in court long enough for it to go bankrupt. The one with the most money to keep going will win—that's leverage. Usually the other side cannot even afford the legal defense. It's the art of the swindle. It's no coincidence that Trump campaigned for the presidency on a promise to "renegotiate" all of the U.S.'s international deals. He meant renege on them, and he has on several.

Cheating is a principle Trump believes in like gospel. There is no doubt he welcomed the illegal help Russia offered in the 2016 election. It's the same reason he's working to prevent and dispute mail-in ballots for the upcoming election, going so far as to block post office funding, get the postmaster general to slow down the mail, and lay the groundwork for not accepting the election results.

It's why he refuses to allow the intelligence community to tell the truth about what Russia did and is planning to do. It's why as president he has moved or dismissed a record number of inspectors general, put together one of the most corrupt cabinets in modern history, reportedly stolen money from his own campaign, and worked to release convicted criminals like Michael Flynn, Paul

---

* He was impeached for this very thing.

Manafort, and Roger Stone, friends who must have dirt on him. It's why he may face charges one day when he's out of office. He can't win fairly, so he doesn't play fairly. But he can't stop. He needs to be a winner, and if he has absorbed any lesson in his life, it is this: Cheating is how you win.

SIX

THE BALANCE SHEET

Rule: Trump will always grab credit and avoid blame.

"No, I don't take responsibility at all."

Of all of Trump's embarrassing statements as president, his answer to a reporter's question about the failed pandemic response may be the most horrifying—and revealing. The line defines him. Never take the blame, but always take the credit.

When I worked with him, Trump rarely changed his mind without some kind of coaxing, and he never, ever admitted to being wrong. That was a hard-and-fast rule. If it looked like he had made a mistake, he would say it was based on information he got from me or someone else, shifting responsibility. If he was all in for one plan and it went sour, he would do a complete 180, pretending that he had been forced into it. Against my advice, he had told me to give Verina Hixon, the woman who put a pool in her apartment at Trump Tower, anything she wanted—until he saw it backfiring and started to blame me for the problem. Anytime he's on one side of a losing argument or failed plan, he will hop to the other side like he's always been there.

In his heart, Donald believes he can do everything better. He is not unique in this. Many people are like that, wanting to take over and fix the problem. The difference is that most people know their limitations and will step aside for someone with more knowledge or expertise. Trump doesn't have that ability to recognize his limitations, because in his mind he can never be incapable and he can never be wrong. Even when things went well, in a contract that was a total win for us, Trump would undercut the negotiated settlement by saying he would have done better. Sometimes it felt like he left negotiations up to other people so he could say this after the fact, touting his own dealmaking skills without ever having to use them.

In the mid-1980s, when Atlantic City first got going for him, Donald assigned his younger brother, Robert, to work on the Trump Plaza Hotel and Casino. The move was mostly so that Robert could report everything back to him, but it was also for self-protection. Robert, both a family member and a not particularly aggressive man, was someone Trump could blame for everything and anything that went wrong. It helped that Robert would never fight his older brother for the credit or publicly deny the blame. Robert described himself as a workhorse, which is very telling. He never said he saw Donald as the show horse in that equation, but he didn't have to.

In October 1989, three Trump casino executives—Steve Hyde, Mark Etess, and Jonathan Benanav—were tragically killed in a helicopter crash. (In the aftermath, Trump falsely claimed that he was supposed to have been on the helicopter.) After the accident, Donald threw some blame about his Atlantic City problems the late executives' way as well. Even after Jack O'Donnell, VP of

Trump Plaza at the time, begged him to stop, telling him that it was hurtful to their widows and families, Donald still did it. "They're dead," Trump said, according to O'Donnell. "What does it matter, really?"

Trump then managed to run his casinos into the ground, paying himself millions in salary and shifting his debt to their ledgers, and replaced the excellent team with less qualified people who would blindly follow orders. Casinos are built to print money, and somehow Donald, the great businessman, couldn't figure out how to make money off them.* Every success in Atlantic City was Trump's own; every failure was Robert's or belonged to someone else at the company. According to Jack O'Donnell, at one meeting over the Taj Mahal—which was hemorrhaging money—Trump lambasted Robert in front of other executives. Robert finally reached his limit; he walked out, had his assistant grab some boxes, and took a helicopter home. Though Trump denies that Robert ever quit, the brothers didn't speak for many years.

For the period when Ivana was installed to run Trump's Castle, she also shouldered some blame. Ivana worked hard down there, learned a tremendous amount, and had the wherewithal to admit what she didn't know or couldn't handle. She was not experienced in business, but apparently she was well liked by those who worked for her.

---

* When Marvin Roffman, a business analyst who specialized in gambling, explained to the *Wall Street Journal* that the Taj Mahal, Trump's third casino, was so expensively designed that it was impossible for it to make money, Trump threatened to sue his employer. Roffman was fired three days later. Of course, Roffman was vindicated when the Taj Mahal missed its first debt payment a few months after opening and was bankrupt in a little over a year. (Roffman was awarded a $750,000 arbitration judgment against his employer and Trump.)

In my time with Trump, I witnessed countless instances of him shifting responsibility to others, including me, but one stands out all these years later. Shortly after we opened Trump Tower, in the early 1980s, there was a bomb threat called into the main office. The caller claimed that the bomb was in the atrium, which was always packed with employees, pedestrians, shoppers, and tourists. Trump called me into his office, telling me that security had just briefed him about the threat and I should call the police. I called the NYPD and then met with the building's security team as we waited for the police to arrive. The cops asked a lot of questions, and then I took them through the atrium, where they conducted a thorough search. From their demeanor, it was clear they were not concerned. They said they were not recommending evacuation. "We don't see a credible threat here," they told me, concluding it was most likely a hoax. But the ultimate decision to evacuate was Donald's.

I stepped into the elevator to head back to the twenty-sixth floor to brief Donald, not realizing I was heading into an ambush. When I got there, his door was open, so I just walked in without knocking.

"What's up, Barbara?" he asked. "What'd the cops say?"

"The cops searched and didn't find anything," I said. "They see no reason to be alarmed. Probably a hoax."

"Okay, great," he replied. "That's that, then, right?" He left that hanging, almost for me to fill in the empty space.

"Well, you know," I said, "there are some things we should probably talk about. There's a one-in-a-million chance that it could be real. The injuries, the damage. We should talk about it." To Trump's credit, he didn't mention the bad publicity that this would generate, but he also didn't want to discuss the potential damage at all.

It was clear that Donald did not want to evacuate and was latching onto any reason I offered. He kept going back to what a "pain in the ass" it would be and how we couldn't empty the building every time some wacko makes a phone call. We were wrapping up the conversation, and I could see his mind was moving on to other things. So I stood up to leave, expecting him to tell me to report to security that we weren't going to evacuate. Then he said, "I don't know, Barbara. You decide."

I was stunned. By that point, I was used to Trump delegating decisions to me, but nothing like this. His building? His employees? All those visitors? It was far too much for my shoulders. I was also infuriated. How dare he put me in that position? It was clear to me that there was no real danger, and if I had thought otherwise, I would've insisted we get everyone out. But still. He pawned it off onto me so that, if god forbid something did happen, he wouldn't have to take the hit. *I don't know,* I could picture him saying. *I was really concerned about it, but I talked to my executive VP, who met with the police and security, and she said not to evacuate.*

So I told him what he wanted to hear: *Don't evacuate.* It weighed on me, not just that day but for a long time afterward. Did I do the right thing? Did I just do what my boss wanted? Why did I allow him to put people's lives into my hands like that? Trump has that effect on people—pressuring them to cross lines. He has this malignant influence that makes you question yourself.

———————

DURING THE CORONAVIRUS epidemic, Trump wanted the accolades for saving "millions of lives" while not doing anything about it. During the first lockdown in the spring, when there was a question as to whether Trump would force the country to reopen by Easter, he claimed it was "the hardest decision" he would ever have to make. I remember watching him, certain that he would find a way to pawn it off on someone else. Sure enough, he left the "hardest decision" to the individual states. There was no way he was going to take on that monumental decision and the culpability that could come from it. Yet all the while, he was milking the moment to show a strength and resolve he did not possess.

Since the beginning of the pandemic, Trump has avoided providing national direction because he doesn't want to take responsibility. Rather than leading, Trump has left everything up to the governors because that's what he does—avoids the big decisions. This way, nothing can get pinned on him. But if anything good happens, he knows he can just swoop in and take credit after the fact. If somehow COVID hadn't stuck around in the summer, he would have been all over TV and Twitter claiming recognition for its disappearance. He would've campaigned for reelection on that very fact. When instead the cases got worse in the bottom half of the country in the summer, he denied it and then blamed the states for reopening too early. Of course, we all remember that he was the one encouraging, insisting, even threatening them to do exactly that.

He has lied about the severity of the pandemic, blatantly insisting things are improving when easily available statistics prove the opposite.* Trump continues to argue the debunked case that the U.S.'s terrible numbers are due to our high number of tests, because

---

* In early September 2020, journalist Bob Woodward shared tapes of interviews with Trump that show the president knew the coronavirus was deadly back in February. At the time, the president was publicly saying it was no worse than the flu and it would go away on its own. Trump's own words to Woodward prove he *knew* the lies would cause needless sickness and death, which makes his downplaying all the more monstrous.

it allows him to frame something awful as something positive. Then he silences those, like Dr. Anthony Fauci and Dr. Deborah Birx, who try to communicate the truth. He can't fire his scientific experts without tremendous blowback, so he undermines them. To keep his hands clean, he has his minions like Peter Navarro smear them. In mid-July, Navarro put out an op-ed in *USA Today* that said Fauci had been wrong about "everything I've interacted with him on." It was a hit piece, and it had Trump's name all over it. Just as we know Trump dictates statements for others to issue (like the statement about Don Jr.'s 2016 Trump Tower meeting with a Russian lawyer, which his lawyers have admitted he wrote), I am sure Trump told him exactly what to say. In August he promoted Dr. Scott Atlas, a radiologist with no infectious disease experience, as his new coronavirus adviser. Atlas has doubted the effectiveness of masks, promoted a widely debunked theory on "herd immunity," pushed for less testing and faster school openings, and falsely claimed that children can't pass on this virus. It's no coincidence that Atlas's beliefs track with what Trump would like the public to believe.

In the same press conference where Trump gave his now-infamous "No, I don't take responsibility at all" answer, PBS's Yamiche Alcindor asked him about his disbanding of the White House pandemic office. We've come a long way from President Truman's "The buck stops here." Here's the exchange:

Yamiche Alcindor: My first question is, you said that you don't take responsibility, but you did disband the White House pandemic office and the officials that were working in that office left this administration abruptly, so what responsibility do you take [for] that? The officials that worked in that office said that the White House lost valuable time because that office was disbanded. What do you make of that?

President Trump: I just think it's a nasty question, because what we've done is—and Tony [Fauci] had said numerous times that we've saved thousands of lives because of the quick closing. When you say 'me,' I didn't do it. We have a group of people I could ask, perhaps in my administration, but I could perhaps ask Tony about that, because I don't know anything about it. You say we did that. I don't know anything about it.

Alcindor: You don't know about the reorganization that happened at the National Security Council?

Trump: It's the administration. Perhaps they do that. People let people go. You used to be with a different newspaper than you are now. Things like that happen.

This exchange is pure Trump. Alcindor's questions are straightforward and factual, but Trump's response reveals how he sees the truth itself as a personal attack. So he attacks back. The fact that Alcindor is a woman of color likely makes him feel all the more justified in doing so. He has to make sure no blame gets on him. Throughout the pandemic, Donald has attached blame to just about everyone: China, the World Health Organization (WHO), the CDC, President Obama, the states, the governors, the Democrats, the media, even his own administration. Everyone but himself. But it's his negligence and dereliction of duty that have resulted in a level of sickness and death once unimaginable in this country. He didn't cause the virus or bring it here, but his incompetence and incessant need to avoid accountability have made it so much worse than it needed to be.

As Trump hides from the negative or spins it away from himself, he greedily tries to absorb all the positive he can. My mind goes to two stories that illustrate how he would do this. Back on the Grand Hyatt, in the late 1970s, it was a few days before Christmas, which meant bonus time. This was when I was still employed by HRH, not by Trump. Donald was in one of HRH's offices on the top floor of the Hyatt talking with the project manager, Ed Sullivan. I was passing by on the way to my little Fort Knox office when I heard Ed's voice.

"Barbara," Ed called out.

I popped my head in. "Hello, Donald. What's up, Ed?"

"Donald's got something for you," Ed said, gesturing to him.

"Yeah. Barbara," Trump said. He stood up and handed me an envelope. "Here you go. Artie thought it was too much, but I insisted. I said, 'No, no, no, Barbara's been amazing. We gotta take care of her.' I pushed for you. So here you go and merry Christmas."

"Thanks, Donald," I said, "I really appreciate it." I wasn't sure what was going on, as I'd never really seen this side of him. He gave me a friendly pat on the shoulder and walked out. After he left, I opened the envelope to find a $4,000 bonus, which was pretty generous, more than 10 percent of my salary. "No shit," Ed said. "Hell of a guy." It was a sarcastic remark, but I didn't know why or care.

"Thanks, Ed," I said. "I'm sure you had something to do with it too." He just smiled.

Here's the thing, though: Trump *hated* Christmas bonuses. We all knew that he had to grudgingly approve every single one. HRH was typically generous with them; it was good for morale, which always inures to the bottom line, something Trump never understood. But if Trump had had his way, there would have been no bonuses, so he was very stingy with what he gave to his own people. Later, at the Trump Organization, I always gave my secretary a second Christmas bonus out of my own pocket.

So why was he making a production of handing me a bonus check, claiming HRH wanted to give me less? The gesture itself was strange, since bonus checks usually just came along with our paychecks. I assume that when Trump saw HRH was proposing a $4,000 bonus for the young female mechanical superintendent, he went nuts. He probably refused, while Artie and Ed insisted I was valuable and deserved it. They probably argued a little, but Trump decided it wasn't worth it. It killed him, though, so he had to get something out of it. By handing the check to me himself and claiming he fought for it, he was showing me what a good guy he was. Since I didn't know him that well, I gave him the benefit of the doubt. But a few years later something happened that opened my eyes.

While we were building Trump Tower, HRH finished the concrete structure in record time, due in large part to the hard work of the concrete foreman, Eddie Bispo. Eddie was often there late into the night, supervising the work, six days a week, in summer heat and winter cold. HRH's project manager and superintendent approached me with the suggestion that we give Eddie a bonus of $5,000 to show our appreciation. I agreed. Trump, to put it mildly, did not.

"No fucking way!" Donald screamed when we suggested it. "What?! We're just gonna *hand* him five grand? Why? Let *his* people give him a bonus!" We were standing around Trump's desk at the Crown Building. We knew it was going to be an uphill battle, but we had power in numbers. We proceeded to bombard Trump with reasons why it was a good idea and continued pressing. "Listen, Donald," I said, "it's the right thing to do."

"This guy works his ass off," the project manager said. "He deserves it."

At some point in the conversation, Trump stopped protesting and I saw a little glimmer in his eye. "Well, if we're gonna do it, let's make a big thing out of it."

"What do you mean?" I asked. I didn't like where this was going; I'd seen this before. Trump had no choice, so the only thing to do was to get something out of it for himself.

"You know what would be something? Let's get one of those gigantic checks," he said, "and have a big ceremony where we have all the guys there and I present it to him. Maybe some cameras. What do you think?"

Silence around the desk. I forget who spoke first, but we all looked at each other.

"You're out of your mind," the super said. "You can't do that."

"Yeah, we're not doing that, Donald," I said.

"No way," the project manager said.

It was an awful idea, and it took longer to talk Donald out of the giant check than it did to convince him to give Eddie his bonus! In the end, HRH had a regular-sized check drawn, which the project manager gave to Eddie, who no doubt gave Trump a big thanks when he saw him on-site. After this incident, I flashed back to the scene of Trump giving me my bonus on the Hyatt and it all made sense. He had made a big to-do out of it so he could get credit for something he never wanted in the first place.

IN THE LATE 1980s, Trump and Steve Roth of Vornado Realty Trust jointly owned a controlling share of stock in Alexander's. I was put in charge of developing or selling the properties within the Alexander's portfolio and got involved in negotiations over an Alexander's store in the Menlo Park Mall in New Jersey. Nordstrom, a high-end department store, was looking to come into the New York metro area. They were very interested in building a new store on the Menlo Park site, and the mall's owner, the J.W. O'Connor & Company, was dying to have them occupy the Alexander's space. A Nordstrom would change the character (and increase the value) of the mall considerably. Alexander's didn't own that store, but they had a lease with seven years remaining on it; if O'Connor wanted that space for a Nordstrom, they were going to have to buy us out of the lease.

When I entered the negotiations, there was already a lowball offer, something like $5 million, on the table. I set up a meeting with Jerry O'Connor, the J in J.W., to let him know I'd be taking over the negotiations and that Alexander's would not be accepting the $5 million. By meeting with O'Connor, I was hoping to get a read on what I could get out of him. As I sat across from him at his Manhattan office, it was clear to me how much he wanted that Nordstrom, at the time the most popular retailer in the country. Nordstrom would change the whole character of the mall, turning it into a high-end shopping center.

O'Connor was cordial enough, but I felt an underlying resentment in how he dealt with me, like he was annoyed we had him over
a barrel. His company was spending a fortune to redo the Menlo
Park Mall, and Alexander's was way too low end—and ugly—for
what they were planning. Without Nordstrom, they had nothing,
so they needed to get us out. They couldn't wait seven years for
the lease to expire; they couldn't even wait two.

After my meeting with O'Connor, I reported back to Trump
that I was going to try to sell the lease for $20 million. Trump just
laughed at me, dismissing it as a preposterous number. "Knock
yourself out, Barbara," Donald said. "If you sell it for twenty, I'll
give you a nice bonus." That was the extent of the conversations
I had with Trump about the entire transaction. He didn't know
whether it was a fee or a lease, whom I was selling to, or even
O'Connor's name, referring to him only as "the Irishman." The
chairman of Alexander's, Robin Farkas, was also keen to make a
deal. Farkas was a soft-spoken guy in tailored suits who had an air
of old money about him. He said we'd be lucky to get $10 million.

"I think I can get twice that," I told him.

"Okay, Barbara," he said, laughing at me. "Good luck." He
bet me a lunch it couldn't be done.

O'Connor had introduced me to the executive I'd be dealing
with from that point on, a friendly and rotund guy with whom I
hit it off. When we met, he raised the offer to $10 million, which
I ultimately rejected; I don't think they dreamed we'd turn that
down. During the many meetings and conversations that followed,
I put everything I had into getting the highest possible price for
that lease, not only because it was my job but in anticipation of a
large bonus—maybe 10 percent of Donald's commission. In each

meeting with O'Connor and his people, they tried to convince me that they had the upper hand, but I saw through that. We had the leverage; Alexander's had an ironclad lease, and the only way out of it was for us to agree to let them buy us out. It was an arduous and exhausting process, the biggest deal I've ever done by myself, but I never stopped pushing.

When all was said and done, I sold the lease to J.W. O'Connor & Company for twice as much as anyone expected, unheard of for a seven-year lease and exactly what I'd told Trump and Farkas I could get: $20 million. Farkas took me to lunch at the Harvard Club, as per our bet, but also to celebrate. I told him about my agreement with Trump and asked him if, when the $800,000 commission check was cut for Trump, I could personally deliver it to Donald. "No problem," he said. The day the check arrived on my desk, I waltzed into Donald's office, a big smile on my face. I was confident, jubilant even, considering the size of the deal and the fact that no one had thought I could get that much. Excited about the prospect of maybe an $80K or $100K bonus—more money than I'd ever received at one time—I had been fantasizing about spending it in fifteen different ways.

"What's up, Barbara?" Donald was looking down at something on his desk.

"Farkas sent me your commission check," I said, placing it in front of him, on top of his papers. "Here you go—eight hundred grand."

He looked up, blank faced.

"For the Alexander's lease I sold," I said, wondering if he was confused. "Menlo Park."

"Wait," he said. "Hang on. I don't get it." He looked down at the check and then back up at me. His eyes opened wide, almost in alarm, and his face got very red. "What the hell are you doing with this check?"

"Oh," I said, on the defensive, "I asked Farkas to let me give it to you because I made the deal, and remember you promised me a bonus—"

"What?! He shouldn't have done that!" Trump yelled. He took the check aggressively off the desk, as if I might snatch it back. "I don't know what the fuck he was thinking," Donald said. "Who the hell do you think you are?" His voice kept rising in volume, and he was getting a little scary.

I was dumbfounded, then alarmed that I had set him off. "I'm sorry," I said, "I just thought since you said you were going to . . . I thought you'd be happy. Remember you said if I got it for twenty million, you'd give me a bonus?"

"Get the fuck out of here," he said, "and don't ever pull a stunt like this again."

I turned around and walked away, afraid to anger him further. It was clear that I had crossed some line and that there'd be no bonus for me either. All I got for my efforts was a nice chewing out. In the end, nothing mattered except that the money was Donald's. As far as he was concerned, I had nothing to do with it.

I knew rich people didn't get rich by giving things away, but I still felt blindsided. Of all the times Donald screwed me over, this one stung the most. I *earned* that money. Trump would not just settle for taking credit for the sale, which the Alexander's board and Roth were ecstatic about; he had to cheat me out of money, too.

The check represented the deal, the credit, and he felt it belonged entirely to him.

Hogging the credit continues to be a driving Trump instinct. In April 2018, Trump was giving a speech in Florida when he made a reference to his new national security adviser, John Bolton, who was at the event. At the mention of Bolton's name, the crowd erupted in applause. The U.S. military had just completed what was viewed as a "successful" strike on Syria, which Bolton was given credit for. As the applause continued and became even more rapturous, with standing ovations, a look came over Trump's face. "I'm a little jealous," he said. "Are you giving him all the credit? You know that means the end of his job." It seemed as if Trump was joking, but I know that face: He was serious. It was the thing that ended Steve Bannon as well—no one upstages the boss. Bolton would go on to clash constantly with Trump, and the high profile didn't help. He would be out after a year and a half.

The flip side of wanting to take all the credit is that Trump also needs scapegoats to hold the blame.

As president, Trump has invoked a wide group of people as the reasons for his failures—Hillary Clinton, President Obama, Democratic House leaders like Nancy Pelosi and Adam Schiff, James Comey and Robert Mueller—as well as institutional ones like the "fake news" and the "Deep State."

The Deep State is a conspiracy theory that didn't start with Trump but became very useful to him as president. When he took office in January 2017, the Republicans also held both houses of Congress. Since the Democrats weren't nearly strong enough to be blamed for anything, Trump needed somewhere to point to, to explain his failures. He needed something large, preferably shadowy and amorphous, to serve as his foil. The Deep State fit the bill. It was a supposedly secret network of bureaucratic officials who joined together to keep Trump from winning the election and who continued to undermine him from their various offices in government agencies. The Deep State was a sinister entity he could use to unite his followers in anger and hate while deflecting all blame onto it. He had nothing to show for his first two years: no wall, no infrastructure deal, no health care alternative. After the 2018 midterms, when the Democrats gained control of the House of Representatives, Trump must've been relieved. Now he had easier targets. He could use Pelosi and Schiff, as well as Alexandria Ocasio-Cortez and the rest of the "Squad," as scapegoats.

Trump's political persona doesn't really work without enemies. Neither did his business persona. If you're on the inside of Trump's circle and you try to make something his responsibility, you're gone. If you're on the outside and you try to make it Trump's responsibility, you are a target. Sometimes I thought he just kept people on in order to have someone to blame. People are just pawns in some large game to him, used and sacrificed for his own benefit.

Subrule: Everything's a transaction and everyone is a part of it.

I want you to do us a favor though.
—DONALD TRUMP, 2019

This is an extension of the rule that Trump always takes the credit but never the blame, because it relates to how Donald uses people to keep score. He is engaged in a constant competition in which he needs to raise his total and lower others', ensuring he's always on top. "All life is a negotiation," according to Trump, "and every negotiation is a zero-sum game. There's no such thing as a 'win-win'; someone will win and someone will lose." Michael D'Antonio, one of Trump's biographers, said Donald told him, "I don't believe in win/win. I believe in I win."

Trump has long been obsessed with winning. When HRH and I were negotiating with the subcontractors, once we got to their best number, we would tell them we were going to bring them in to see Donald. Before they went in, we advised them to add a small percentage to their asking price for Trump to knock down; Donald had to feel like he had won something. (There were a few times when Trump actually got an even better deal than we had.) Trump loved these "negotiations" because they bolstered his sense of winning. Life to him is just a series of transactions: trading off, maneuvering, and getting a leg up on everyone else.

As the Grand Hyatt and Trump Tower bonus check stories show, Trump puts a lot of effort into trying to make people feel like they owe him. He collects people, favors, and IOUs, hoping they'll pay off for him at some point. He stakes a great deal on relationships, not because of friendship or affection, but because he believes that people are tools to help him win. Donald cannot conceive of someone doing a favor without a payoff on the other side. He is about exploiting relationships, not nurturing them. It's why a person can be Trump's trusted friend one day, archenemy the next, and then—if Donald sees a benefit—a friend once again.

It's no surprise that he's taken this transactional mentality into politics. In 1987 he toyed with running for president; from my perspective it was a publicity ploy. After stringing along a few New Hampshire political folk who were trying to draft him to run, he flew up to New Hampshire and gave a speech, where the first thing he did was say he was not running, disappointing the few who thought he was serious. It's telling that in his first foray into politics, Trump manipulated both the situation and the people who had faith in him. In his 2000 campaign for the Reform Party ticket for president, he went further, trying to make money out of it. He teamed up with motivational speaker Tony Robbins and merged his campaign stops with a speaking tour ($100K per appearance) and book signings. "It's very possible that I could be the first presidential candidate to run and make money on it," he said. He was right, though not because of any particular skill or genius; he'd be the first to make money on running for president because no one had ever been unscrupulous enough to do so. His penchant for corruption is so total that he is willing to benefit where others just won't.

Of course, in 2015 he actually ran, hoping to bring attention to himself and his dying brand. Running for the highest office in the land was just another transaction to him.

Trump's politics, just like his business and personal lives, are transactional. When I knew him, he was a socially liberal Democratic New Yorker and not shy about it. He took mostly moderate positions but was progressive on women's reproductive rights and LGBTQ rights and supported candidates in this mold. Now he wants to ban abortions, protect guns, save the Confederate flag, and take away LGBTQ rights. Some people change their politics as they age, but Trump's shift can be directly tied to his political ambitions. He saw an opportunity in the Republican Party, so he aligned some of his beliefs with theirs. Once he actually won the job, the die was cast, so he had to make the best of it. He turned the presidency into a perch from which to make money, gain influence, punish enemies, and—as always—collect more favors. Any of his previous schemes about benefiting from politics and government were small potatoes.

In September 2019, when a whistleblower filed a complaint that Trump had tried to withhold aid from Ukraine in exchange for an "investigation" into the supposed corruption of his primary political rival, Joe Biden (and his son), the world saw how Trump treats running the country as just another arena for transactions. All that talk about whether or not there was an explicit quid pro quo with the Ukrainian president had me wanting to scream: Trump's *life* is a quid pro quo! It is the nature of all his relationships. The Ukraine call felt normal to Trump; he saw nothing wrong with holding back congressionally approved money from an ally for political gain. He is used to this kind of carrot-and-stick dealing, and he understood so little of government that he apparently thought the money approved by Congress was his to hold back for any reason he wanted. He kept labeling the call "perfect." To him, it was. It looked and sounded like so many other calls he has made in his life.

This what's-in-it-for-me mentality has infected all of his presidency. He openly talked about stealing oil from Iraq, complained about European countries not paying enough to NATO, and asked why we have to pay for our military presence in South Korea. He suggested the military should only go if and where the U.S. was paid to send it, saying, "All these countries need to start paying us for the troops we are sending to their countries. We need to start making a profit." As if the United States military were some kind of mercenary army we should rent out to the highest bidder. As for NATO and the international alliances that have kept things together since World War II, he just doesn't see the point of it. He has risked our standing in the world because he doesn't understand our role. If we're not getting benefits in the way he understands—money, power, control—then we're getting "screwed over."

Donald Trump seems to understand only the language of money and trade-offs, which in business makes him crafty. But as a president, it makes him completely amoral. That thinking is what has allowed him to forgive Saudi Arabia for its genocidal bombing of Yemen and the murder and dismemberment of journalist Jamal Khashoggi inside the Saudi consulate in Istanbul, Turkey.* When he refused to call off an arms deal with Saudi Arabia after the killing, he said, "I don't like stopping massive amounts of money coming into our country." Can you imagine any other U.S. president—or even politician—saying something so depraved?

There are also his own business interests to consider; he has talked more than a few times about how Saudis give his businesses plenty of money too. ("They pay cash," he has bragged.) Money is the only relevant factor in the relationship, and it apparently overrules human life. Based on what he has said and how he has taken no retaliatory action against the Saudis, it doesn't even seem to be a hard call for him. In December 2019 a shooting on an air force base killed three U.S. sailors and injured eight. Six months later the military revealed that the attack, on American soil, was conducted by a member of an Al Qaeda offshoot (AQAP) from

---

* The Saudi government has denied involvement.

Saudi Arabia. The way Trump handled it was not by issuing a formal declaration, making a threat, or imposing sanctions, but by saying it would not affect the United States' relationship with the Saudis. He also has obvious business connections to Russia—whether through his long-planned Trump Tower Moscow or some other projects that have yet to come to light.

He tried to convince China, America's biggest rival, to buy soybeans from American farmers in order to help Trump's 2020 election prospects. All other countries are just more transactional partners to him—not to America, *to him*. He admires the despots, who make him feel good about himself, while he insults the other liberal democratic leaders, who refuse to kowtow to him. Because of this, the United States has become a force *against* democracy and human rights in the world. His single-mindedness and self-interest have isolated us from our allies and helped split us into two at home. His incessant need to stoke and invent divisions in this country is a transaction meant to benefit him: his poll numbers, his reelection, his image, his future business opportunities. Just as he once pitted executives against each other at the Trump Organization for his own personal benefit, he is doing so again with the nation.

IT'S NO SURPRISE that Trump's transactional mentality has also seeped into his marriages. In discussing the prenuptial agreement he made Marla Maples sign, Donald said, "It's, it's a lousy thing. I hate the concept, but it's totally necessary. And I think a million dollars is a lot of money. . . . I guess I look at everything like a deal. I mean, you know, it's just one of those things."

Suffice it to say he does not hate the concept at all, as Ivana and Melania signed them as well. If prenuptial agreements didn't exist, Donald would have paid someone to invent them. He even tried to sell the broadcast rights to his wedding with Melania before the bride refused. "Three hours in prime time. That's $25 million in advertising!'" he said. Everything—even his wedding—is up for sale.

If you are not of use to him, you don't exist. It's why he had no conscience about kicking tenants out of buildings—they were in his way. It's a what's-in-it-for-me mentality across the board. Cheating me out of my bonus on the Menlo Park Mall was not just a one-off. He betrayed and took from his own people, some very talented ones, over the years.

I remember what he tried to do to Louise Sunshine, who was not only the outstanding head of sales for Trump Tower but the driving force behind many political favors Trump got over the years. It was Louise's connections that really brought Donald into Manhattan real estate and yielded tens of millions of dollars in apartment sales at Trump Tower. Donald rewarded Louise for her work with a 5 percent ownership interest in Trump Plaza, an apartment building Trump was erecting on Third Avenue. I bet he later regretted it.

Not too long after, Louise ended up being liable for $1 million in taxes. Though it would seem inconceivable that a 5 percent share could accrue such a large tax, Trump controlled the numbers. He then proceeded to demand the money from Louise, knowing she didn't have that kind of cash lying around. He proposed buying her out so that she wouldn't have to come up with the money. It must've killed Trump that someone stood to make millions of dollars "off of him." Louise wanted to hold on to her share. She was very good friends with the owner of a major corporation, who had plenty of cash available. He gave Louise the million she needed. After that, she and Donald parted ways. Later, they must have realized they each had something to offer the other and became friends again.*

Trump has repeatedly said no president or politician in history has ever been treated more unfairly, a typical exaggeration that is pretty revealing. Even though he skirts all blame and tries to swallow all credit, he still thinks the balance sheet isn't in his favor. That's the subtext of just about all his complaints. As a white man in America, born into money, who has gotten everything he ever wanted, who has gotten away with countless questionable and unethical actions, who became president of the United States without an ounce of experience, he thinks the world is very unfair to him.

---

* In a 2016 interview for *Frontline*, Louise said, "Donald and I were were able to work things out very amicably."

SEVEN

NO FRIEND TO THE COMMON MAN

**Rule: Trump disdains exactly the type of person
who supports him.**

*The oddity in all of this is the people Trump despises most, love
him the most. The people who are voting for Trump for the most
part . . . he'd be disgusted by them.*
—HOWARD STERN, LONGTIME FRIEND OF DONALD TRUMP

D onald Trump has built a fierce loyalty amid a segment of
the public he holds in contempt. In fact, the greatest con
Trump has pulled in a life full of them has been convincing his
voters that he's somehow one of them. The diehards, those who
still won't give up on him, are mostly rural and exurban, poor
to working class, with no college degree, and almost exclusively
white. Trump would otherwise have nothing to do with them as
people. But he shamelessly embraces and panders to them as
voters, while doing nothing for them, and in many ways acting
against their interests.

He has ripped away environmental and industry regulations to help corporations at the expense of regular people and passed tax cuts that did virtually nothing for the working class while enriching the 1 percent. This is what he knows; getting money out of the government, through tax breaks, abatements, zoning bonuses, and the like is just part of the real estate business. Someone who's learned to take from the public in order to profit will not magically become a selfless public servant at the age of seventy, especially when he's put in charge. The idea is nonsensical.

While he and his circle have regular, daily testing for coronavirus, he has done everything he can to hinder it for the rest of us and convince us the virus is not so bad. Beyond that, he has tried to destroy the Affordable Care Act (also known as Obamacare), which has insured tens of millions of people, made false promises about some imaginary health care policy that would guarantee insurance for preexisting conditions, imposed tariffs that hurt American consumers, tried to dismantle the Consumer Financial Protection Bureau, which has recouped billions of dollars for citizens scammed by financial institutions, and threatened cuts to Medicare, Medicaid, and Social Security.

Donald grew up rich and became richer and has never done anything in his life solely for the public good. The New York attorney general found that the Trump Foundation was nothing but a shell game, and his apparent grifting of other charities has been reported in various outlets. In every way possible he has made sure that "regular folk" are blocked off from him. His world is personal drivers, exclusive clubs, private planes, and parties. But without the MAGA-hat-wearing white male, he has no political career. So he created this charade. Friend to the common man? Give me a break: Trump can't *stand* the common man.

Trump has projected an image of himself as a "man's man," more comfortable with construction guys than their bosses, but it's a crock. Whenever he tries to pull this, I'm reminded of what happened when we finished Trump Tower. On a construction project, when the last floor is poured or the last piece of steel is set, the building is considered to be topped out. It is traditional to raise a flag at the highest point and then to have a "topping-out" party. Generally, it consists of a few minutes of speeches from the bosses and sandwiches for all the tradesmen on the job. The topping out is a moment of solidarity among them and a celebration for a job well done.

For the Trump Tower topping out in the summer 1982, the party had to be, of course, the best in the world. Through his political connections, Donald managed to get Mayor Koch and Governor Hugh Carey to agree to attend, which was unheard of. Trump's version of a topping-out ceremony was to be a champagne party on the roof with an orchestra and news cameras and important people—not construction workers. He actually balked at inviting the workforce at all. When Aldo, the tall, redheaded project manager for HRH, brought up the party, Trump was excited. Another PR opportunity. "That's great!" Trump said. "Let's really do it up."

I looked across the desk at Aldo. Trump's tone meant we weren't on the same page.

"Lots of men working on the site now, several hundred," Aldo said. "So it's going to take some work to pull it off, catering for everyone and all that."

Trump's face changed. "What are you talking about?" he asked. "Construction workers? I don't want the construction workers."

"The party's *for* the construction workers, Donald." I explained. "That's the point. It's *their* topping-out party."

Ignoring me, Donald turned to Aldo. "Aldo, we can have just the foreman, and then you can have another party for the workers."

A small smile crept across Aldo's face, but he did a good job hiding it. We were both amused at Trump's ignorance, especially for someone who bragged about being in the business since he was a kid. I wasn't surprised Trump wanted to use the topping-out party for self-glorification, but he had the audacity to think we could do it without the workers? Wow. After some back-and-forth, and more complaining on Trump's part, he reluctantly allowed the men who built Trump Tower to attend their own topping-out party.

The party included the workers, the mayor, the governor, journalists, and news cameras, along with a thousand balloons, souvenir ashtrays, and coffee cups of shiny black ceramic with TRUMP TOWER in gold lettering. This was standard: Everything at the Trump Organization was designed or redesigned to produce something of value to Donald, usually publicity. In the end, the topping-out party was just another thing Trump used as a promotion of himself. And because he's one of the luckiest people alive, he got more press out of it than even he expected. Mayor Koch was speeding in his limo to make it on time, and his car got into a fender bender with a local driver. Koch was then rescued by a patrol car and shuttled to Trump Tower, sirens blaring. The story was picked up by the wire services and ran in all the papers. It was only fitting; Trump Tower's topping-out party was news because of the important people who attended. If it was up to Trump, the men who built it wouldn't have been there at all.

I can hear the pushback, implying that he has changed: *That was decades ago!* I know! That's true. He still went to jobsites and flew commercial back then. He was not yet a household name, and he was still married to his first wife. But you think forty years spent in gilded apartments, private clubs, his own plane, and properties with his name on them put him *more* in touch with regular people?

———————

If I had to be like Robert, I'd kill myself. . . . I couldn't stand to be out of the limelight. I couldn't stand it.

—DONALD TRUMP

THIS DIG AT Robert, which Donald made to an employee, is typical of the ways Trump put his brother down. But the condescension was meant to hide something that most of us knew about Donald. No matter what Donald thought or said about his younger brother, there was something Robert had over Donald. Trump long had a desire to be seen as aristocratic—a Kennedy type—but money is not all it takes to travel in that set. No matter how rich he became, Trump was never accepted by the upper crust. In fact, high society rejected Donald and Ivana, and it killed him. But Robert, through his wife, Blaine—wellborn, well-bred, a fixture of the social scene in New York City—was welcomed by the same elite that shunned his older brother. Robert had something

Donald would never have, an entrée to society that no amount of money could buy.

Donald used to always talk about "class" and "high class," trying to elevate himself from what he really was, a man with no pedigree, the son of that "vile Fred Trump from Queens." When Donald Trump brought his business into Manhattan, his goal was to secure a place among the upper ranks of society. But no matter his net worth, his coarse speech, crude manners, and tacky style offended them. He was not let into their clubs—both figurately and literally—and he resented that. After years of trying and failing to be one of them, Trump ultimately rejected the notion that there was a class of people above him. He simply rewrote the script so that he could see himself as American royalty, right up there with the Kennedys and the Bushes. The Trump name, according to him, "used to mean hotels and golf courses and now it means class and dignity and the presidency and power."

As for the lower classes, Trump has long disdained them, though he knows enough to hide his contempt. Construction workers on the job would see him walking around glad-handing laborers and were fooled by it. But it was all for show. Trump felt scorn for most people who actually worked for a living. He has said that he has respect for only a few people in this world, and the common man (and woman) is likely not among them. That's why it is so easy for him—in business and in government—to screw them over.

When he first started with his father in the outer boroughs, Donald was already learning the practice of forcing tenants out of their homes. If these people stood in the way of more lucrative prospects, they had to go. That attitude has followed Trump's career all the way into politics, where people remain either tools or obstacles.

Trump has always pushed the limits of the law and in some cases has exceeded them in order to get what he wants. All this talk of Trump not being above the law goes against one of the main lessons of his life: *He has* always *been above the law.* It's comparable to his fellow billionaire grifter Leona Helmsley saying that taxes are for little people. When Hillary Clinton attacked him for not paying federal taxes, his response was "That makes me smart," which tells you what he thinks of everyone else. Trump thinks laws are meant for "stupid people" who don't have the wealth or savvy to get away with breaking them. The punishment was never sufficient enough to deter him—and that was assuming you could even get him to accept the punishment.

Donald has spent his career threatening the weak, pandering to the powerful and connected, hiring the best lawyers, and putting his thumb on the scale of justice in ways we don't even know about. Like playing fast and loose with the tax laws, this too is a family legacy. Fred Trump was part of the "Brooklyn machine" in the 1950s and '60s, a corrupt group who had at least as much power as the elected leaders. In the 1990s, as the *New York Times* discovered, Fred Trump set up a management company, All County Building Supply & Maintenance, which was technically owned by his children.* The company did all the maintenance for the Trump buildings and grossly overcharged, and Fred "used the padded invoices

---

* Their late cousin John Walter, whom I knew well, also had a 20 percent stake in this scam. His home address was actually the one used for the company. John was quite religious, and I was pretty shocked to find out he was involved in this crooked enterprise.

to justify higher rent increases in rent-regulated buildings, records show." That money—taken from working-class people in Trump Village and other Trump properties—was funneled to Donald and his siblings, apparently to avoid any gift or estate tax. So besides screwing the working people of Trump Village, they were doing it to the taxpayers as well.

The ultimate example of his contempt for the people in his buildings was the battle for 100 Central Park South. Trump was always on the lookout for underutilized buildings in good residential areas that he could buy cheaply, and he did this with some success. The plan either was to renovate them or, ideally, tear them down and build luxury condos on the site. The problem for Trump was that there were always tenants living in the buildings, and their right to remain there was protected by law. In addition, they were often in rent-controlled or rent-stabilized apartments they didn't want to give up. In New York City, for many decades, the government has limited the amount by which landlords can raise the rent each year in those apartments. Because the permitted rate has not been near the rate of inflation, over the years these rents stayed far lower than what the landlords could get on the open market. The result was that tenants in many buildings were paying ridiculously low rents and the landlords could do nothing but wait for them to move out or die.

Some residents are given a fair price and move out, while those who refuse to leave are called holdouts. Tales of holdouts are legendary in New York. A holdout caused Macy's to put a notch in one of their stores, creating an eyesore and preventing them from building a proper plaza. Another holdout left a house sitting in the shadow of a massive office building on Third Avenue, with the same effect. Buildings with holdouts are a nightmare to develop, so they tend to sell very cheaply, which Trump knew well. Developers who take these buildings on need to have open pocketbooks and reserves of patience, because it might take years for them to be able to build out their projects. The saying goes that the saved money from getting the property cheap "buys a lot of aspirin."

In 1981, Trump pulled the trigger on a deal for a great location: 100 Central Park South, a fifteen-story building across from Central Park, which he envisioned as his next luxurious project. It was adjacent to a decaying hotel, the Barbizon, which was part of a package deal. It cost Trump $63 million, financed by a $50 million bank loan, for two buildings on Central Park. Even back then that was a steal. He intended to tear down the buildings and claimed he was going to turn the site into the most luxurious apartments ever built on the storied Central Park South, selling for unheard-of prices. Trump was going to outdo himself with a "new 165-unit tower, with penthouse apartments scheduled to go for millions apiece."

The building was about 80 percent full of tenants at the time, which would have presented a major problem for any other developer. But Trump knew his way around clearing a building. He had just finished turning the Commodore into the Grand Hyatt after emptying out every retail tenant with a lease and single-room-occupancy resident. On 100 Central Park South, he first offered to sell the building to the tenants for a price nowhere near what they could afford; it was his way of sending a message that he had no intention of selling. Then he went the other way, trying to buy them out cheaply. When that failed, Trump dug into his bag of tricks. As he had done in the past, Trump brought in

a "management" company who told him the building would be
free of tenants in a year.

Trump and his managers engaged in a number of actions that
would later be deemed illegal by the city and state government.
They tried to evict tenants for nonpayment of rent though the residents had canceled checks proving they had paid. Trump's managers demanded that tenants restore their units to their original
condition "within 10 days or face immediate eviction." under a
wild interpretation of an obscure law that had not been enforced
for thirty years. According to court documents, the superintendent testified: "They [the management company] didn't want any
repairs done. No cleaning. No accepting of packages."

Trump had this unshakeable notion that when services got
unacceptable in a building, the tenants would have no choice but
to move out. So he made living there a nightmare. He stopped the
heat and gas, wouldn't fix the plumbing, and had his people leave
reeking garbage around. One time I walked into Trump's office
and he was having a discussion with the building manager, Sal.
When I walked in, Trump and Sal were kicking around ideas about
ways to enrage the tenants at 100 Central Park South, including
putting raw chickens in the elevator shafts. This was the same Sal
who almost demolished a building on Third Avenue without permits because Trump told him to. Trump believed he was righteous
in forcing these people out. It was his building, landlord-tenant
laws be damned.

Among other things on 100 Central Park South, Trump told
his managers to cover up the windows in the empty apartments
with tin to make the building look run-down and empty, giving
the tenants another impetus to move. This was a throwback to the

Brooklyn days, when they used to drip paint out the windows and over the bricks to make buildings look unattractive. He wanted us to use similar tactics to make the Alexander's stores and the Ambassador Hotel unsightly. These ideas show a major flaw in Trump's thinking. Though he thinks he understands people better than anyone else, he doesn't. These tactics don't make people capitulate to him, or hope he'll swoop in as their savior and work his magic. They just end up hating him more and digging in their heels.

Another scheme Trump devised for 100 Central Park South was to move homeless people into empty apartments, petitioning the city for permission and even taking out ads in the paper pitching his idea. Many of the tenants were "people living on fixed incomes, such as Social Security checks, who have made their homes there for 20 years or more," but they were not destitute. The city turned him down, but the threat scared the hell out of the tenants, who saw Trump would stop at nothing to get them out.

He used his lawyers as well, suing individual tenants and the tenants' group, knowing his resources vastly outweighed theirs. For someone like Trump, the courts aren't about justice—they're about beneficial delay. Trump and his lawyers knew how to exploit the inefficiencies of the courts and regularly gamed the system. If he lost a case, he would just appeal. For many years I observed Trump's dealings directly on this matter. He'd sue a contractor, tying him up in the legal system until it was clear that it would be cheaper to settle—for a fraction of what he was owed. Some just gave up, knowing that to continue would mean bankruptcy. Donald uses the delaying tactic to this day, most notably with the public demand to see his taxes. He has managed to string this out for five years now, and since he became president, he has used the power of a subservient Justice Department to countersue, maneuver, and delay.

But Trump's tactics ultimately fell flat against the holdouts of 100 Central Park South. They banded together, had the will to fight him, were able to hire good lawyers, and got the press on their side, casting Donald as the villain. There were certainly some well-off people who lived there, but the majority of them were "middle-income people and retirees, living on $900 a month Social Security payments." In their suit against Trump, which included harassment claims, the depth of Trump's venality came out. Trump had investigators poking around residents' financial records and "instructing employees to obtain information about the private lives [and] sex habits of the tenants." In the end, Trump was mostly defeated; the city required him to offer the apartments to the tenants for a below-market price and to let the rest remain as renters. He renovated the building and combined it with the much bigger one next door to create yet another testament to his greatness, another eponymous edifice, Trump Parc.

THE SO-CALLED REAL Americans whom Trump pretends to care about as president have been his dupes and victims for decades. He has long bullied them to get what he wants; his career as a builder and developer was built on those tactics. We can argue whether or not this is disqualifying for a big-city real estate developer in a business known for playing dirty. Unlike Trump, other developers typically obey the laws put in place to protect tenants. They try to work things to their advantage, but it's within bounds that, in my experience, Trump does not recognize or respect. It's simple: If Donald didn't feel like doing something, he didn't do it. He knew that all enforcement mechanisms were weak, and if he gamed the system with delays, bluffing all the way to court, he could prevail. If the outcome damaged the regular people, so be it. They were just collateral damage.

But we are not talking about developers and landlords anymore. What is acceptable conduct for the president of the United States and the leader of the free world? The bare minimum that citizens are entitled to expect of their president is that he care about their well-being. But Trump can't clear even this remarkably low bar.

Now that he is president, Trump is no longer tempered by the curbs that act as a restraint on an ordinary—albeit very rich—citizen. He has the ultimate power, more than enough to engage all his worst tendencies. His attitude that the laws are for other people still governs his actions, but the terrifying truth is that he is now *in charge of* those laws. And the damage has been incalculable. Now we are *all* collateral damage.

EIGHT

THE OTHER

**Rule: Trump believes in the superiority of
the white Christian male.**

*There is nobody—nobody—that has more respect for women
than I do.*

—Donald Trump

*You know, it really doesn't matter what they write as long as you've
got a young and beautiful piece of ass.*

—Guess

It is true that Trump put a woman—me—in charge of construction for his biggest project at the time, Trump Tower. And he did it when that was pretty much unheard of. It is also true that he is a world-class objectifier and degrader of women. Trump works in extremes. Very often, the things he does contradict each other.

During the 2016 campaign, Trump held up my hiring as proof of how he'd be "great for women." Candidate Trump would tell his audiences about me, using me as some kind of marker of how progressive he was. His daughter Ivanka repeated the story, praising her father for breaking the glass ceiling for women in construction. The ceiling is still intact, but if there were any cracks, I made them. I suffered the indignities of discrimination, intimidation, and sexual harassment, not Trump. I worked mornings and nights and weekends, twice as hard as the men around me for less money. But, of course, Trump took all the credit. And he didn't even mention my name. It was no oversight. I was something he used to confirm his greatness, not a person in my own right.

Trump didn't hire me out of some desire to advance the cause of women. He did it because I was the best person available from the crew who worked on the Grand Hyatt. He also knew that I would work harder, smarter, and cheaper than a man, because I already had. Putting a woman in such a high position—he made me a vice president—and bragging that I was the first woman to be in charge of a major construction project was something that made him look good. His supporters still refer to it as proof of how forward thinking he is on women.

When I began as head of construction on Trump Tower, I started getting some publicity—a feature article about me in the *Daily News* (with a large photo of me on-site in a hard hat) and an appearance on a game show, *To Tell the Truth*. Soon after, the attention dried up. I think Trump put the kibosh on it because he couldn't have anyone, much less a woman, taking any of his spotlight. Overall, my hiring was a great opportunity for me but an absolute windfall for him. Not only was Trump Tower a huge success, but he could claim my running the construction gave him feminist credentials. Irritatingly, Trump and his daughter both talk as if my hiring were part of some larger pattern, as though I was the first of a slew of women Donald placed in high construction positions. He had senior marketing and sales executives who were female, but I believe I am the one and only female engineer Trump ever employed.

Unfortunately, women have not really risen in the construction business, either in number or position, from where they were forty years ago when I started working for Trump. Over the course of working on Trump Tower, I saw three or four women working in the trades out of about eight hundred men. While I successfully got the general contractor to hire equally among the races, I failed at getting the subs to hire women. Even today, when I meet with the bosses of a subcontractor, I'll ask about women in their crews. They always answer that the women they do have are among the best workers, but then undercut it by claiming "women don't want to do the work" or "they're not really cut out for this." All of this is as wrong now as it was then. I have devoted much of my time to studying and speaking about the status of women in construction and find little has changed over the decades. Back then, companies like the Trump Organization did not have employment manuals or hiring guidelines. We didn't even have an HR department. Trump's executive assistant, Norma, and the chief accountant handled all that. The laws have changed and companies are now required to adopt policies about discrimination, racism, and sexual harassment, but I'm not sure how effective they are, especially in the construction industry.

As for Trump, there was a definite line he crossed in the late 1980s—as his first marriage started to unravel—in how he treated and spoke of women, different from his typical boorish behavior. During their marriage, Ivana seemed to have a restraining effect on him, as did the other women in his life: Norma, his mother, sales executive Louise Sunshine, and I. Other women came and went, but none stood up to him or acted as the kind of curbs we did. In the early days Norma would have stopped him from doing a lot questionable things, but I felt she ultimately became his enabler, like so many others.

As his marriage fell apart, Donald's behavior changed, beginning with how he treated his wife. When I first met them in the late 1970s, Donald and Ivana were sometimes sweet with each other and he would occasionally defer to her. By the time of their divorce proceedings in 1990, Donald had turned ugly and obnoxious. He denigrated Ivana's looks and desirability, saying no one would want to "touch those plastic breasts" and he didn't want to sleep with a woman who'd had children (even his children!). His cruelty toward his wife was coupled with a further objectifying of women in general. The breakup with Ivana seemed to unleash a part of him that had been kept partly at bay until that point. Over time he became cruder and cruder in private and in public; and the press ate it up, which delighted him.

"Barbara," Trump said to me more than once, "you have to understand there's no such thing as bad press. All press is good press." In 1990, when the tabloids were obsessed with the Donald/Ivana/Marla drama, he exulted in the attention. I remember the day of Marla Maples's famous *New York Post* cover, with the headline: "Marla Boasts to Her Pals About Donald: 'Best Sex I've Ever Had.'" When I came into his office that morning, he was in a great mood, a big smile plastered on his face.

He held the newspaper up with one hand and waved it in the air, asking me, "Did you see this?" I had. What bothered me the most was that he had children who were undoubtedly being taunted by other kids. But Trump acted like he couldn't have cared less. This was an unfaithful husband, and the woman who broke up the kids' parents, reveling in their sex life. Though Trump denied he planted the story, I would've bet anything that he was lying. Since then, reporters at the paper have confirmed Trump concocted the whole thing.

There was a similar atmosphere of braggadocio when he landed on the cover of *Playboy* a few weeks later. It showed him in a tuxedo shirt and pants standing next to a young woman who was naked, except for his jacket draped around her like a stole. He left the magazine on his desk and asked people if they'd seen it. This was during business meetings, in an executive office, and it was horribly degrading. He was still married, and I thought it made him look like a clown.

"Isn't that something?" he said to me, referring to the magazine.

"To be honest, I actually really hate it," I told him.

"What do you mean?" he said, almost laughing. "It's great! It'll be great for business!"

"You're wrong, Donald," I said. "It's bad for business. It makes you seem unprofessional." Donald wanted to be taken seriously, we all wanted to be taken seriously, and this just embarrassed us.

"Oh, you don't know anything. It's great!" Trump had no clue, nor would he have cared, that he'd created the textbook hostile work environment by repeatedly talking about that magazine to other men in front of me. He clearly relished the attention and the implications that he was some kind of ladies' man. I got so sick of that disgusting magazine, which circulated in the office for weeks when it belonged in a locker room.

After the divorce from Ivana, Donald would regularly make lewd comments about women, usually unprovoked, sometimes in business settings. I remember doing interviews with the various architectural firms for the Los Angeles project. During one meeting, Trump asked a local architect named Richard about various LA neighborhoods, what they were like, and then, like it was a perfectly normal segue, what the women looked like. Then Donald started talking about women in Los Angeles, how the women in Marina del Rey had "tighter asses" than the women in Beverly Hills or Bel-Air because they had to "try harder." This came completely out of nowhere, and Richard looked over at me with a pained look, though neither of us said a word. Trump felt he had the freedom both to judge women in this way and to talk about them openly with other people, even in a business environment.

In his office, I'd hear him on the phone as one of his aliases leaking to the press the names of women he was supposedly dating (he wasn't) and making statements about which actress wanted him and which model called him (they hadn't). For Trump, women were just another trapping of success, a possession. He also used his supposedly busy sex life as an excuse for his financial problems, blaming his losses on the fact that he was paying more attention to women than his business. I remember a ride home from a city planning board meeting during the Riverside South project. We were in a limousine, with an outside lawyer and a woman from the civics we barely knew, when Donald started complaining about his problems in Atlantic City. He was deflecting blame away from himself, onto his brother and other people down there. Then he said he couldn't concentrate on work because he was "fucking women two and three at a time." Everyone just broke eye contact right then, kind of looked out the windows. The limo felt very small all of a sudden. It was embarrassing, but, of course, Trump would never understand why it would be.

Obviously, Trump's sexism also spilled into his obsession with appearances. He was extremely conscious of and vocal about how women looked, even those who worked for him. Women were not just objects in his world but *reflective* objects. He treated wives as trophies, as though their appearance was the only attribute that really mattered. Even his daughter was a reflection on him. I remember him saying that depending on how things worked out for him, Ivanka would be known either as a local beauty, a national beauty, or an international beauty.

Another time Trump was scheduled to have a lunch meeting at the Plaza with a very accomplished and important woman whom he called "ugly." He made me join him, even though I had no reason to be there. When I protested, Donald made it clear to me that he could not be seen at his corner table (in the Edwardian Room) dining alone with this woman. It would hurt his image. She did not serve the purpose of women in his world—to make him look good.

Conversely, Donald judges other men by the attractiveness of their wives and girlfriends—his disparaging remarks about Ted Cruz's wife during the 2016 campaign being just one of many such instances. Men who like their women young and beautiful—those are his kind of guys. I recall being at a meeting in his office with other executives when Donald started talking about someone's girlfriend being young. Then he mentioned a friend of his who he said "likes them very young . . . *really* young, if you get what I mean." We all knew he was talking about teenagers—and he was making a joke of it. No one said a word. We looked at each other, disbelief and disgust on our faces. I couldn't not say anything. "That's not funny, Donald," I said. "Really, that's just horrible."

"What, it's not me!" he said defensively. "I'm just saying."

I didn't register the name back then, but after reading about the allegations against Jeffrey Epstein, I realized Donald must have been referring to him. The two had been friends in the late '80s, and Trump told *New York* magazine in 2002, "I've known Jeff for fifteen years. Terrific guy. He's a lot of fun to be with. It is even said that he likes beautiful women as much as I do, and many of them are on the younger side." After Epstein's former girlfriend and accomplice, Ghislaine Maxwell, was arrested and charged with trafficking and sexual abuse in 2020, Trump's only comment was "I wish her well." I can't imagine the upside to expressing support for someone accused of such heinous crimes.

By 1987, when I returned after my first hiatus from the Trump Organization, women did hold some relatively high positions in the company, though not on the construction side. As far as I could tell, Donald did not discriminate in hiring, or no more so than anyone else did in those days. He may have even preferred hiring women, and he always treated me the same as he would a man. While he gave me and the other female executives a level of respect, that was not true for many other women in lower staff positions. I saw Donald ogle them and speculate about their private lives. And it was clear that he was only interested in the more attractive ones. Eventually, all the personal assistants and secretaries in the company started to look the same. His executive assistant,

Norma, served as a one-woman human resources department and, I believe, made sure that they all met Donald's standards for beauty. I don't want to deride their work—they seemed mostly intelligent and competent—but it was obvious that they had to have a certain level of attractiveness to get the job.

My secretary, whom I hired myself, did not fit the Trump mold. I loved her and thought she was quite beautiful; she just didn't look like a model. When I asked her to help with getting coffees and sodas for the attendees of an important meeting, Trump told me to replace her. That was the culture he created in that office, and the fact that I went along with it that day made me ashamed of myself.

Trump believed women were property like paintings. He didn't care much for art, so the beautiful women in his employ were his "decorations." Trump would criticize his female employees for their looks. There was one woman who worked with Donald whom he would regularly demean about her weight and how distasteful it was. At some point she went on a diet and lost a tremendous amount of weight. But Donald still made fun of her, saying she was really just a "thin version of an unattractive woman." He would tell us that since she'd lost weight, she was badgering him to get her dates with people he knew, who, to his mind, were way out of her league. "Who does she think she is?" he'd say dismissively. He just couldn't help himself.

A woman's appearance was so important to him; he talked about it constantly, commenting on it when it wasn't appropriate. Anything else about women—their intellect, their accomplishments, their (nonsexual) desires, especially their childbearing—was not important. Once when I was talking to Trump on the phone from home and holding my infant son, the baby started making

noises. Trump got really angry and said, "Give the baby to someone else!" Once an employee who worked for me on the West Side
Yards project asked me to approach Donald to find out what our
policy was for maternity leave; she needed time off due to her preg-
nancy. The next time I saw him, at the end of a meeting, I brought
it up casually. "Oh yeah, Jane in marketing is having a baby. She
wanted to know much time off we give—"

"Who is that? I don't know her," Donald said.

"You know her. She's working PR with Billy."

"Yeah, yeah that one," he said, and it was clear he didn't like
her. "What does she even do? What do I need her for?" He was
starting to get angry now.

"What do you mean, what does she do? I just told you. She
works with Billy and the PR people."

"I don't want any pregnant women working here. Just get rid
of her."

"For god's sake, Donald. You know you can't fire someone
for getting pregnant," I said almost dismissively because it was so
obvious. "It's against the law and—"

"Just do it. Now," he said, which meant the conversation was
over.

I absolutely hated firing her, but I had no choice; I had gotten
a directive. Everyone in the office was excited about her baby, planning to have a little shower. and now I had to terminate her. Since
I had no reason, I did not make one up. I was not going to cover
for Donald this time. "This is illegal," I told her, "and you should
sue him." I knew she wouldn't do anything. She went quietly, and
he agreed to give her two weeks' severance, which was company

policy anyway. Like so many other women Trump screwed over, she knew she was outmatched and just gave up.

Women who disparaged Trump or even just challenged him were "bitches," and more often than not, he'd insult their looks, which he still does. In the early 1990s, after Daryl Hannah said that Trump had no business being compared to her stepfather, a real estate developer, Donald called her a "six" and said she needed a bath. He has repeatedly called Rosie O'Donnell "fat" and "ugly," and he called adult actress Stormy Daniels "horseface" after she revealed she was paid for her silence about their affair. He used this tactic during the 2016 primary campaign as well, saying of rival presidential candidate Carly Fiorina, "*Look* at that face! Would anyone *vote* for that?"

He went so low as to attack the looks of women who accused him of sexual assault, including E. Jean Carroll, who accused him of raping her. "Take a look, you take a look. Look at her . . . ," he said dismissively to an adoring crowd. "I don't think so." He wanted the world to know he would never resort to having sex with someone who looked like her, as if sexual assault were about anything but exerting power. As of September 2020, at least twenty-six women have accused Donald Trump of sexual "misconduct," ranging from harassment to sexual assault and rape.*

The 2017 Women's March, held in Washington, DC, the day after Trump's inauguration, was just the beginning of the mass response to Trump's behavior. I was there that day, among nearly

---

* Though he denies the allegations and has made a lot of threats about suing his accusers, I haven't found any evidence that he did.

half a million people, mostly women, and I had never seen the kind of solidarity I saw that day. I was amazed. Although I knew there were other marches, I was blown away by the images of millions of women all over the world who shared a single goal: getting rid of Trump.

Later that year, the #MeToo movement really took off after the stories about Harvey Weinstein became public. Trump's reaction to the movement was fitting: self-protection. He saw it as a referendum on him, and surely some of it was. He had been accused of decades of sexual harassment and assault, and had been caught on tape bragging about grabbing women, and the country still elected him.

Threatened, Trump had to attack the #MeToo movement itself, talking about how it was going to backfire on women, how men now had to be afraid of being tricked and lied about, and how the whole thing was a "big, fat con job." When Rob Porter, a White House aide, was accused of beating his ex-wife, Trump publicly defended Porter, accusing the ex-wife of lying. Among his most viciously misogynist moments was at one of his rallies when he publicly mocked and attacked Dr. Christine Blasey Ford, who in September 2018 had courageously testified to Congress about Supreme Court Justice nominee Brett Kavanaugh sexually assaulting her.*

He continues to single out, condescend to, and insult powerful women throughout government, especially those who disagree with him, calling Governor Gretchen Whitmer "the woman in Michigan" and Speaker of the House Nancy Pelosi "Crazy

---

* Kavanaugh denied the allegation.

Nancy." You can work your way up and become the most powerful person in your state or the leader of an entire branch of Congress, second in line to be president, but if you're a woman, that's all you ever are to Trump. Even if you're a head of state. He bullied British Prime Minister Theresa May on phone calls and called German Chancellor Angela Merkel "stupid." At a G-7 meeting, Trump threw some Starburst candies at her and said, "Here, Angela, don't say I never give you anything." Immediately after Joe Biden named Kamala Harris as his running mate, Donald pulled out his favorite adjective for women who don't bow to him: "nasty." He's used it on Hillary, Pelosi, Elizabeth Warren, and before any of them, yours truly. Technically, I was the first "nasty" woman, which Donald called me in a May 2016 tweet, reacting to my coming out as a Hillary supporter.

The *Access Hollywood* tape was something of a revelation even for me. I had watched him change over the eighteen or so years I worked with him, but I didn't personally witness that level of behavior. He was talking about outright sexual assault and he was bragging about it. I was fortunately spared some of Donald's boorish moments in the 1980s. He was somewhat protective of me at the time and wouldn't behave like that in front of me. After the fame and money went to his head, around the time of the divorce from Ivana, there was no more self-control and he didn't care about who was in the room when he spoke.

The role women now play in Donald's world is entirely subservient and reflective: Hope Hicks, Kayleigh McEnany, Ivanka, his former personal assistant Madeleine Westerhout. These are conventionally attractive women who loyally serve the boss. It's no wonder that we've seen him get contentious or befuddled by a handful of talented and strong female reporters who stand up to him, from Paula Reid to Kaitlin Collins to Yamiche Alcindor to Abby Phillip, an African American reporter to whom he said, "You ask a lot of stupid questions." He's such a coward in his inability to handle criticism from women that he has twice walked out of news conferences when a female reporter challenged him on a basic fact.

Donald would rather women know their place, as they supposedly did during some longed-for era when men like Fred Trump were in charge. He wants them beautiful, silent, and domestic. The most crystallized example of this was in a May 2020 press conference while Secretary of State Mike Pompeo was being investigated for using assistants for personal errands: "I'd rather have him on the phone with some world leader than have him wash dishes because maybe his wife isn't there or his kids aren't—you know?"*

I'm the least racist person there is anywhere in the world.
                                        —Donald Trump, 2019

IN THE SUMMER of 2020, when there was a movement to stop glorifying Confederate leaders from statues to army bases, Trump saw it as an opportunity and he embraced the Confederacy, which was absurd: What does a guy from Queens care about Southern heritage? He sees it as a wedge issue that he can use to appeal to

---

* Obviously there's too much to fit here on this topic, and this is not an exhaustive list. As I wasn't present for his behavior at the Miss Universe and Teen USA pageants or on *The Apprentice*, I can't comment on that. As I note above, I also think he hid some of his worst behavior from me. But many outlets have covered this extensively, most notably in Michael Barbaro and Megan Twohey, "Crossing the Line: How Donald Trump Behaved with Women in Private," *New York Times*, May 14, 2016.

his base. But the racism that undergirds it, that's genuine. Like his attitude toward women, his views on race are shaped by the fact that anyone who is not white is beneath him.

Donald first hired Roy Cohn for a 1973 Justice Department civil rights suit against Trump Management (both father and son) for allegedly not renting to African Americans in Brooklyn and Queens, or steering them away from their "white" buildings. They were investigated by the FBI and sued by the Justice Department. The Trumps countersued for $100 million, claiming they only discriminated against welfare recipients, not African Americans. But the government had all the evidence it needed. To prove that there was discrimination based on race in Trump Management's rental practices, the FBI had sent in white and Black couples with the same economic profiles to apply for apartments. The Black couples were invariably turned away or guided to other properties, while the white ones were accepted. The FBI also found rental applications marked with a big C for "colored." Without ever admitting guilt, a strategy Cohn held as gospel, the Trumps settled. From then on their rental practices were closely watched, and they had to advertise in papers that catered to nonwhites.

For those who say that was decades ago, I would argue that Trump's views on race have barely moved—even on this exact issue. In July 2020, President Trump repealed an Obama-era law to help desegregate communities and tweeted: "I am happy to inform all of the people living their Suburban Lifestyle Dream that you will no longer be bothered or financially hurt by having low income housing built in your neighborhood." Not very subtle. He hasn't changed one bit; he just has a much wider reach and far more power. In August 2020, the morning after Joe Biden selected

Kamala Harris, an African American woman, as his running mate, Trump again drew from this racist well, even more directly, with this tweet:

> The "suburban housewife" will be voting for me. They want safety & are thrilled that I ended the long running program where low income housing would invade their neighborhood. Biden would reinstall it, in a bigger form, with Corey [sic] Booker in charge!

Playing to supposedly scared "suburban housewives" (code for white) by threatening an invasion led by the only Black male Democratic senator? It's all right on brand.

Trump is not just racist—he accepts, vindicates, and inspires racism by making no attempt at concealing it. When Fox News' Chris Wallace asked him recently about the push to rename some military bases like Fort Bragg, Trump said, "What are we gonna name it? You're going to name it after the Reverend Al Sharpton?" This is a snapshot of how he exacerbates and exploits underlying racial tension in this country. Trump has defended Confederate monuments more virulently than even the Mississippi state legislature, which voted with broad bipartisan support to remove the Confederate battle emblem from its state flag.

Trump understands how race can be used to stir up people's resentment and gain supporters. His entry into politics was built on the back of a racist lie: that Barack Obama, a U.S.-born citizen, was actually born in Kenya (and possibly a Muslim) and was thus an illegitimate president. Birtherism was a vehicle for Trump to use racism to denigrate Obama, raise his own profile, and enter the political arena. He saw race (and religion) as an opening, and the first Black president with the foreign-sounding name was just too irresistible a target for him. I don't know what's more horrible, that he did it or that it worked. It took only two days for Trump and his minions to start doing a birther number on VP candidate Kamala Harris as well. Even his pitch to African American voters during the 2016 campaign was incredibly racist: "You're living in poverty, your schools are no good, you have no jobs, 58%* of your youth is unemployed—what the hell do you have to lose?" The fact that he thought this would somehow endear him to Black voters gets at the depth of his warped, racist thinking.

Most of the people I know who have spent time with Trump also think he's a racist. There is little doubt among us; it is treated as an accepted fact. When I worked with him, I was aware of his attitudes toward all minorities and they upset me. Of course, he was not alone in this. In the 1970s, '80s, and well into the '90s, prejudice against African Americans—as well as Latinos, immigrants, and LGBTQ people†—was very common in the real estate and construction fields.

In the early 1980s, it had not been very long since African Americans were even *allowed* to work on jobsites. They were kept out by the selectivity of the construction unions, which really only brought in new workers who were relatives or friends of members—who were, incidentally, all white. Over time, laws and customs changed. During the construction of Trump Tower, we

---

* This is a wildly misleading statistic, as it counts students, obviously a large percentage of "youth," as unemployed. (See "Trump's Economic Speech: CNN's Reality Check Team Vets the Claims," CNN Business, August 8, 2016.)

† I've also heard Trump joke about homosexuals, herpes, and even AIDS.

had several African American workers, but they were mostly laborers and concrete masons. And Donald made clear to me on a number of occasions that he wasn't happy about it.

A few racist incidents with Donald regarding employing people of color stick out in my memory. During the building of Trump Tower, we were doing concrete work on the second floor, which had to be poured and ground smooth. The floor was still open to the sky, and the public could see what was happening from the street and overlooking windows. One day there was an African American worker running a grinding machine over the concrete. Donald called me and HRH's project manager, Aldo, to his office at the Crown Building. "What is that Black guy doing over there?" he asked, referring to the mason tender. Aldo described the operation, thinking Trump was interested in the work the man was actually doing. No such luck.

"Get him off there right now," Donald said, "and don't ever let that happen again. I don't want people to think that Trump Tower is being built by Black people." He was dead serious. At the time, I was genuinely surprised. I thought it was blatantly racist, not to mention irrelevant. Who would care? I guess he did. In Trump's mind, African American workers were inferior to white workers, and he didn't want it out there that they were working on his building.

I told Donald that he was being ridiculous and he waved me off. What was the point of arguing? It was easy enough to take care of, and I simply had the man do something else. Not too long after, Trump was walking with me around the jobsite at lunchtime. There was a chain-link fence separating the entrance into the project from the street. At the time, there were men leaning against it, several of them African Americans. Trump grabbed one of the assistant superintendents from the general contractor's crew and told him to get the men out of sight. Again, he didn't want it known that African Americans were working on his building.

It happened in his casinos too. In *Trumped!,* former Trump Plaza COO Jack O'Donnell quotes Trump as saying Blacks were lazy and he didn't want them counting his money (he only wanted "short guys that wear beanies" for that, meaning yarmulkes). When Donald and Ivana were visiting Trump's casinos, African American employees were actually removed from the floor so Trump wouldn't see them, because it was known that he didn't want them in such highly visible positions.

After the racist fence episode at Trump Tower, Donald did something that really shook me and finally made me face the reality of who and what he was. I was interviewing architectural students for the job of plan clerk, ideally an intelligent and enthusiastic worker willing to do mundane jobs like keeping my drawings up to date in exchange for experience. One afternoon, I had set up a meeting with a student at the Crown Building. When I arrived, I saw a young African American sitting in the lobby, and I brought him in to my office to interview him for the position.

Right after he left, someone came to tell me Trump wanted to see me. When I got to his office, he was livid. He stepped forward and closed the door behind me. "I never ever want to see that again," he said. His face was red, which was not a good sign.

"What do you mean?" I didn't even know what he was talking about.

"I don't want people thinking Black people work here," he said. "Don't you ever do that again."

"What do you mean? I was interviewing him for a position. I need a plan clerk for—"

"Barbara, I don't want Black kids sitting in the lobby where people come to buy million-dollar apartments!" Donald really lit into me, telling me not to hire the young man. As it happened, I wasn't going to hire him (not because of Trump), but I always wonder what I would have done if he had been my choice. I probably would've fought Donald, although I don't think I would have won. Racism was accepted practice in the industry back then, and I didn't have enough clout to prevail over Trump on the issue. I didn't like it, I didn't endorse it, and I didn't condone it. Some of the other executives also disdained Trump's conduct and let him know. Trump would just laugh it off.

By the late 1980s, I saw more people of color working within the Trump Organization or on the periphery, some even in visible positions at the Plaza or at Trump Tower, though mainly as doormen and waiters. Most people who worked for Trump, the same ones who used to tell racist jokes, suddenly acted as though they had always respected people of color. Trump tamped down on his public bigotry for a few years, probably because he knew it would be bad PR. But then something happened that brought his racism right into the papers.

One night in 1989, a horrible crime was committed in Central Park. A woman jogging by herself was attacked, raped, and left to die. The story was front-page news, even national news, and there was this palpable fear and anger in the city. There was obviously a lot of pressure for an arrest, and five teenage boys, Black and Latino, were soon charged with the crime. Trump ran a full-page ad (really an open letter) in four major New York City newspapers calling for the return of the death penalty for "roving bands of wild criminals [who] should be forced to suffer." It was less than a year after the 1988 election, in which he had flirted with running, and he was still talking about how he should be president. The ads' very presence garnered their own wave of publicity for Trump, which was no doubt the point. His "tough on crime" stance, which is just coded racist language, was all an effort to beef up his political profile. Trump doesn't spend money like that just to express himself.

Many of the executives at the company disapproved of the way he was speaking about these young boys, who were just high school age. No one knew yet that they were falsely accused, but they hadn't even had their day in court. Trump saw an opportunity to stir up the "law and order" folks, just as Richard Nixon had successfully done when running for president and as Trump himself would do when he ran for president in 2016.

Even after the young men were all exonerated—after years in prison—on the basis of DNA evidence and the perpetrator's confession, and given a giant settlement from the city, Trump still wouldn't concede that they were innocent. He called the settlement a disgrace and said people still believed they were guilty, which is just not true. Anyone with a basic grasp of the facts was aware they were innocent. But Trump doesn't care about facts. *Never, never, never admit*, Cohn taught him—no matter what the evidence says.

As president, Trump has used racist language to achieve racist ends. During the mass Black Lives Matter (BLM) protests in the wake of George Floyd's murder by Minneapolis police in May 2020, he immediately attacked the movement. He has called BLM a symbol of hate, called protesters "thugs," and publicly threatened "when the looting starts, the shooting starts." As I write this in August 2020, in the wake of the Jacob Blake shooting by police in Kenosha, Wisconsin, he continues to attack mostly peaceful protesters while excusing right-wing violence.

You can also see Trump's bigotry in the way he goes after Black women in power, from DC Mayor Muriel Bowser ("incompetent") to Rep. Frederica Wilson ("wacky") to senator and vice presidential candidate Kamala Harris, whom he's called "awful," "phony," and "a mad woman." He feels safest going after them, at the intersection of gender and color, where he thinks he will get broad support, certainly from many of the white men without college degrees who make up much of his base. Trump also told four female Democratic congresswomen of color, newly elected during the 2018 midterms and known as the "Squad," to go back to where they came from. It didn't matter that three of the four—Reps. Alexandria Ocasio-Cortez, Rashida Tlaib, Ayanna Pressley—were born in the U.S.* They weren't white, so to him they were "other," from some foreign place.

This all leads to the next form of bigotry in Donald's arsenal: nonwhite foreigners, especially immigrants.

When Mexico sends its people, they're not sending their best. They're not sending you. They're not sending you. They're

---

* The fourth, Rep. Ilhan Omar, was a refugee from Somalia who came to the U.S. as a twelve-year-old and became a U.S. citizen twenty years ago, at age seventeen.

sending people that have lots of problems, and they're bringing
those problems [to] us. They're bringing drugs. They're bringing
crime. They're rapists. And some, I assume, are good people.

—DONALD TRUMP

Trump built his candidacy on the back of a bigoted attack on President Obama, but he launched his campaign by going after immigrants from Mexico. "Some, I assume, are good people," he said, implying he doesn't know of any. Trump has used the term "infested" to describe what immigrants are doing to our country, which echoes the language of genocide and specifically the Holocaust. He is very comfortable with this rhetoric because he believes it. But as with his racism, he is also leaning into it to appeal to the anti-Mexican sentiment found among many of his followers.

Trump's biggest campaign proposal in 2016 was to build a giant wall along the U.S.-Mexico border, to be magically paid for by Mexico, which was just another PR ploy. Trump knew what it would take to build a wall, and he probably had no intention of really doing it, though he has wasted over $11 billion (and counting) of taxpayer money to keep up the charade. During that campaign he also went after an American-born judge of Mexican descent assigned to the suit against Trump University, claiming the judge's heritage meant he couldn't be impartial—literally the judge's job—because of Trump's wall proposal.

During Trump's presidency, his and his administration's response to Hurricane Maria, which devastated Puerto Rico, seemed intentionally cruel and indifferent. He essentially blamed the people and not the failed government response for the problems caused by the storm. For good measure, he also attacked Mayor

Carmen Yulín Cruz of San Juan—a Latina—for calling him out on his ineptitude. Adding insult to injury, Trump staged a ridiculous photo op of himself throwing rolls of paper towels into a crowd of people who had suffered a death toll that matched 9/11. Puerto Rico is a territory of the U.S., and Puerto Ricans are citizens, though they can't vote for American presidents, which also likely influenced Trump's behavior. His response paled in comparison to his sympathetic reaction to the hurricane that had caused damage to Florida and Texas the previous month. Miles Taylor, the former chief of staff at the Department of Homeland Security (DHS), told NBC's Hallie Jackson that Trump proposed trading Puerto Rico for Greenland, because "Puerto Rico was dirty and the people were poor."

In the run-up to the midterm elections in 2018, Trump fanned the hatred and fear of anti-Latino and anti-immigrant racists by claiming that a group fleeing Honduras for a better life was actually a caravan of dangerous criminals coming to invade the U.S. (After the election, his concern magically disappeared.) And, of course, his most horrific and inhumane action as president has been to arrest, detain, and separate Mexican and other Latino immigrant families, taking babies from their mothers and locking them all up in cages. According to Taylor, Trump told DHS officials that he wanted to shoot, maim, and tear-gas migrants at the border.

Though Mexicans seemed to be his favorite targets, Trump also conveyed his utter disdain for African (and Latino) countries by referring to some as "shitholes," saying that Nigerians should "go back to their huts," and that Haitians have AIDS. At the same meeting he said he wished more Norwegians would come to the U.S.

Then there is his distaste for Muslims, which dates back to at least 9/11, when he insists that he saw thousands of "Arabs" celebrating in Jersey City when the Twin Towers fell. He continues to make this claim though not a shred of evidence has ever been put forth to support it. He knows certain people have a twisted view of Islam, and he can feed into their bigotry. During the 2016 campaign, Trump attacked the Muslim parents of a U.S. soldier who died in combat after they spoke at the Democratic National Convention. He further denigrated the mother, suggested that maybe she was not allowed to speak. As a candidate he also promised a ban on all Muslims coming into the United States, and as president has tried—and failed in the courts—a few times to implement one.

Bigotry and bias control Donald's view of the world, even the so-called positive stereotypes, which are just as damaging, like saying the Japanese (whom he seems to despise) are smarter than Americans. He has fixed ideas about what groups are the best with money, the sternest bosses, the cleanest. Donald organizes the world based on nationality and ethnicity and comports himself as though his bigoted notions are facts.

When we were in the swing of construction on Trump Tower, and I was ready to hire a residential manager, Donald came across a candidate who may have worked for Fred in Brooklyn. He was 100 percent German, and Trump was thrilled. Donald believed Germans were especially clean and orderly, and without consulting me or Louise, he just gave this man the job. In a room full of executives, he stressed that because the guy was German, he was "very clean." Trump then joked that "this guy still reminisces about the ovens, so you guys"—meaning the Jewish executives—"better watch out for him." Every one of us was horrified. We just looked at each other, and I shook my head. No laughs, not even a smile.*

The German building manager turned out to be an outright disaster for us. He lacked the finesse necessary to deal diplomatically with the wealthy apartment owners, and he was as clueless as he was clumsy. Unpleasant, unsmiling, and condescending to some of my crew, this guy also knew nothing about construction. After two weeks, my assistant and I went to see Donald to tell him the guy had to go. "Okay," Donald said. "Fire him." My assistant did the deed, nicely but firmly. But it didn't take. The German left the meeting and marched across the street to Trump's office and, lo and behold, got himself rehired.

Incensed, I confronted Donald, but he argued that we hadn't really given the guy a chance. Another week of working with him went by, and there was no improvement. Once again, I told Donald he had to go. With Trump's permission, we fired him for a second time. The German again went across the street to the Crown Building to make his case to Donald, who—unbelievably—rehired him again! It was too ridiculous to even get angry about. I had to get through to Trump, and I finally did, getting rid of the residential manager for good. It took three attempts to get rid of a guy whose only qualification was that he was German.

I could see that Trump really bought into the Aryan race mindset. While the Trumps' Germanness was kept under wraps in the years following World War II (they claimed to be Swedish), Donald eventually embraced and bragged about it. Trump believed that he

---

* I have heard Donald's cousin jokingly refer to him as "Der Führer."

was superior because of his whiteness, his Christianity, his gender, his genius, and his looks.

Perhaps not surprisingly, Trump also has strong feelings about Jewish people. A lot has been made of Trump's support of Israel and the fact that he has a Jewish son-in-law, Jared Kushner, neither of which proves anything. Trump supports Israel for the same reason almost all Republicans do—because the Evangelicals insist on it.* (Trump admires the dictatorial style of Israel's leader, Benjamin Netanyahu.) I heard from a close relative of Trump's that when Ivanka married Kushner in 2009, the family—including Donald—was horrified at having a Jewish man in the family. Trump's late assistant confirmed to me that Trump was initially opposed to the union, though he came around. Perhaps he saw a silver lining in an alliance with the Kushners, since Jared's father was a shady real estate developer too.

As with all groups, Trump regularly talked about "the Jews" as if they were a bloc. He thought Jewish people were all crafty, unsavory, and good with money, a centuries-old caricature that is directly connected to the most heinous acts of anti-Semitism. Trump initially thought that I was Jewish, and he seemed disappointed when he learned I wasn't. I guess it made me less of a "killer" in his mind. But it meant, to him, that I was the "right kind"; he didn't have to be careful around me with anti-Semitic comments. At work, Trump was surrounded by Jewish people, starting with Roy Cohn and virtually all his lawyers and executives. I deduced from Donald's comments and behavior that although

---

* Evangelical Christians are almost entirely pro-Israel, though not necessarily pro-Jewish. They want the Jews to control the Holy Land (Israel) because it's a prerequisite for the Rapture—which, incidentally, will send all Jews who refuse to convert to hell.

Jews were useful to have on your side, they were not to be fully accepted.

None of this is disconnected from his not-so-subtle support of white supremacy (or the "alt-right," if you buy the rebranding). After a hate group rally led to the murder of a peaceful protester in Charlottesville, Virginia, in 2017, Trump failed to condemn the violent white supremacists who marched to the rallying cry "Jews will not replace us." Instead, Trump equivocated, claiming there were "fine people on both sides." This was not a slip. Trump dragged his feet on denouncing David Duke or even the KKK; he has gone out of his way *not* to condemn white supremacists because he knows they make up a significant part of his base, and he seems to share a good deal of their sentiments. Alt-right leaders have said that Trump's election gave them the license to come out of the shadows; Trump isn't just riding that wave—he is the primary force making it rise.

Racism and xenophobia are a useful tool Trump digs out when he thinks it behooves him. In the past few months, Trump and his administration have continually branded the coronavirus as something foreign, specifically Asian ("kung flu," "Chinese virus"). Before the virus had spread so completely, he repeatedly extolled the job Chinese president Xi Jinping had done keeping it at bay. But once the virus became a pandemic, and he could benefit by othering it, Trump seized upon the opportunity to exploit race once again.

To Trump, the world that isn't white, male, and Christian is necessarily beneath him. Trump's prejudice is an integral part of who he is, as a person and a politician. Many of his followers like that he's saying aloud what they are thinking. For years, these people have been marginalized because society has passed them by. Trump has played to their racial grievances and encouraged their basest instincts, and they feel justified in their feelings, liberated. They are empowered. Now they are bold and unafraid because they feel like they are right. And how do they know? Because the president of the United States feels exactly the same way.

NINE

SEARCH AND DESTROY

Rule: Trump's default is attack mode.

My scare value is high. My arena is controversy. My tough front is my biggest asset.

—Roy Cohn

In late 1980, I was negotiating final payments with all the subcontractors for work done on the Grand Hyatt, while also taking bids for Trump Tower. Since I had a very big project in the pipeline, offering the opportunity both to make money and gain notoriety for working on a celebrated building, I had the upper hand with all the subs. I was working with Donald's favorite tool: leverage. Sometimes with a partner from HRH and sometimes alone, I negotiated final payment with all the subcontractors for work done on the Hyatt.

Sometimes a sub would start saber-rattling with me, refusing to budge on the price for their work. I'd say $200K and he'd say 300. I'd go up to 225, and he'd stick with 300. When it looked like we were at an impasse, I'd march him down the hall to Donald's office, where he and I would conduct something of a routine. "Donald," I'd say, after introducing the sub, "he wants 300, I offered him 225, which I think is a good deal, and he won't take it. Maybe you can move him."

I always left wiggle room so Trump could sweeten it, play good cop. "Listen, Barbara's a good negotiator," Trump would say. "She only thinks of what's best for me, but just because I'm a nice guy I'll give you another 15. Let's make a deal at 240. What do you say?"

If the sub stood firm, Trump would open a drawer in that giant bloodred desk and pull out a picture. It was a grainy black-and-white eight-by-ten photograph of Donald's friend and personal lawyer, Roy Cohn. "All right then, but I gotta tell you," he'd say, holding up the picture. "This is my lawyer, and he loves suing contractors. You really wanna go against this? I have him just waiting in the wings." With his haunting eyes, boxer's nose, and scarred face that not even a mother could love, there's really no one else to compare him to: Roy Cohn looked like the devil.

Cohn was notorious, a genuine American villain who had been chief counsel to Senator Joe McCarthy during his Communist witch hunt in the 1950s. In the decades since, Cohn had become a famously ruthless lawyer who knew where the bodies were buried—figuratively and literally. His mob ties, political connections, and shady clients gave him enormous power and reach, especially around New York City. Cohn was not just a lawyer to Trump but a mentor, and except for Fred, maybe the greatest influence in Donald's life.

After Cohn defended the Trumps against the Justice Department's charges of racist housing practices in 1973, he stayed on as Trump's rottweiler for any legal issues arising from construction and real estate, for lawsuits filed by or against Donald, and for the prenuptial agreement with Ivana. Donald used Cohn—or Cohn's picture—for all kinds of things. Though I didn't see much of Roy, aside from occasionally crossing paths with him at black-tie events, I knew how important he was to Trump. He was like Trump's hidden beast, coming up from under his rock when summoned.

The one time I worked with Cohn directly was when we had a dispute with the electrical contractor on the Grand Hyatt over his final payment. I was in the office telling Trump about it when he said, "We should get Roy on this." Right then, he called Cohn—and took him off speakerphone, which was something Trump rarely did. I heard only one end of the conversation, which concluded with Donald telling Roy, "I'm sending over Barbara Res. She's great. She does all my construction for me. She's great." Then Donald hung up and said to me, "I want you to talk to Roy. Go see Norma. She'll give you the address." Though most people were scared of Cohn, I'd always been curious; I was looking forward to meeting him.

Cohn's office was one floor of a brownstone he lived in on the Upper East Side of Manhattan. I didn't know what to expect, but when I got there, I was stunned. You literally could not see the floors. Cartons of papers everywhere, file boxes stacked up to a person's height, trash and packaging, random knickknacks, and household items all over the place, like the Collyers' mansion. Roy Cohn was a hoarder.

There were about a dozen people in his office, and one of them took me over to Roy. I was surprised by his appearance as well. In photos he had this dramatic face, but in person he was just a short and ugly guy. Cohn and I had a brief chat in the hallway, and then he introduced me to the associate I'd be working with. We both knew this was just going to be a threat of a lawsuit. The associate drew up the legal papers, which was all that needed to be done. I sent the papers to the electrical contractor and called him up, told him that Roy had everything ready to file the lawsuit. Then I asked if he wanted to come in one more time, and miraculously, he did and we made a deal. The photograph and some paperwork were all we needed. That was Cohn's power—and Donald wielded it frequently.*

Trump has had a longtime penchant, even love, for suing people, and Cohn was the perfect tool to do this. Over the years, I watched Trump sue, countersue, try to sue, or threaten to sue just about everyone. *USA Today* did an investigation before the 2016 election and found that Trump was party to 3,500 lawsuits up to that point, "unprecedented for a presidential nominee." When I was working on Trump Tower, I pretty much kept us out of court by making fair payments to the contractors and getting Trump to agree to them. Disputes in construction are commonplace, and so litigation isn't rare. But no matter the disagreement, Trump insisted that a lawsuit be initiated right away against his potential opponent so he could be the plaintiff. He could not abide the notion that someone would strike first—legally or otherwise.

Suing was just the cost of doing business with Donald, as HRH president Irving Fischer had warned me my first day working on

---

* Cohn was disbarred in 1986 for what the New York State Court called "reprehensible" and "unethical" conduct. He died a few months later.

the Grand Hyatt. Trump used it as a point of intimidation and to get what he wanted, but it also arose out of his wicked temper. Considering how long he's been in the public eye, it's surprising that people don't really know this about Donald Trump. He manages to hide or deflect his full-blown anger in public, but it comes out in other ways: through snide or scathing remarks directed at reporters, impulsive decisions, Twitter outbursts, and long ugly diatribes at his rallies. In private it's much worse: volcanic, explosive, frightening. Because I know about his anger, and his almost innate need to attack, very little of what Trump does scares, confuses, or surprises me.

Trump's attacks against Hillary Clinton were never normal political fodder. They were intense, arising out of his deep loathing of a highly accomplished woman who dared to go up against him and question his fitness. There was this *Who the hell does this woman think she is?* kind of attitude toward her, especially at the debates: the audacity of a woman thinking she could run the free world, not to mention do it better than he could! His verbal assaults on Hillary were vicious, and they had a different tenor from anything he would have directed against a male opponent. You couldn't miss the hostility in how he spoke of Hillary, the confidence with which he encouraged his followers and surrogates to go after her, the pleasure he took from the "Lock her up!" chants, and the physical intimidation he used during that second presidential debate, which came from a very angry place.

But Trump's an equal opportunity aggressor. He hated that John McCain was treated as such a hero; it ate at him to the point of rage. Donald somehow took it personally, because everyone knew he got out of Vietnam because of alleged "bone spurs."

When Trump first said that despicable thing about McCain, who spent five years as a POW in a North Vietnamese torture camp—"I like people who weren't captured"—it had the sound of a prepared line, like something he'd been holding on to for the right moment. He probably didn't realize how outraged people would be, but no way was he going to apologize. Since Senator McCain remained a critic of Trump's administration, even casting the deciding vote against Trump's last Obamacare repeal in 2017, it became even easier for Trump to ramp up the attacks. He went after McCain to the senator's dying day and, grotesquely, even after.*

The Trump I knew was consumed by revenge, heaping it on anyone who had crossed him, even when it did nothing but hurt himself. He had a long-standing battle with billionaire Leonard Stern, who owned much more real estate than Donald as well as some newspapers. Trump began a feud with Stern after one of the newspapers he owned printed some facts about Trump Tower: what it cost, how the resale value of the condos was falling, and how Donald had lied about the number of apartments sold. Donald naturally resented Stern, who had a better reputation and more experience than he did. Since Trump had nothing on him, he came up with an attack that was naturally below the belt. Trump claimed that Stern's wife Allison had asked Donald out, a preposterous lie. He got one of the papers with whom he traded in gossip to report that he rejected Allison; Stern called the story "childish and sick." The Sterns wisely did not give it any more fuel, and it sputtered

---

* As this book went to press, the *Atlantic* released a story (verified elsewhere) that Trump had insulted captured or dead war veterans, calling them "losers" and "suckers." There has been a brief spurt of outrage, but I doubt it moves the needle. The comments and behavior surrounding McCain are well known and appeared to have little effect on Trump's base.

out. But in the meantime, Trump worked hard to create the illusion that this billionaire's wife, along with so many others whose interest he invented, wanted Trump.

Everyone can see how vengeful Trump is as president, whether it's his continuous attacks on Hillary, FBI Director James Comey, former Attorney General Jeff Sessions, or President Obama. After Obama ribbed him at a couple of White House Correspondents' Dinners, Trump's attacks on him took on an obsessive quality. These only seemed to intensify after Trump took office. Trump treats Obama's very existence—his good looks, his education, his legislative accomplishments, his popularity—as a personal slight. Some of Trump's actions as president to undo Obama's policies don't even make sense from a conservative point of view; they emerge wholly from spite. He has to take revenge against the man who succeeded in all the ways Trump has failed as president. The fact that Obama is Black just makes it easier for him, as there's a ready-made group of racists ready to cheer him on.

Revenge is at the heart of so many of Trump's actions in office: his attacks on FBI Director James Comey and special counsel Robert Mueller, his evisceration of Jeff Sessions's political career, his insistence on insulting people he hired after they leave, and his cruelty toward "Democratic" states or cities. One example among many: In 2018, Trump tried to cut off FEMA funding to help Californians who had suffered after the devastating wildfires because the state didn't vote for him.

Trump's most visible retaliatory actions as president were reserved for anyone who was "against" him in his impeachment trial. Once he was acquitted by the Senate, Trump went after the career bureaucrats and military officers who spoke up regarding his corrupt dealings and the far less than "perfect" phone call with the Ukrainian president: former Ambassador Marie Yovanovitch, who stood in the way of Trump and his cronies' corrupt dealings in Ukraine; Dr. Fiona Hill, the former National Security Council (NSC) adviser who called him on his lies about Russia and Ukraine; and Lt. Col. Alexander Vindman, a decorated veteran, who testified about what he heard on the call and what he saw in the White House.

Trump struck back cruelly at both Alexander Vindman and his twin brother, Lt. Col Yevgeny Vindman,* moving them out of the NSC and having them escorted out of the White House. Alexander Vindman was left with no choice but to retire early after he understood that the administration would never allow him to get the promotion he was due. Throughout the ordeal, Vindman was a patriot, an inspiration, and a class act. His poise and courage did America proud; so of course, Trump had to ruin him. The ultimate dig at Donald Trump is to behave with dignity, to refuse to sacrifice principle for profit, to stand up for what one believes in no matter the personal consequences. He can't stand for that. He can't even conceive of it.

Trump also devised a way to never have to answer for what he's done by labeling the press "the enemy of the people." He's brandished the term constantly, indifferent to the damage it does to our democracy and its echoes of Hitler and Stalin. He does it to serve and protect himself, a fact he admitted to *60 Minutes'* Lesley Stahl. "You know why I do it?" he said about insulting the media. "I do it to discredit you all and demean you all so that when you write

---

* Lt. Col. Yevgeny Vindman filed a whistleblower complaint in August 2020.

negative stories about me no one will believe you." His attacks on the press satisfy his need to always be on offense while also allowing him to lie and cheat with impunity.

When Trump first bought the Plaza Hotel in 1988 for $390 million* ($868 million in today's dollars, a staggering amount for a hotel), he knew people were whispering and laughing at how he had overspent, so he had to respond. He took out a full-page ad in the *New York Times* explaining it was like the *Mona Lisa* and that's why he paid so much. The Plaza was and is a beautiful hotel and a New York institution, but the *Mona Lisa* it was not. He claimed he spent $50 million in renovations, but I would estimate it was closer to $10 to $20 million. Many of his Plaza stories strain the truth, if they don't outright stomp it to death.

When Donald bought the Plaza, Ivana was down in Atlantic City managing Trump's Castle casino. After the purchase, he immediately relocated his wife to New York and named her president of the hotel. (The rumor was that he wanted to keep his mistress, Marla Maples, in Atlantic City.) Donald announced that we were going to do a complete restoration of the Plaza, an important project that would be complicated by the Trumps' inexperience with construction and incessant interference. The work was further complicated by the fact that the Plaza was also a New York City landmark, putting us on the radar of the preservationists, who hold enormous sway with the City Planning Commission and have the power to kill a project.

---

* This is according to the Plaza and most news outlets. Trump's website has it at $407 million. In 1995, Trump sold the Plaza to a Singaporean developer and a Saudi prince at an $83 million loss.

Not only were we redoing the rooms, but we were rebuilding some of the Plaza's major public spaces, changing and upgrading mechanical systems and structural elements, and painting and decorating the entire hotel. I set up a small satellite office on-site that I quickly outgrew, soon moving to a spacious suite that I filled with drawings and paperwork.

Trump said he would restore the Plaza to its original splendor, but unsurprisingly, this was a very loose use of the term "restore." The architects fought to preserve the authenticity of the hotel but kept losing to Trump, who rebuilt or covered up almost everything in the place that was original. Sure, he *talked* about restoring the mosaic tile floors, but he ended up installing cheap carpeting from India, an inexpensive copy of something Ivana saw in a decorating magazine. We installed a green marble tile in the bathroom that was a poor substitute for Antique Verde, the Vermont marble we had in the residential lobby at Trump Tower; it was actually a copy from China, not even an Italian green. When I first saw the samples, it was obvious to me that they were very different from what Trump was picturing, and I made certain to get his approval. I laid out the marble tiles and let him know their associated price tags. He pointed at the cheapest one and said, "Go with the Asian."

Once we got under way with the renovation, I could see that there were problems between Donald and Ivana. They couldn't agree on a single thing. Paint colors, finishes, furnishings, materials—they argued about everything. The difficulties stemmed not only from design disagreements but the fact that Ivana was speaking back to Donald instead of just reverently acquiescing, as she had in the past. For her to try to hold her own with Donald, as an equal might, made him nuts. It seemed like Donald would disagree with her just to put her in her place.

But it was never a fair fight. Trump knew he had the upper hand and could reduce his wife to tears, either in private or in public. In fact, when he first installed her as president of the Plaza, he said in a press conference that he was paying her "one dollar a year plus all the dresses she can buy," an incredibly belittling and demeaning comment. It devastated her, cut her feet out from under her on day one. Even though Ivana had no more business running a luxury hotel than leading General Motors, Donald did name her as the president, a position that should have commanded respect—and serious money. But he had to try to reduce her to what she was in his eyes: just a woman, or less, the boss's wife.

Part of the reason for Trump's viciousness went back to something that occurred near the beginning of Ivana's reign at the Plaza. There was a reception for her in the hotel's main ballroom, and all the employees who were able to leave their posts were there. Ivana was an icon to them, and they were fawning all over her. She was especially congenial to the lower-level employees, even more so than Trump, who liked to kibitz with the workers, who flattered him while he excoriated their bosses. When Trump arrived at the reception, he was totally ignored. No fuss over him, no one moving out of the way, no circling around to hear his stories. Ivana was the star and Trump was treated like her second. I remember glancing over at him and seeing that look on his face, a mix between a pout and a snarl. I knew exactly what it meant: Someone had upstaged him and he was pissed.

About a year into the project, matters between Donald and Ivana started to spill into the Plaza. Their marriage was falling apart, and the acrimony between them was apparent. This was before their issues were public, before Marla Maples was a household name, before the papers were reporting daily on all the ins and outs of the "triangle." But to those who worked with him and who needed to get him to sign off on decisions, it was clear that Trump was extremely distracted—not just by his marital problems and the new woman in his life, but by a mad buying spree that left him bouncing from project to project, idea to idea. He was constantly changing his mind, and it was impossible to get him to focus.

One thing that did catch his attention was the Grand Ballroom. When you walked in, you were on a raised balcony looking down onto the ballroom floor. The balcony's massive wood railing was original to the building in 1907; it had been painted maybe fifty times, and it looked awful, all bumps and scratches. Trump decided we should bring it down to its original wood and then paint it properly, which would require stripping off eighty years of paint. We all told him it was a bad idea; the painters weren't even sure it could be accomplished, much less how to do it. The general contractor, HRH, the painter, and I all agreed that it could be made to look great with a good sanding and maybe some stripping. But Trump insisted. It was impossible to give a fixed estimate for this kind of work—it was all priced on time and materials, the most costly and inefficient way to do construction work. They tried stripping it chemically, but that left uneven and inconsistent results. They tried sanding it, which looked decent but was not the perfect finish Trump demanded. So they ended up using these huge heaters that looked like oversized hair dryers to melt the old paint off. This went on forever until they finally got the rail down to close to the original layer, and then they repainted it. It cost a fortune and was another example of how flawed Trump's thinking was. He thought something small like an imperfect handrail would reflect poorly on him. Meanwhile, throughout the hotel, Trump was making choices that actually did make him look bad, often using lesser materials and knockoffs and failing to restore some of the more beautiful and impressive elements of the Plaza, like the original glass ceiling in the Palm Court restaurant and the ceiling in the Fifth Avenue lobby.

Ivana's inexperience—combined with Trump's stinginess—also kept creating unnecessary problems. Early on, Ivana bought heavy wool uniforms for the room service waiters, a poor choice for people stuck in a small hot room until the food was ready to deliver to guests. The famous chef Alain Sailhac, whom Ivana lured away from Le Cirque, told me he had begged Donald to have the room air-conditioned—the waiters were starting to smell—but Trump said no. Even in a $400 million hotel, Trump didn't spend money where he didn't think it would show. When I came on the job, the chef immediately took me aside and begged me to try again with Donald. I got the air-conditioning approved, and Sailhac never forgot it. Whenever I was in the restaurant, he came out to greet me, telling my companions how I'd saved him.

Though Donald and Ivana seemingly couldn't see eye to eye on anything, one thing they did agree on was gold. We installed a lot of new ceiling and wall moldings, which were custom made in Canada and might have been quite beautiful if a little restraint had been used. The moldings in the public rooms and meeting spaces were to be gold leafed, though not with actual gold leaf, which is very expensive. Instead, we used something called Dutch Metal, which looks like gold—for a while. But it is actually brass in leaflike sheets, very cheap, costing a small fraction of the price of gold, and it tarnishes quickly. Again, Trump didn't understand that that would make him look bad.

Everything seemed to come to a head in the fall of 1989. One afternoon, Trump wanted to take a tour of the finished guest rooms, so we took the short walk from Trump Tower to the Plaza, with Donald barely saying a word. We met up with my assistant; the in-house decorator, George, a short guy with a mustache; and someone from Plaza security to let us into the sample room. It was obvious that Donald was wound tight and ready to erupt even before we got to the room. In retrospect, I think it was his unhappiness with his marriage combined with his regret that he had put Ivana in charge that put him in such a foul mood. The fact that he was in serious financial trouble added to it, and I imagine walking around a hotel he'd sunk $400 million into only reminded him of that.

We all walked in and watched quietly as Donald looked around at the sample room that was the model for all the others. His reaction built slowly, with him mumbling disgruntledly, to louder complaints about how everything looked like shit. "Fucking Ivana," he said as he manhandled some of the furniture, all knockoffs that he had approved. But it was when he saw the TV armoire that he really went ballistic. "What the fuck is this?" he said. Ivana had designed the armoire. It had pocket doors that slid back so you would not see them while watching TV. Trump walked over to the armoire and pulled out the door, which was a little unsteady. It was cheaply made, to be honest, and it got stuck a little as he moved it. "Look at this shit," he said as he tried to slide the door back in. "What is this shit?!" he said again, louder, and everyone in the room got tense. Then Donald became so enraged that he literally pulled the door off the armoire, breaking the hinge and cracking the wood. He threw it down on the floor, startling everyone in the room. "Fucking Ivana!" he screamed again. I looked over at George and saw that he was petrified.

Donald was already at his peak, and I still had to show him the bathroom, which was actually quite nice considering he'd opted for the cheaper finishes. The fixtures were white and good quality, and the green marble, even though it was milky, complemented them nicely. But Trump's temper, already boiling, inflamed again. "What the fuck is this?" he said, pointing at the marble. "What is this cheap shit, Barbara?"

"It's the Chinese marble. You approved it." That made him even more furious.

"Do you know how this fucking shit makes me look? I wouldn't have approved this shit."

"Yes, you did," I said. I tried to stay even-keeled, but he was actually scaring me.

"You're making me look bad! With all this cheap shit!" he screamed, his face beet red and his lips white. "Who told you to buy this?"

"I showed it to you with all the other marble, and you picked this one," I said. "This was the cheapest, and it's what you said to use. So don't blame me." I had never seen such anger and hatred on his face; for a moment, I believed he might hit me, and I was ready to just go down. But he kept on rambling, and instead of cowering like the decorator did, I went right back at him. "You wanted the cheap marble, Donald. It was less than half the price of the Vermont. What can I tell you? You get what you pay for."

He looked at me with absolute disgust and then, somehow, it was over. I went up to my office in the hotel, and Donald returned to Trump Tower without me.

Not long after the tumultuous walk-through, on my way from my home office to the Plaza, I spotted a young man I knew, Billy, walking into Trump Tower. Billy was a big fan of Trump's and had ingratiated himself with Donald while trying to get a job. I had no idea what Billy was doing there, and when I tried to chat with him, he barely gave me the time of day. From my people at the Plaza, I learned he had been snooping around the hotel. I smelled a rat.

Shortly after, I got a message to appear in Donald's office. I put two and two together and got paranoid, imagining Trump was going to replace me at the Plaza. Before my meeting with Trump, I went over to Ivana's office to—in my mind—say goodbye. This was the winter of 1989–90, around the time Marla Maples had confronted Ivana in Aspen, though I knew nothing about this at the time. At a resort in the Colorado ski town, Marla went up to Ivana, and in front of her young children said, "I'm Marla and I love your husband. Do you?"

I knocked on the doorframe and Ivana looked up. "Hi, Ivana, can I come in?" She nodded. "I just wanted to say—well, I think Donald is about to fire me," I said, taking a step into the office. She looked up, and then her perfectly made-up face started contorting. It was like something just snapped in her and she started sobbing. I froze, not expecting this at all. She sat there, dressed in her haute couture at her beautiful desk in her fabulous spacious office, her makeup smearing as tears rolled down her face. I had never seen her like this and didn't know what to say. "Ivana? What's wrong?" I asked, understanding obviously something else was going on.

"You don't know what he is like," Ivana said. "You think you do, but you don't. You only spend the day with him. I am with him twenty-four hours, every day." Ivana and I had been pretty close, and Trump had been terrible to her lately. I had sensed all this, witnessed a lot of it, but until that moment, I hadn't known how heavily it weighed on her.

"I'm sorry, Ivana. You're right," I said, taking a seat in front of her desk. "He doesn't appreciate you."

She grabbed a tissue and started carefully dabbing at her eyes.

"You work so hard here," I said. "I know you do. I see it."

"Thank you. No matter what happens, Barbara," she said, still through tears, "you'll be okay. You are strong and you can walk away."

I was too taken aback to speak. At some point Ivana calmed down and started talking about how "I think we are so alike. You and me. So alike. You will be fine."

When she composed herself, Ivana thanked me profusely and promised me the very best of recommendations. I thanked her back and walked out of there feeling awful for her. I didn't know about the Aspen confrontation, but I'd heard about a blonde Donald had been seeing, and it seemed as if Ivana had too. On top of insulting her, demeaning her at work, and cheating on her, Trump would later try to hold her to an unfair prenuptial agreement, which gave her nowhere near the $25 million settlement she eventually got. She had to fight like a dog to get what, I felt, was rightfully hers. I could tell Trump resented Ivana, and he repeatedly talked about how he regretted bringing her into the business. But Ivana actually helped to make him: She smoothed the waters for him, acted as his hostess, stood in for him at social events, worked hard on his various projects, and perhaps most important, gave him class he did not have.

I went back to Trump's office for the meeting that I had been dreading, but it turned out to be a nonevent. Trump was not at all unhappy with my work at the Plaza, and there was not a word about Billy. I later learned that Billy was tasked with finding out how things were going with the hotel, and he gave Trump a glowing review of our work. That tearful meeting was the last time Ivana and I saw each other on the job. I worked for Donald, and once they split up, I couldn't divide my loyalties; I had to be on his side. But my sympathies always rested with her.

As the tantrum at the Plaza demonstrated, Trump would often get angry with people who were simply doing what he asked for. If he didn't like the result, he'd go nuts, although he was the one who made cheap choices and gave impulsive directives—serious ones, like telling his people to start demolition on the Third Avenue project without a permit, or idiotic ones like objecting to Braille in the Trump Tower elevators.

As my years with Trump went on, I noticed how he became nastier to the people who worked for him, curt and outright abusive. Some employees respected him, others didn't, while many hated his guts. He had a serious temper and would lash out when things were not going his way. Roy Cohn taught Trump to always be on the attack and never admit you're wrong, advice he took to heart. But the combination of the two made him insufferable.

ANGER IS THE underlying reason for many of Trump's actions as president and almost all of his tweets. Anyone who has watched a Trump tantrum firsthand understands the tweets—the all caps, the exclamation points, the swinging from topic to topic—as his rage in text form. Twitter was built in a lab for Donald: As a coward, he needs to lob attacks safely from his couch. As a liar, he needs to spread falsehoods on a massive scale. As an impulsive person, he needs to not have to explain or answer for his words. During my days with him, he'd have to go through a whole song and dance to get good press: schmooze with newspaper publishers, offer information to gossip columnists, or invent personas like John Barron.

Those days are long gone. Twitter lets Trump talk to the world effortlessly: With the press of a button his message goes out unvarnished and unfiltered. It's the control, the instantaneousness, and the reach that he loves, something he couldn't even have imagined back in his days calling *New York* magazine. Some supporters think he'd be better off without Twitter, but it's obviously his lifeblood. He can only go on Fox News so many times, and even they, once in a while, throw a fact-check at him. To maintain his influence and power, Trump requires an outlet where he can present his version of events, lie with impunity, and endlessly attack his detractors. You can't disregard the tweets, because Twitter has just allowed Donald to be more himself.

Trump thrives on anger and grievance, and he can never let up. He is also the thinnest-skinned bully in the world. Donald can't take the slightest bit of criticism or pushback, whether it's from the media or from his own circle. Trump's people know that any news that reflects poorly on him—whether it's about poll numbers or Russia or white supremacists—will enrage him because his ego is that fragile. When he's in a corner, which he has been from day one as president, he has to attack. It's why he worked so hard to not just prove he didn't collude with Russia on the election, but to try to show it was the Democrats and Ukraine who cheated. (Four years later, he still has flunkies in his administration and Congress trying to prove this lie.) He had to make believe that not only were Michael Flynn and Roger Stone innocent, but they were *set up*; that Comey and Mueller were not only wrong, they were corrupt, part of the Deep State. Not that he disagreed with Obama, but that his predecessor was spying on him.

Trump's minions and supporters eat it up because they feel empowered by his attacks, which are often against their perceived enemies. And the more he sees them respond to it, the more he does it. It's why right now, in the fall of 2020, when he should be concerned about almost nine hundred Americans dying each day from COVID-19 on his watch, he's pretending there's a need for federal agents in Portland to stop peaceful protesters. He thinks the videos of his storm troopers beating, tear-gassing, and arresting law-abiding citizens inures to his benefit. It's why he keeps talking about sending the National Guard into American cities. These images and threats put him in a fighting position, let him claim he's the "law and order" candidate, which is a joke: Trump continually flouts the law and has just about destroyed the order.

Trump understands two types of relationships: the subservient and the adversarial. If you're not in the first group, then you're in the second. Donald's cousin John Walter told me that Fred taught his son tricks to use when negotiating. Fred said to set things up so the sun shines in his adversaries' eyes through the blinds. Fred also kept around the office a special chair with one shorter leg to put them literally off-balance. He would even do this to potential hires to put them off guard. I once asked Donald about this and he confirmed it. That controlled disadvantage is the ideal Trump playing field.

Trump's desire to always be on offense wreaked havoc in his business. As a boss, Trump cultivated chaos, criticized his own teams, and divided them against each other. He would give the same assignment to two or more people, thinking that one would come up with a solution, not realizing how much confusion this caused. Donald loved pitting people against each other—reports are he does this in the Oval Office as well—and somehow thinks the resulting chaos benefits him.

I became aware of this tendency when he tried to do it with me and my Trump Tower crew. When he told one of us that some-one had said something negative about another, we always got together and verified it. We assumed that, coming from Donald, it was invented, and usually it was. He has gotten it into his head that people perform better when they're fighting with each other, but it's also a tactic of self-protection: He's trying to ensure that his people will never band together in common cause against him. By design, his staff doesn't work together; things don't get done or they get done twice. It almost guarantees that things are going to get screwed up and his employees are going to be unhappy.

In Atlantic City, Trump made sure that Ivana, who was running Trump's Castle, and Steve Hyde, who ran Trump Plaza, were always competing with each other. It was unfair to compare an executive of such pedigree and experience to Ivana. So besides running the business, Steve had to compete in a silly contest, which allowed Trump to keep Hyde in his place. When the Castle's grosses were higher than Trump Plaza's, Trump goaded Hyde. Not only did

Hyde have to navigate this nonsense, but he also had to deal with being compared to the boss's wife, which diminished and humbled him. Again, Trump somehow thought this worked to his benefit, that Hyde would be less inclined to challenge him. Certainly, Trump could not have expected that it would make Hyde any more effective. Donald always wants his people scared and on the defensive, often letting the work suffer, because he needs to protect himself.

"YOU THINK YOU'RE so fucking smart, but these people are walking all over you," Trump would say to me from time to time, but always in private. He didn't take me apart in front of other people as he did with some employees—maybe aware that I wouldn't stand for it. Until he did.

Through most of the 1990s, I was in charge of Trump City West, a 6-million-square-foot proposed development on the site of the Ambassador Hotel in Los Angeles. Over the years my involvement changed: I began as an in-house executive at the Trump Organization and later became a consultant for the project. (I maintained my position as executive VP for Trump.) Trump City West would have been great for the area and the city at large. Ultimately, nothing came of the project except lots of travel, aggravation, and lawsuits. We had a prolonged battle with the Los Angeles School District, which wanted the site for a high school. There were other better, cheaper sites, but the school board was stubborn and powerful. Through their political connections,* they were able

---

* The most influential was current California congresswoman, and Trump foe, Maxine Waters. She ended up being the deciding factor against us.

to get the money from the state to take the property by eminent domain. Eminent domain allows government agencies to condemn and take private property for public use to provide essential services when substitute property cannot be found.

Though his name was on it, Donald really had very little to do with the Ambassador project. He once held a press conference in Los Angeles, and he interviewed the architects and the lawyers. The few decisions he did make were mostly ineffective and costly, such as bringing in Johnnie Cochran and another lawyer, a former politician, who was close to the mayor and did nothing for us. Even his deposition showed how uninformed and uninvolved he was with the project.* Meanwhile, I was the one who worked with the lobbyists, met with state lawmakers in Sacramento, spoke to the state assembly and major business groups, flew back and forth to LA, talked with the partners, and oversaw the design work.

At one point Trump insisted on talking to an important ally in California, Councilman Nate Holden, face-to-face before Nate and I went up to Sacramento to argue our case. I flew Nate across the country for the meeting, but the best Trump could do was make time for him on the helicopter trip to Atlantic City. Along for the ride with me, Donald, and Nate were Robert Trump and Harvey Freeman. This is a perfect example of how disengaged Trump was with the project: that he thought this was an acceptable way to meet with a very important legislator, whom we needed and who was worth flying five thousand miles round trip.

Shortly after we pulled out over the Hudson River, the helicopter began to shake, and I could see Nate's face drop. "Don't

---

* This is the Bitting/bidding story discussed in Chapter 3.

worry, Councilman!" Robert said. "This is where the ocean water meets the fresh water, and certain air currents arise that cause disturbances!" *Really, Robert?* I thought, though I didn't say a word. From the corner of my eye, I could see into the cockpit and noticed the copilot manically pumping something that looked like a stick shift. Then the pilot got on the microphone and told us he had lost some instruments and we needed to make an emergency landing. By now, the helicopter was making an alarming rumbling noise. The pilots were very calm and reassuring, but it was scary as hell. Donald loves to tell the story that Nate, an African American, turned white, but as I recall Donald was pretty white himself, and none of us were too comfortable.

After Robert's brief meteorology lesson, no one spoke another word. It was less than a year after the helicopter crash that had killed our three executives, which was all on our minds. When we finally got on the ground at Teterboro, a small airport in northern New Jersey, the relief was palpable. After all that, Trump had spent maybe five minutes talking about the project with one of the most essential players in the city. This is what much of Donald's "involve-ment" consisted of—useless efforts that wasted time and money.

The entire Ambassador project was an outlier from the start. Trump didn't know anything about California. He just liked the idea of having a stake in Los Angeles, maybe because Marla Maples was interested in acting, maybe because of his fascination with Hollywood and show business. When the site was first put up for sale, I went out to LA and looked at it and told Donald I didn't think he should buy it, and he passed. Then the group who bought it seduced him into joining them as a partner and developer with flattery, the promise of big fees, and the allure of creating a massive project on the West Coast. They formed an entity called Trump Wilshire Associates, consisting of an American entrepreneur and three companies from the U.K. and Ireland.

The Ambassador story is very complicated, enough for its own book. Over a seven-year period we engaged in several protracted lawsuits and appeals related to the Los Angeles School District's condemnation of the site through eminent domain. The state approved the allocation of the money, and the school district deposited the money with us, based on the evaluation of what they thought it was worth.

After the real estate market started sliding in 1991, the big project we had planned was no longer viable. The value of the property was decreasing significantly from what it had been the day it was condemned. We just wanted to sell it at a fair price and get out. The law required that the school board pay us the true value of the property—significantly more than we'd paid for it—which it did not want to do. What the court would decide was anybody's guess, but it was most definitely more than the school board's evaluation, so it was in their interest to negotiate before the court's ruling came down. We were trying to sell the property, but all the while we presented the idea that we still wanted to develop it and could return the school board's money. (In fact, we had used that money to pay off a loan and we could not have paid LAUSD back.) It became a game of chicken.

Unfortunately, one of our partners was going under, desperate to get some money out, and willing to sell at any price. Their VP, a guy named Finbar, approached Donald and claimed the school board had called him to say they wanted to make a deal but didn't want to negotiate with me.

There was zero percent chance that this was true; the school board wouldn't have known Finbar if they tripped over him. Finbar was a large and jolly Irish guy who was friendly on the surface but actually sneaky and self-important. Maybe he thought I was holding out for an unrealistic price when his company would have taken anything. They were bleeding to death and couldn't wait for an infusion. He was cornered like a rat and, to save himself, acted like one.

Donald called me and my assistant, Steve, into his office and told us Finbar's story. "It's not true, Donald," I said.

"Well, you don't know," Trump said. "You can be very difficult, Barbara. Maybe they did."

"They didn't. Trust me. They don't even know who Finbar is."

"Still, I think I'm gonna let him take it over."

"No, you can't," I said. "It's a big mistake."

"Why?"

"Finbar is a blowhard," I said. "You can't believe anything he says. Secondly, he and his group are totally desperate. He will make a terrible deal or let them know how desperate we are. And the minute that happens, Donald, the school board will walk away. Mark my words. Right now they think we can pay them back. If they learn that we don't have the money, we are screwed."

Donald ignored me and let Finbar take over the negotiations.* We ultimately arrived at a price we could all live with. After weeks of lawyers drawing up papers, and spending countless dollars, we went into the final meeting ready to sign. However, when we

---

* I ultimately learned in his sworn court testimony that Finbar invented the whole thing. I can't prove it, and Finbar has passed away, but my gut tells me that Trump was in on the phony story too.

sat down, the first thing out of the school board representative's mouth was: "We have no deal." This came out of nowhere and was devastating to us. I was totally astonished that a government agency would do something so unethical. They knew. Finbar had showed his hand.

Then, to put another nail in our coffin, Finbar made it obvious just how desperate we were, blurting out, "Is there another number we can do?" That told them we would sell at any price. Exactly what I'd said would happen happened. So we had no deal. Trump was angry, and since it was his fault, he needed someone else to saddle with the blame.

Now the price would have to be determined by the court. But because of Finbar's antics, the school district knew we could not pay it back, and they abandoned the condemnation altogether, knowing that we would not return the deposit, that they would get it for their ridiculous estimate.

They got the seventeen acres, but we had the chance to develop a much smaller project, like a shopping mall, on the remaining six acres if we could prevent the district from forcing a sale of the property to get its money. To prevent this, it was clear, the answer was for the Ambassador company to go into bankruptcy, which would put their creditors on hold and give them time to reorganize.

There was a big meeting in the conference room at Trump Tower: all the partners and a Realtor I had brought in from California to discuss realistic development possibilities. The problem was that Trump didn't want any part of a bankruptcy. His name was all over this thing, and people believed it was actually his. Donald loves having people think properties are his until something goes wrong. A bankruptcy here would be a personal failure, not like the gambling business going sour, which he could spin as "gaming the system." This was his failure as a developer. He couldn't have it.

Somehow the discussion in the meeting went back to the legal cases, and Trump turned on me like a rabid dog. He did what he knows best—attack. He ranted about how we were in the situation we were in because "Barbara fucked it up," lighting into me for the mess that he (and Finbar) had created. I'd always felt mostly immune to Donald's attacks, but this was different. Not only was I the direct target of his rage, but he was blaming me for his mistake, while also undermining and embarrassing me in front of the partners, people who were paying almost all of my salary.

"Calm down," I said at one point. "You know, there are drugs you can take for this, Donald." He turned red and I thought he would explode, but as I recall, he didn't say anything in response and went on with his diatribe. What I said was totally inappropriate and disrespectful, but I was just too livid to think straight. Everyone who works for Donald has to create some line for themselves, and he had crossed mine. Shortly after that meeting broke up and I said goodbye to the partners, I went to Trump's office. I sat down across from him at his desk.

"Look," I said, "I think it might be time for me to leave."

"What, why?" He was shocked and a little shaken. His people don't quit.

He'd insulted me, ridiculed me in public, blamed me for things that were his fault. I was rightfully angry, but my decision was not just based on emotion. I could tell this was not going to be a Trump project for much longer, and I was better off leaving sooner rather than later.

The partners knew me well and trusted me. If they had anything for me, they would seek me out later, which they eventually did. But as long as Trump was in charge, it would be a nightmare of Trump's unending abuse, which I was not built to take.

"I don't see any need for me here anymore," I told Donald. "They don't need to pay fees like mine to do a shopping mall. I don't see it for you either." I didn't call him out for degrading me. Instead, again, I made sure to keep our relationship intact.

"Are you sure?" he asked, still incredulous. I think he was worried he was losing his fall guy.

Was I doing the right thing? This project constituted most of my income. I was scared, but I knew this was what I had to do.

"Yeah, I'm sure," I said. "We've had a good run. It's time for me to go."

And I walked out of Trump's office for the last time.

EPILOGUE

In February 2016, during the Republican presidential primary, I wrote an op-ed in the *New York Daily News* about some of my experiences with and opinions of Donald Trump. While not glowing, it was factual and certainly within the bounds of public commentary. The morning it was published, I received a call from a man named Michael Cohen, identifying himself as Trump's lawyer. Even though I had never heard of him, I immediately sensed he was a jerk. After calling me a "liar" in his thick Long Island accent, he said that what I had written constituted libel. I knew this was bullshit, but I wasn't going to engage. I told him I was very busy with work at the time and that I'd have to call him back.

Later that day, Rhona Graff, Trump's secretary, who had been a friend of mine during my days at the Trump Organization, called me. The conversation was short. She told me Trump was very upset by my "slander."* I told her I disagreed, that what I had written was honest and fair.

---

* This was her mistake. Libel refers to published statements; slander is about spoken ones.

As for Cohen, I never bothered calling him back.

I did some TV and print interviews and wrote a few more op-ed pieces. Then in May, soon after Trump locked up the Republican nomination, I appeared on *All In with Chris Hayes* on MSNBC. In answering a question about Trump, I said, "He has to be stopped," a sound bite that was memorable enough to spread on TV and online.

The next day, I got another call from Rhona, who said that if I didn't "stop," she would release some pandering emails I had written Donald about five years earlier when I was looking for a job. I took this as a threat. Though I imagine Rhona was just following Trump's orders, it was extremely harsh, coming from a so-called friend. The emails were not something I was proud of, but I was certainly not afraid of the public seeing them. I hadn't talked to Trump for many years, so I wasn't aware of what he had turned into. Looking for work, as consultants do, I approached all my former bosses to see if anything was available. I was very complimentary to Donald in my emails, laying it on thick, knowing what Trump wanted to hear. All my other former bosses—to whom I wrote normal business letters—called or sat down with me. Trump wouldn't let get me past Rhona; he couldn't even be bothered to talk to me on the phone.

It's typical that Trump would threaten to use these emails to shut me up. In his mind they gave him the upper hand, allowing him to claim that I "begged" him for a job, which bore no relation to the truth.* Without even giving me time to "stop," Trump

---

* Trump loves to claim people were "begging" him for jobs. He did this with Robert Mueller in order to claim that the former FBI director had a conflict of interest in the Russia investigation. Of course, it was not true.

released the emails to a tabloid with which he had a relationship. The tabloid then published a very negative story about me, which quoted Trump saying he had "gotten rid of me." Later, Trump went off on me at a press conference and a few times at rallies, and his campaign tried to paint me as a "disgruntled employee" who was fired. I sued the tabloid, and the article is no longer available.

It is in the interest of Trump's followers to believe his fabricated versions of events. They don't want to hear that someone who knew Donald very well, who was once an important executive, a trusted employee, now finds him to be a dangerous and odious person, a danger to his country and its citizens. His people and his followers came after me then, and they will certainly vilify me once again, as will Trump. I can handle it. I've dealt with worse.

———————

I REMEMBER A colleague of mine on Trump Tower who would occasionally show me a *New York Times* article he thought might interest me. One day he came in with an article about narcissists. He said it reminded him of someone and passed it around the office to see if we agreed.

> *Delusions of grandeur*
> *Always the victim*
> *Lacking in empathy*
> *Entitled and manipulative*

The only thing missing was Donald's picture.

* * *

Selfishness informs all of Trump's behavior. It is the characteristic that undergirds all the rules in this book. I remember
an interview Donald gave on September 11, 2001—only hours
after the World Trade Center came down and took the lives
of thousands of people—about how he now had the tallest
building in downtown Manhattan. What kind of mind comes
up with something like that? And, even then, who would say it
out loud in the hours after such death and destruction? Only
someone devoid of the most basic empathy. Only someone who
wasn't even aware how it would sound to a normal person.
There are countless examples of how Donald Trump sees the
world entirely through his own interests, but his words that day
remain, by far, the clearest one.*

As I've argued throughout this book, Trump has become
the worst version of himself. I watched this evolution and, in the
process, have grown to detest a man I once thought of as something
of a mentor and friend. The Trump who is plastered across our
twenty-four-hour news feed is not the same person I met or first
started working for. But as I have shown, the seeds were always
there.

Sometimes when I read or hear about something horrible or
preposterous that Trump has said or done—this summer the
news broke that he actually looked into getting himself on Mount
Rushmore—I remember another Donald. One day in the summer
of 1990, when the Los Angeles School District got the money to

---

* On top of everything else, it wasn't even true.

condemn the Ambassador, I was in my office and Trump came in. It was quite rare by then that he would leave his own office. He knew what had happened, took a seat on my couch, and asked how I was doing. My dream project was now nothing but a headache, an interminable lawsuit, and I was distraught. Donald told me he understood that I was depressed and that I should be. He said he got depressed too sometimes, and it was natural. *Something will come along*, he said. *Try to be positive*. I know Donald, I know when he's pretending or lying, and I could tell that at that moment he was being sincere. He didn't have to do that.

Not long afterward, he put me in charge of the West Side Yards project. By this point Trump had changed, but because our relationship preceded his new persona, there was still a trace of affection left in him for me. Now it's hard for me to remember this without feeling sad. We had something then, a closeness that I don't believe is possible with those around him today. Who, now, does Trump protect or even respect?

I will always have mixed emotions about Donald. Even when he was at his worst in the early days, he was human and even sometimes humane. That version of him has been so thoroughly subsumed—by his yes-men, his ignorance and arrogance, his focus on appearances, his lies and cheating, his desire for credit and avoidance of blame, his disdain for (and manipulation of) the working people of this country, his denigration of anyone who isn't a white Christian male, and his incessant need to attack. It is impossible even to glimpse any of the positive attributes of that earlier Donald.

After Trump was elected, I was devastated. I wrote an open letter—which the *Huffington Post* published—to the president-elect. In the letter I outlined how I thought he could become an excellent president and even win my support. I needed something positive to hold on to, to believe that maybe this could work after all. My heart held out hope, but my brain knew better. He wouldn't even read it. Everything he's done since then has been the exact opposite of how I hoped he would behave and lead. It doesn't surprise me.

I wrote this book to share the personal knowledge and experiences of someone who knew him well, to add to the vast trove of Trump stories, hopefully in a useful way. The nation has become so accustomed to Trump the racist, Trump the sexist, Trump the liar and criminal, that even his most egregious acts no longer shock us. And that is the heart of the problem.

The world needs to understand the depth of Trump's depravity. It's not a show; it's real. We have witnessed nearly four years of him learning how to abuse the power of the presidency and get away with it. Now we have to ask ourselves, "What else is he capable of doing?" Is it only his pure cowardice that has kept us out of a nuclear war? If he is reelected, what kind of country will we ultimately live in by the time he's gone? What will be the fate of immigrants, people of color, LGBTQ folks, the marginalized, and the poor?

We know Trump was happy to let people suffer with coronavirus as long as it was contained in the "blue" states. He was willing to let the elderly and infirm die if it avoided hurting his economy and his prospects for reelection. Whom else will he sacrifice, persecute, deprive, and neglect? Four years ago we could not have imagined what we now almost take for granted about him and our country. Unimaginable things can never happen—until they do. Donald Trump represents a serious and growing danger to our democracy, our way of life, and our future.

So, what are we going to do about it?

ACKNOWLEDGMENTS

I WOULD LIKE to acknowledge my publisher, Graymalkin Media, for believing in the value of my story, encouraging me, and bringing my book to fruition. I would also like to thank the editors who reviewed the book, making improvements in the presentation; my dear friends Roberta Kalan and Barry Berg, who worked with me on Trump Tower and the Plaza and who helped jog my memory; my sister, Elaine Lappe, and my former husband, Peter Res, who were there for me throughout the times I worked for Trump and patiently listened to all my stories and provided advice and sympathy to me, at the time, for dealing with him—and now helped me recall certain events and confirm others. I could not have written this book without them. Finally, my children, Res and Peter G. Res, who are a constant inspiration to me to reach higher and try harder to realize and achieve what I am capable of doing.

NOTES

INTRODUCTION

Page xi: **The person I hired:** Donald J. Trump, *The Art of the Deal* (New York: Ballantine Books, 2015), 173.

4: **I recognized this characteristic:** Mark Abadi, "Trump Won't Stop Saying 'My Generals'—and the Military Community Isn't Happy," *Business Insider*, October 25, 2017.

4: **"my Justice Department":** Jordan Phelps, "Trump Launches New Attack on His Justice Department," ABCnews.com, April 26, 2018.

10: **"What lurks in him is apparent":** Michael D'Antonio, *The Truth About Trump* (New York: Griffin Books, 2016), xix.

CHAPTER ONE: THE (GOOD) OLD DAYS

Page 12: **The real story was:** Gwenda Blair, *The Trumps: Three Generations of Builders and a President* (New York: Simon & Schuster, 2001), 523.

12: **"the largest construction job":** Wayne Barrett, *Trump: The Greatest Show on Earth: The Deals, the Downfall, the Reinvention* (New York: Regan Arts, 2016).

40: **"may well be the most pleasant":** Paul Goldberger, "Architecture: Atrium of Trump Tower Is a Pleasant Surprise," *New York Times*, April 4, 1983.

CHAPTER TWO: A PARADE OF YES-MEN (AND WOMEN)

Page 50: **"Everybody is too scared":** Philip Rucker, Yasmeen Abutaleb, Josh Dawsey, and Robert Costa, "The Lost Days of Summer: How Trump Fell Short in Containing the Virus," *Washington Post*, August 8, 2020.

51: **They came back with "better" polls:** Maggie Haberman and Annie Karni, "Polls Had Trump Stewing, and Lashing Out at His Own Campaign," *New York Times*, April 30, 2020; Asawin Suebsaeng and Lachlan Markay, "Trump Aides Know His Polls Are Terrible—And Tell Him Otherwise," *Daily Beast*, June 14, 2020.

51: **He would eventually replace:** Steve Benen, "Despite Crises, Trump Retains Pollster to Criticize Pollsters," MSNBC, June 9, 2020.

52: **Trump's former personal:** Jacqueline Thomsen, "Ex-Doctor Says Trump Dictated Letter Claiming He Would Be 'Healthiest' President Ever," *The Hill*, May 1, 2018.

52: **Dr. Jackson spoke repeatedly:** Dan Merica, "Dr. Ronny Jackson's Glowing Bill of Health for Trump," CNN Politics, January 16, 2018.

52: **Soon after, he got:** Aaron Blake, "The Lengthy List of Allegations Against Ronny Jackson, Annotated," *Washington Post*, April 25, 2018.

54: **Ironically, the *New York Times* architectural:** Goldberger, "Architecture: Atrium of Trump Tower."

59 footnote: **Anonymous notes in:** Anonymous, *A Warning* (New York: Twelve, 2019), 222.

61: **In his first year in the White House:** Olivia Nuzzi, "My Private Oval Office Press Conference with Donald Trump, Mike Pence, John Kelly, and Mike Pompeo," *New York* magazine, October 10, 2018.

62: **"I tell Mike":** Donald Trump, "Remarks by President Trump, Vice President Pence, and Members of the Coronavirus Task Force in Press Briefing, March 27, 2020.

62: **Trump did the same thing:** Michael D. Shear, Noah Weiland, Eric Lipton, Maggie Haberman, and David E. Sanger, "Inside Trump's Failure: The Rush to Abandon Leadership Role on the Virus," *New York Times*, July 18, 2020.

63: **Now that he's in the White House:** "Remarks by President Trump, Vice President Pence, and Members of the Coronavirus Task Force in Press Briefing," whitehouse.gov, April 20, 2020.

63: **Cliff Sims, a White House communications:** Cliff Sims, *Team of Vipers: My 500 Extraordinary Days in the Trump White House* (New York: Thomas Dunne Books, 2019), 233.

64: **Though CNN reports that he told it:** Daniel Dale, "Trump Walks Out of News Conference After Reporter Asks Him About Veterans Choice Lie He's Told More Than 150 Times," CNN Politics, August 9, 2020.

64: **An August 2020 investigation:** Robert Draper, "Unwanted Truths: Inside Trump's Battles with U.S. Intelligence Agencies," *New York Times Magazine*, August 8, 2020.

66: **Later, she wouldn't pay:** Christopher Dickey and Michael Daly, "The Party Girl Who Brought Trump to His Knees," *Daily Beast*, April 13, 2017.

70: **He's on record saying:** Brett Samuels, "Trump Learns to Love Acting Officials," *The Hill*, April 14, 2019.

71: **Though he is too dumb to know:** Timothy Bella, "Jared Kushner Clarifies After Saying He's 'Not Sure' He Can Commit to Date for Presidential Election," *Washington Post*, May 13, 2020.

72: **Reports from inside the White House:** Rucker et al., "The Lost Days of Summer."

72: **"99 percent harmless":** Roni Caryn Rabin and Chris Cameron, "Trump Falsely Claims '99 Percent' of Virus Cases Are 'Totally Harmless,'" *New York Times*, July 5, 2020.

72: **"I'm not going to get into":** Veronica Stracqualursi and Sarah Westwood, "FDA Commissioner Refuses to Defend Trump Claim that 99% of Covid-19 Cases Are 'Harmless,'" CNN Politics, July 5, 2020.

73: **"Every one of these doctors said":** Donald Trump, "Remarks by President Trump After Tour of the Centers for Disease Control and Prevention, Atlanta, GA," whitehouse.gov, March 6, 2020.

CHAPTER THREE: THE BEST WORDS

Page 75: **"it would take an hour-and-a-half":** Lois Romano, "Donald Trump, Holding All the Cards The Tower! The Team! The Money! The Future!" *Washington Post*, November 15, 1984.

75: **moon is part of Mars:** Adam Gabbatt, "Trump Attacks NASA and Claims the Moon Is 'a Part' of Mars," *Guardian*, June 7, 2019.

75: **the Continental army took over:** Suyin Haynes, "President Trump Said Revolutionary War Troops 'Took Over the Airports' in His Fourth of July Speech," *Time*, July 5, 2019.

75: **that nineteenth-century abolitionist:** Dan Merica, "Trump: Frederick Douglass 'Is Being Recognized More and More,'" CNN Politics, February 2, 2017.

75: **who didn't know England was:** "Donald Trump 'Unaware UK Was Nuclear Power,' Says Former Aide," BBC News, June 18, 2020.

75: **thought Finland was part of:** Rachel Sandler, "Trump Once Asked If Finland Is Part of Russia, Bolton Book Says," *Forbes*, June 18, 2020.

75: **believed "clean coal":** Joe Romm, "Trump Thinks Clean Coal Is When Workers Mine Coal and Then Actually 'Clean It,'" *ThinkProgress*, August 23, 2017.

75: **said that windmills cause cancer:** Zachary B. Wolf, "Trump's War on Windmills Continues," CNN Politics, December 23, 2019.

76: **suggested we nuke hurricanes:** Jonathan Swan and Margaret Talev, "Scoop: Trump Suggested Nuking Hurricanes to Stop Them from Hitting U.S.," *Axios*, August 25, 2019.

76: **recommended injecting disinfectant:** "Coronavirus: Outcry After Trump Suggests Injecting Disinfectant as Treatment," BBC, April 24, 2020.

76: **"This job is a lot harder":** Sims, *Team of Vipers*, 71.

76: **This is a man who admits:** Alex Shephard, "Donald Trump Doesn't Read Books," *New Republic*, May 17, 2016.

76: **Not surprisingly, but still somehow:** Philip Rucker and Carol Leonnig, *A Very Stable Genius: Donald J. Trump's Testing of America* (New York: Penguin Press, 2020), 184.

76: **John Bolton said he was:** John Bolton, *The Room Where It Happened: A White House Memoir* (New York: Simon & Schuster, 2020), 7; Dexter Filkins, "Rex Tillerson at the Breaking Point," *New Yorker*, October 16, 2017; Rebecca Morin, "'Idiot,' 'Dope,' 'Moron': How Trump's Aides Have Insulted the Boss," *Politico*, September 4, 2018.

77: **"Chris," Trump said, "you and I are so smart":** Michael Lewis, *The Fifth Risk: Undoing Democracy* (New York: W. W. Norton & Company, 2018).

78: **"The president got bored with it":** Alexander Burns, Jonathan Martin, and Maggie Haberman, "As Trump Ignores Virus Crisis, Republicans Start to Break Ranks," *New York Times*, July 19, 2020.

78: **Yet Trump continues to equivocate:** *CNN Newsroom* transcript, July 18, 2020, CNN.com, http://transcripts.cnn.com/TRANSCRIPTS/2007/18/cnr.07.html.

80: **who had just won a crooked election:** Henry Meyer, "Russian Observers Charge Fraud in Putin's Landslide Re-Election," *Bloomberg*, March 19, 2018.

80: **DO NOT CONGRATULATE:** Carol D. Leonnig, David Nakamura, and Josh Dawsey, "Trump's National Security Advisers Warned Him Not to Congratulate Putin. He Did It Anyway," *Washington Post*, March 20, 2018.

80: **He regularly skips the written:** Carol D. Leonnig, Shane Harris, and Greg Jaffe, "Breaking with Tradition, Trump Skips President's Written Intelligence Report and Relies on Oral Briefings," *Washington Post*, February 9, 2018.

80: **So, just as we:** Rucker and Leonnig, *A Very Stable Genius,* 132; Anonymous, *A Warning* (New York: Twelve, 2019), 29–30.

80: **"You cannot focus the commander in chief":** Anonymous, *A Warning*, 30.

81: **"I didn't think these briefings":** Bolton, *The Room Where It Happened*, 84.

81: **"He just rants and raves":** Adam Entous, "What Fiona Hill Learned in the White House," *New Yorker*, June 29, 2020.

84: **"flood the zone with shit":** Sean Illing, "'Flood The Zone with Shit': How Misinformation Overwhelmed Our Democracy," *Vox*, February 6, 2020.

84: **"He continued to believe":** Carl Bernstein, "From Pandering to Putin to Abusing Allies and Ignoring His Own Advisers, Trump's Phone Calls Alarm US Officials," CNN Politics, June 30, 2020.

84: **"I'm highly educated":** Donald Trump, "User Clip: Trump: I Know Words," C-Span, March 7, 2017.

85: **"We put it in very powerfully":** "Remarks by President Trump in Press Briefing," whitehouse.gov, August 10, 2020.

85: **Years ago it was:** Adam Withnall, "Donald Trump's Unsettling Record of Comments About His Daughter Ivanka," (London) *Independent*, October 10, 2016.

85: **commenting on baby Tiffany's:** Lee Moran, "That Time Donald Trump Speculated About His 1-Year-Old Daughter's Breasts on TV," *HuffPost*, August 25, 2018.

85: **As a candidate he made:** Matt Flegenheimer and Maggie Haberman, "Donald Trump, Abortion Foe, Eyes 'Punishment' for Women, Then Recants," *New York Times*, March 30, 2016.

86: **As president he took:** "Trump on Northern Syria Pullout: U.S. Will 'ONLY FIGHT TO WIN,'" *Axios*, October 7, 2019.

86: **confessed to Lester Holt:** "Watch Lester Holt's Extended Interview with President Trump," NBC News, May 11, 2017.

86: **revealed sensitive intelligence matters:** Greg Miller and Greg Jaffe, "Trump Revealed Highly Classified Information to Russian Foreign Minister and Ambassador, *Washington Post*, May 15, 2017.

87: **He thought he was allowed:** "Transcript: Vindman and Williams Testify in Front of the House Intelligence Committee on Nov. 19," *Washington Post*, November 19, 2019.

88: **He once wrote:** Trump, *The Art of the Deal*, 77.

88: **He had a connection through:** Michael Kranish, "Trump Has Referred to His Wharton Degree as 'Super Genius Stuff.' An Admissions Officer Recalls It Differently," *Washington Post*, July 8, 2019.

88: **His former fixer:** Grace Ashford, "Michael Cohen Says Trump Told Him to Threaten Schools Not to Release Grades," *New York Times,* February 27, 2019.

91: **"I'm speaking with myself":** Eliza Collins, "Trump: I Consult Myself on Foreign Policy," Grand Old Primary Series, *Politico*, March 16, 2016.

91: **"I don't want to talk to anyone":** Rucker and Leonnig, *A Very Stable Genius*, 165.

92: **Gary Cohn, Trump's first:** Woodward, *Fear: Trump in the White House* (New York: Simon & Schuster, 2018), 58.

CHAPTER FOUR: A TALE OF TWO TOWERS

Page 95: **"doesn't sleep anymore":** Donald J. Trump, "Remarks by President Trump, Vice President Pence, and Members of the Coronavirus Task Force in Press Briefing," whitehouse.gov, March 27, 2020.

95: **"in the White House":** "Trump Says He's 'in the White House, Working Hard' During the Government Shutdown," *The Week*, December 22, 2018.

95: **Though he hounded President Obama:** https://trumpgolfcount.com; Daniel Dale and Holmes Lybrand, "Fact Check: Trump Has Spent Far More

Time at Golf Clubs Than Obama Had at Same Point," CNN Politics, May 25, 2020.

96: **It has been widely reported:** Jonathan Swan, "Scoop: Trump's Secret, Shrinking Schedule," *Axios*, January 7, 2018; Jen Kirby, "Trump Reportedly Works 11 AM to 6 PM During the Week," *Vox*, January 8, 2018.

96: **According to National Security Adviser:** Bolton, *The Room Where It Happened*, 93.

104: **The contract actually stated:** Andrew Leonard, "Donald Trump: The President We Deserve," *Salon*, April 20, 2011.

105: **Trump hired a company that took out:** Aaron Couch and Emmet McDermott, "Donald Trump Campaign Offered Actors $50 to Cheer for Him at Presidential Announcement," *Hollywood Reporter*, June 17, 2015.

105: **It was a set they built:** D'Antonio, *The Truth About Trump,* 263.

107: **Anybody that can do:** Emily Cochrane, "'That's My Kind of Guy,' Trump Says of Republican Lawmaker Who Body-Slammed a Reporter," *New York Times*, October 19, 2018.

109: **In fact, according to Harry:** Harry Hurt III, *Lost Tycoon: The Many Lives of Donald J. Trump* (Brattleboro, VT: Echo Point Books & Media, Reprint 2016).

109 footnote: **Trump did a similar thing:** Kaitlan Collins, Jeremy Diamond, and Jeff Zeleny, "Longtime Trump Aide Fired over Financial Crime Investigation," CNN Politics, March 13, 2018.

109: **He would later deny it:** Libby Cathey, "Contradicting Trump, Barr Says He Went to White House Bunker for Security Not 'Inspection,'" ABC News, June 9, 2020.

110: **"the most feared":** Betty Goodwin, "Just the Facts / Powerful Hollywood Lawyer Bertram Fields Judiciously Tackles the Bard's Authorship," *San Francisco Chronicle*, April 3, 2005.

111: **Myerson had represented:** UPI "Myerson Guilty of Overbilling Clients," April 29, 1992.

113: **"Wouldn't it be great":** Kathryn Watson, "Trump Says He Wants the Country 'Raring to Go by Easter,' Later Says It Will Be Based on 'Hard Data,'" CBS News, March 24, 2020.

113: **"I've felt it was a pandemic":** Donald Trump, "Remarks by President Trump, Vice President Pence, and Members of the Coronavirus Task Force in Press Briefing," whitehouse.gov, March 17, 2020.

114: **There's evidence that the Trump:** Dan Diamond, "Trump Officials Interfered with CDC Reports on Covid-19," Politico, September 11, 2020.

116: **both sold at huge losses:** Julie Satow, "That Time Trump Sold the Plaza Hotel at an $83 Million Loss," *Bloomberg Businessweek*, May 23, 2019.

116: **drove the short-lived United States Football League:** Jeff Pearlman, "The Day Donald Trump's Narcissism Killed the USFL," *Guardian*, September 11, 2018.

116: **Trump lost so much:** Russ Buettner and Susanne Craig, "Decade in the Red: Trump Tax Figures Show over $1 Billion in Business Losses," *New York Times*, May 8, 2019.

119: **while Trump was trying to buy:** Hurt, *Lost Tycoon*.

121: **He was nearing bankruptcy**: John Cassidy, "Donald Trump's Business Failures Were Very Real," *New Yorker*, May 10, 2019.

121: **As Trump himself admitted:** "Donald Trump Admitted He Was Worth 'Minus $900 Million' in His Book," *The Week*, October 3, 2016.

122: **the income Trump promised from the casinos:** "For Donald Trump's Gambling Bets, Some Wins and Losses," CBS News, December 15, 2015; Peter Grant and Alexandra Berzon, "Trump and His Debts: A Narrow Escape," *Wall Street Journal*, January 4, 2016.

122: **But his interests in the Grand Hyatt:** Richard D. Hylton, "Trump Discussing Empire's Breakup to Pay Off Banks," *New York Times*, April 25, 1991.

122: **The banks gave:** "Trump Allowance: $450,000 a Month," Associated Press, June 25, 1990.

123: **"All you folks have":** D'Antonio, *The Truth About Trump*, 233.

123: **In *The Art of the Comeback*:** Michael Kruse, "The Lost City of Trump," *Politico*, July/August 2018.

CHAPTER FIVE: LIE, CHEAT, AND SOMETIMES STEAL

Page 127: **I believed him when he said the Metropolitan:** Christopher Gray, "The Store That Slipped Through the Cracks," *New York Times*, October 3, 2014.

127: **I believed him when he said he didn't know the demolition:** Charles V. Bagli, "Trump Paid over $1 Million in Labor Settlement, Documents Reveal," *New York Times*, November 27, 2017.

127 footnote: **Louise Sunshine claimed:** Callie Wiser, "The *Frontline* Interview: Louise Sunshine," *Frontline*, September 27, 2016.

133: **He had Press Secretary:** Rachel Chason, "Sean Spicer Says He 'Absolutely' Regrets Crowd-Size Briefing," *Washington Post*, September 19, 2017.

133: **Trump and Spicer even:** Gregory Wallace, "National Park Service Edited Inauguration Photos After Trump, Spicer Calls," CNN Politics, September 9, 2018.

134: **The *Washington Post*, which has been tracking:** Glenn Kessler, Salvador Rizzo, and Meg Kelly, "President Trump Has Made More Than 20,000 False or Misleading Claims," *Washington Post*, July 13, 2020.

134: **lying (over a hundred times):** Salvador Rizzo, "Bottomless Pinocchio: Trump's Claim That He Will 'Always' Protect Those with Preexisting Conditions," *Washington Post*, June 29, 2020.

135: **He got the National Oceanic:** Nick Sobczyk, "NOAA Watchdog Chides Agency for How It Handled Hurricane Dorian's 'Sharpiegate,'" *Science*, July 10, 2020.

136: **Donald's claim that he got:** Nick Gass, "Trump: My Dad Gave Me a 'Small Loan' of a Million Dollars," October 26, 2015.

136: **The *Times* investigation determined that in total:** David Barstow, Susanne Craig, and Russ Buettner, "Trump Engaged in Suspect Tax Schemes as He Reaped Riches from His Father," *New York Times,* October 2, 2018.

136: **When the casinos were tanking:** "Trump Dad Reportedly Helped Son with $3 Million Chip Buy," Associated Press, January 21, 1991.

136: **Fred sent his man down:** "Trump Castle Admits Gaming Law Violation," *Los Angeles Times*, April 10, 1991.

137: **Donald also regularly lies:** "In Lawsuit Deposition, Trump Repeatedly Called Out for Exaggerating Wealth," CBS News, May 23, 2016.

137: **"My net worth fluctuates":** Timothy L. O'Brien, "How Much Is Trump Worth? Depends on How He Feels," *Newsweek*, October 19, 2015.

137: **"So yeah, even my own feelings:** "Trump: in His Own Words," CNN Money, April 21, 2011.

137: **"I've earned billions":** Caitlin Dickson, "Donald Trump for President!" *Atlantic,* February 10, 2011.

138: **He neither developed nor owns:** Jim Zarroli and Alina Selyukh, "Trump SoHo: A Shiny Hotel Wrapped in Glass, but Hiding Mysteries," NPR, November 7, 2017.

138: **which found business improved:** Nikki Ekstein, "The Trump SoHo Hotel Was Struggling to Survive. Then It Dropped the Trump Name," *Bloomberg News*, February 27, 2019.

138: **Overseas, the trend of slapping:** Aaron Williams and Anu Narayanswamy, "How Trump Has Made Millions by Selling His Name," *Washington Post*, January 25, 2017.

138: **Trump is a licenser:** Julianna Goldman and Laura Strickler, "Failed Developments in Trump-Branded Real Estate Led to Lawsuits," CBS.com, October 8, 2015.

139: **Trump cheats as "a way of life":** Maggie Haberman and Alan Feuer, "Mary Trump's Book Accuses the President of Embracing 'Cheating as a Way of Life,'" *New York Times*, July 7, 2020.

139: **The *New York Times* investigation:** Barstow et al., "Trump Engaged in Suspect Tax Schemes."

139: **This holds true:** John Cassidy, "Trump University: It's Worse Than You Think," *New Yorker*, June 2, 2016.

140: **When he wasn't using the Foundation:** John Cassidy, "Trump and the Truth: His Charitable Giving," *New Yorker*, September 24, 2016; David A. Fahrenthold, "How Donald Trump Retooled His Charity to Spend Other People's Money," *Washington Post*, September 10, 2016.

140: **The Foundation was forced to disband:** Luis Ferre-Sadurni, "Trump Pays $2 Million to 8 Charities for Misuse of Foundation," *New York Times*, December 10, 2019.

141: **to one of his own courses:** Mark Landler, Lara Jakes, and Maggie Haberman, "Trump's Request of an Ambassador: Get the British Open for Me," *New York Times*, July 22, 2020.

141: **A recent *Washington Post* investigation:** David A. Fahrenthold, Josh Dawsey, and Joshua Partlow, "Room Rentals, Resort Fees and Furniture Removal: How Trump's Company Charged the U.S. Government More Than $900,000," *Washington Post*, August 27, 2020.

145: **It's the same reason:** Felicia Sonmez, "Trump Says He's Blocking Postal Service Funding Because Democrats Want to Expand Mail-In Voting During Pandemic," *Washington Post*, August 13, 2020.

145: **put together one of the most corrupt:** David A. Graham, "The Unchecked Corruption of Trump's Cabinet," *Atlantic*, May 20, 2019.

145: **reportedly stolen money from:** Dan Alexander, "Trump Has Shifted $1.7 Million from Campaign Donors to His Private Business," *Forbes*, December 6, 2019; Dan Alexander, "Trump Has Now Moved $2.3 Million of Campaign-Donor Money into His Private Business," *Forbes*, August 25, 2020.

CHAPTER SIX: THE BALANCE SHEET

Page 147: **"No, I don't take responsibility":** Remarks by President Trump, Vice President Pence, and Members of the Coronavirus Task Force in Press Conference, whitehouse.gov, March 13, 2020.

148: **Even after Jack O'Donnell:** This story is told by O'Donnell in "The Confidence Man," an episode of *Dirty Money* (dir. Fisher Stevens), Netflix, January 26, 2018.

149: **Trump then managed:** Russ Buettner and Charles V. Bagli, "How Donald Trump Bankrupted His Atlantic City Casinos, but Still Earned Millions," *New York Times*, June 11, 2016.

149 footnote: **When Marvin Roffman:** Joel Rose, "The Analyst Who Gambled and Took on Trump," NPR, October 10, 2016; Michael Kruse, "The Man Who Beat Donald Trump: How Marvin Roffman Told the Truth, Was Punished for It—and Then Fought Back," *Politico*, April 25, 2016.

149: **According to Jack O'Donnell:** John R. O'Donnell with James Rutherford, *Trumped!: The Inside Story of the Real Donald Trump—His Cunning Rise and Spectacular Fall* (New York: Simon & Schuster, 1991), 237.

152 footnote: **In early September 2020:** "Donald Trump & Bob Woodward Covid Conversation Transcript: Trump 'Playing It Down,'" Rev.com, September 9, 2020.

153: **To keep his hands clean:** Peter Navarro, "Anthony Fauci Has Been Wrong About Everything I Have Interacted with Him On: Peter Navarro," *USA Today*, July 14, 2020.

153: **In August he promoted:** Yasmeen Abutaleb and Josh Dawsey, "New Trump Pandemic Adviser Pushes Controversial 'Herd Immunity' Strategy, Worrying Public Health Officials," *Washington Post*, August 31, 2020.

153: **"My first question is":** Yamiche Alcindor and Donald Trump, "Remarks by President Trump, Vice President Pence, and Members of the Coronavirus Task Force in Press Conference," whitehouse.gov, March 13, 2020.

162: **In April 2018, Trump was giving:** "Trump Hails Syria Strikes: Every One Hit Target," AP Archive, April 21, 2018. https://www.youtube.com/watch?v=jFqsACmjltM.

164: **"All life is a negotiation":** Sims, *Team of Vipers*, 113.

164: **Michael D'Antonio, one of Trump's biographers:** *CNN Tonight* transcript, August 15, 2019, http://transcripts.cnn.com/TRANSCRIPTS/1908/15/cnnt.02.html.

165: **He teamed up with motivational speaker:** Jerry Useem, "What Does Donald Trump Really Want?" *Fortune*, April 3, 2000.

166: **Stealing oil from Iraq:** Julian Borger, "Trump's Plan to Seize Iraq's Oil: 'It's Not Stealing, We're Reimbursing Ourselves,'" *Guardian*, September 21, 2016.

166: **He suggested the military:** Rucker and Leonnig, *A Very Stable Genius*, 177.

167: **When he refused to call off:** "Remarks by President Trump at Signing of S. 3508, the 'Save Our Seas Act of 2018,'" whitehouse.gov, October 11, 2018.

168: **He tried to convince China:** Caitlin Oprysko, "Trump Asked China for Help Getting Reelected, Bolton Book Claims," *Politico*, June 17, 2020.

168: **"It's, it's a lousy thing":** ABC interview with Nancy Collins, "Donald Trump Compared Women in His Life to Buildings in 1994 Interview with ABC," https://abcnews.go.com/Politics/video/donald-trump-compared-women-life-buildings-1994-interview-39538139.

169: **"Three hours in prime time":** Jennifer Fermino, "Trump Rings Up Number 3; Weds Melania in Celeb-Filled Seaside $how," *New York Post*, January 23, 2005.

169: **He proposed buying her out:** Lisa Belkin, "Donald Trump's Original Apprentice, Louise Sunshine, Recalls Her 'Magical' Years and the Not-So-Happy Ending," Yahoo News, September 24, 2016.

170: **He gave Louise the million:** Marie Brenner, "After the Gold Rush," *Vanity Fair*, September 1990.

170: **Trump has repeatedly said no president:** David Jackson, "Trump: No Politician in History 'Has Been Treated Worse,'" *USA Today*, May 17, 2017.

CHAPTER SEVEN: NO FRIEND TO THE COMMON MAN

Page 171: **"The oddity in all of this":** Brian Niemietz, "Howard Stern to Trump Supporters: He Hates You and So Do I," *New York Daily News*, May 12, 2020.

172: **Beyond that, he has tried:** "Obamacare: Has Trump Managed to Kill Off Affordable Care Act?" BBC, March 29, 2019.

172: **made false promises about:** ibid.

172: **imposed tariffs that hurt:** Conor Sen, "History Hints at How Trump's Tariffs Will Hurt Americans," *Bloomberg News*, August 8, 2019.

172: **tried to dismantle the Consumer:** Katy O'Donnell, "High Court Gives Trump Power to Fire Consumer Bureau Chief," *Politico*, June 29, 2020.

172: **threatened cuts to Medicare:** Tara Golshan, "Trump Said He Wouldn't Cut Medicaid, Social Security, and Medicare. His 2020 Budget Cuts All 3," *Vox*, March 12, 2019.

172: **the Trump Foundation was:** New York Attorney General, press release, "Donald J. Trump Pays Court-Ordered $2 Million for Illegally Using Trump Foundation Funds," ny.gov, December 10, 2019.

172: **his apparent grifting of other charities is:** Dan Alexander, "How Donald Trump Shifted Kids-Cancer Charity Money into His Business," *Forbes*, June 29, 2017.

175: **If I had to be like Robert:** Joanne Palmer, "How Did Melania Trump Get U.S. citizenship?" *Jewish Standard,* December 22, 2016.

176: **He was not let into their:** Susan Mulcahy, "Confessions of a Trump Tabloid Scribe: How New York's Gossip Pages Helped Turn a Lying Real Estate Developer into a Celebrity Phenom," *Politico Magazine*, May/June 2016.

176: **The Trump name, according to:** Jeffrey Toobin, *True Crimes and Misde-meanors: The Investigation of Donald Trump* (New York: Doubleday, 2020), 97.

176: **He has said that he has respect:** D'Antonio, *The Truth About Trump,* 1.

177: **"That makes me smart":** Dan Mangan, "Trump Brags About Not Paying Taxes: 'That Makes Me Smart,'" CNBC.com, September 26, 2016.

177 footnote: **Their late cousin John Walter:** Gwenda Blair, "Did the Trump Family Historian Drop a Dime to the *New York Times*?" *Politico*, October 7, 2018; Barstow op. cit.

177: **The company did all the:** Barstow et al., "Trump Engaged in Suspect Tax Schemes."

179: **It cost Trump $63 million:** Tony Schwartz, "A Different Kind of Donald Trump Story," *New York* magazine, February 11, 1985.

179: **Trump was going to outdo:** Barrett, *Trump: The Greatest Show on Earth.*

180: **Trump and his managers:** Park South Associates v. Fischbein, 626 F. Supp. 1108 (S.D.N.Y. 1986), January 23, 1986; Schwartz, op. cit.; Jose Pagliery, "Donald Trump Was a Nightmare Landlord in the 1980s," CNN Money, March 28, 2016.

180: **Trump's managers demanded that tenants:** Ron Suskind, "Trump Eviction Dispute Taken to State Hearing," *New York Times*, February 28, 1985.

180: **According to court documents:** Pagliery, op. cit.

181: **Another scheme Trump devised:** Tracie Rozhon, "A Win by Trump! No, by Tenants!; Battle of the 80's Ends, with Glad-Handing All Around," *New York Times*, March 26, 1998.

181: **Many of the tenants:** Max J. Rosenthal, "The Trump Files: The Brief Life of the 'Trump Chateau for the Indigent,'" *Mother Jones*, July 21, 2020.

182: **There were certainly some:** Hurt, *Lost Tycoon*, Kindle edition, location 2141.

182: **Trump had investigators poking:** Sydney H. Schanberg, "Doer and Slum-lord Both," *New York Times*, March 9, 1985; this is also reported in D'Antonio, *The Truth About Trump,* 171.

182: **In the end, Trump was mostly defeated:** Park South Associates v. Fischbein, op. cit.

CHAPTER EIGHT: THE OTHER

Page 185: **"There is nobody":** Tara Golshan, "Trump Justifies His Past Sexism: 'That Was Done for the Purpose of Entertainment,'" *Vox*, October 6, 2016.

185: **You know, it really doesn't matter:** Harry Hurt III, "Donald Trump Gets Small," *Esquire*, May 1, 1991.

188: **"touch those plastic breasts":** ibid.

188: **he didn't want to sleep with:** Nina Burleigh, *Golden Handcuffs: The Secret History of Trump's Women* (New York: Gallery, 2018), 13.

188: **In 1990, when the tabloids:** "Marla Boasts to Her pals About Donald: Best Sex I Ever Had," *New York Post*, February 14, 1990.

189: **Though Trump denied he planted:** Jill Brooke, "The Real Story Behind Donald Trump's Infamous 'Best Sex I've Ever Had' Headline," *Hollywood Reporter*, April 12, 2018.

192: **The two had been friends:** Catriona Harvey-Jenner, "Jeffrey Epstein and Donald Trump: Everything You Need to Know About Their Friendship," *Cosmopolitan*, June 15, 2020.

192: **Trump told *New York* magazine:** Landon Thomas Jr., "Jeffrey Epstein: International Moneyman of Mystery," *New York* magazine, October 28, 2002.

192: **"I wish her well":** Aamer Madhani, "Trump Says of Ghislaine Maxwell, 'I Wish Her Well,'" Associated Press, July 21, 2020.

195: **In the early 1990s, after Daryl:** Andrew Kaczynski and Nathan McDermott, "Donald Trump Called Daryl Hannah 'a Six' Who Needs a Bath During a 1993 Spat," *BuzzFeed*, May 31, 2016.

195: **He used this tactic:** Paul Solotaroff, "Trump Seriously: On the Trail with the GOP's Tough Guy," *Rolling Stone*, September 9, 2015.

195: **"Take a look":** Naomi Lim, "Donald Trump on Accuser: 'Take a Look at Her . . . I Don't Think So,'" CNN Politics, October 13, 2016.

195: **As of September 2020:** Eliza Relman, "The 26 Women Who Have Accused Trump of Sexual Misconduct," *Business Insider*, September 17, 2020.

196: **Threatened, Trump had to attack:** Emma Ockerman, "Trump Just Called the Accusations Against Kavanaugh a 'Big, Fat Con Job,'" *Vice News*, September 26, 2018.

196: **When Rob Porter:** Sam Stein, "In Private, Donald Trump Voices Doubt About Rob Porter's Accusers," *Daily Beast*, February 9, 2018; @realDonaldTrump, Twitter.com, February 10, 2018, 10:33 a.m.

196: **"the woman in Michigan":** David Jackson and Michael Collins, "Trump to Mike Pence: 'Don't Call the Woman in Michigan,' aka Gov. Gretchen Whitmer," *USA Today*, March 27, 2020.

196: **"Crazy Nancy":** @realDonald Trump, Twitter, September 2, 2020, 9:12 a.m.

197: **He bullied British Prime Minister:** Adam Payne, "Trump Said to Be 'Humiliating and Bullying' Toward Theresa May in Phone Calls That Left Her 'Flustered and Nervous,'" *Business Insider*, June 30, 2020.

197: **called German Chancellor Angela Merkel:** Bernstein, "From Pandering to Putin to Abusing Allies and Ignoring His Own Advisers."

197: **At a G-7 meeting:** Cristina Maza, "Donald Trump Threw Starburst Candies at Angela Merkel, Said 'Don't Say I Never Give You Anything,'" *Newsweek*, June 20, 2018.

197: **He's used it on Hillary:** @realDonaldTrump, Twitter.com, May 16, 2016, 11:46 p.m.

197: **Technically, I was:** ibid.

198: **"You ask a lot of stupid questions":** John Bowden, "Trump Rips Reporter for 'Stupid Question' on Mueller Probe," *The Hill*, November 9, 2018.

198: **The most crystallized example:** John Bowden, "Trump on Pompeo: I'd Rather Have Him Working Than Doing Dishes 'Because Maybe His Wife Isn't There,'" *The Hill*, May 18, 2020.

198: **"I'm the least racist person":** Jordan Fabian, "Trump Says He Is the 'Least Racist Person Anywhere in the World,'" *The Hill,* July 30, 2019.

199: **From then on their rental:** Jennifer Rubin, "Trump's Racist Housing Tweet Is Par for His Family," *Washington Post*, July 30, 2020; Michael Kranish and Robert O'Harrow Jr., "Inside the Government's Racial Bias Case Against Donald Trump's Company, and How He Fought It," *Washington Post*, January 23, 2016; David A. Graham, Adrienne Green, Cullen Murphy, and Parker Richards, "An Oral History of Trump's Bigotry," *Atlantic*, June 2019.

199: **"I am happy to inform all"**: @realDonaldTrump, Twitter.com, July 29, 2020, 12:19 p.m.

200: **"The 'suburban housewife'"**: @realDonaldTrump, Twitter.com, August 12, 2020, 7:59 a.m.

200: **Playing to supposedly scared:** Jamie Ross, "Trump Vows to Save 'Suburban Housewives' from Cory Booker in Dog-Whistle Tweet," *Daily Beast*, August 12, 2020.

200: **When Fox News' Chris Wallace:** Interview with Chris Wallace, *Fox News Sunday*, July 19, 2020.

201: **"You're living in poverty:** Tom LoBianco and Ashley Killough, "Trump Pitches Black Voters: 'What the Hell Do You Have to Lose?'" CNN Politics, August 19, 2016.

203: **In *Trumped!*, former:** John R. O'Donnell, *Trumped!*, 115.

203: **When Donald and Ivana were visiting:** Congressional Record volume 162, number 145 (Monday, September 26, 2016), Senate, pages S6073-S6074.

205: **"roving bands of wild criminals":** Donald J. Trump, "Bring Back the Police," *New York Daily News*, May 1, 1990.

206: **"when the looting starts":** @realDonald Trump, Twitter.com, May 29, 2020, 5:53 a.m.

206: **"When Mexico sends its":** Michelle Ye Hee Lee, "Donald Trump's False Comments Connecting Mexican Immigrants and Crime," *Washington Post*, July 8, 2015.

207: **Trump has used the term "infested":** Abigail Simon, "People Are Angry President Trump Used This Word to Describe Undocumented Immigrants," *Time*, June 19, 2018.

207: **wasted over $11 billion:** John Burnett, "$11 Billion and Counting: Trump's Border Wall Would Be the World's Most Costly," NPR, January 19, 2020.

207: **During that campaign he:** Nina Totenberg, "Who Is Judge Gonzalo Curiel, The Man Trump Attacked for His Mexican Ancestry?" NPR, June 7, 2016.

208: **Miles Taylor, the former:** Hallie Jackson, "Ex-DHS Official: Trump Wanted to Trade Puerto Rico for Greenland," MSNBC, August 19, 2020.

208: **According to Taylor, Trump:** Roger Sollenberger, "Trump Wanted to 'Maim' and 'Tear Gas' Migrants at US-Mexico Border, Former DHS Official Claims," *Salon*, August 28, 2020.

208: **Though Mexicans seemed:** Michael D. Shear and Julie Hirschfeld Davis, "Stoking Fears, Trump Defied Bureaucracy to Advance Immigration Agenda," *New York Times*, December 23, 2017.

212: **Instead, Trump equivocated, claiming:** "Full Text: Trump's Comments on White Supremacists, 'Alt-Left' in Charlottesville," *Politico*, August 15, 2017.

CHAPTER NINE: SEARCH AND DESTROY

Page 218 footnote: **Cohn was disbarred:** Martin Gottlieb, "New York Court Disbars Roy Cohn on Charges of Unethical Conduct," *New York Times*, June 24, 1986.

218: *USA Today* **did an investigation:** Nick Penzenstadler and Susan Page, "Exclusive: Trump's 3,500 Lawsuits Unprecedented for a Presidential Nominee," *USA Today*, October 23, 2017.

220: **When Trump first said that:** Ben Schreckinger, "Trump attacks McCain: 'I Like People Who Weren't Captured,'" *Politico*, July 18, 2015.

220 footnote: **As this book went to press:** Jeffrey Goldberg, "Trump: Americans Who Died in War Are 'Losers' and 'Suckers,'" *Atlantic*, September 3, 2020.

220: **He got one of the papers:** Mark Alpert, "The Battle of the Billionaires," *Fortune*, September 25, 1989.

221: **In 2018, Trump tried to cut off:** Noah Bierman and Eli Stokols, "Trump Sought to Withhold California Wildfire Aid Because State Didn't Vote for Him, Former DHS Official Says," *Los Angeles Times*, August 17, 2020.

222: **He does it to serve and protect:** Dan Mangan, "President Trump Told Lesley Stahl He Bashes Press 'to Demean You and Discredit You So . . . No One Will Believe' Negative Stories About Him," CNBC, May 22, 2018.

225: **In fact, when he first installed:** "All the Dresses She Can Buy," editorial, *New York Times*, March 29, 1988.

230: **Marla went up to Ivana:** "Ivana Trump Recounts the Donald's Public Affair with Marla Maples," *Daily Beast*, October 8, 2017.

233: **Trump's people know that any:** Asawin Suebsaeng and Erin Banco, "Trump Advisers: He Was 'Triggered' by Talk of White Supremacy," *Daily Beast*, August 28, 2020.

EPILOGUE

Page 248: **I remember an interview:** Mark Abadi, "Trump Had an Unusual Reaction to 9/11 Just Hours After the Attacks," *Business Insider*, September 11, 2019.

250: **We know Trump was happy:** Katherine Eban, "How Jared Kushner's Secret Testing Plan 'Went Poof into Thin Air,'" *Vanity Fair*, July 30, 2020.

ABOUT THE AUTHOR

BARBARA A. RES is frequently interviewed on television and in the media as an
expert on Donald Trump, having worked
directly with him for eighteen years. Res
was first hired by Trump as vice president
in charge of overseeing construction of
Trump Tower. She later became executive
vice president in charge of development and construction at the
Trump Organization. She started working with Trump on his first
development project in Manhattan, the Grand Hyatt Hotel.

Res is a trailblazer, having worked in construction as an engineer in the 1970s, when few women worked in that field. With
over forty years in construction and development in the U.S. and
Europe, she is a licensed professional engineer and has held virtually every position in the contracting and subcontracting trades.
She is also an attorney licensed in New York and New Jersey as
well as a mediator and arbitrator for the American Arbitration
Association, and she travels the world as a public speaker. She
has been awarded the Townsend Harris Medal by City College of
New York, the college's most prestigious alumni award, and the
Emily Warren Roebling leadership award by Professional Women
in Construction. She is a native of New York City and the mother
of two. She currently lives in New Jersey.